Analyzing redistribution policies

T0323345

To
MY PARENTS

Analyzing redistribution policies

A study using Australian data

NANAK KAKWANI

*World Institute for Development Economics Research
Helsinki, Finland*

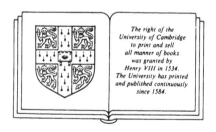

The right of the
University of Cambridge
to print and sell
all manner of books
was granted by
Henry VIII in 1534.
The University has printed
and published continuously
since 1584.

CAMBRIDGE UNIVERSITY PRESS

*Cambridge
London   New York   New Rochelle
Melbourne   Sydney*

CAMBRIDGE UNIVERSITY PRESS
Cambridge, New York, Melbourne, Madrid, Cape Town, Singapore,
São Paulo, Delhi, Dubai, Tokyo

Cambridge University Press
The Edinburgh Building, Cambridge CB2 8RU, UK

Published in the United States of America by Cambridge University Press, New York

www.cambridge.org
Information on this title: www.cambridge.org/9780521126311

First published 1986
This digitally printed version 2009

A catalogue record for this publication is available from the British Library

Library of Congress Cataloguing in Publication data
Kakwani, Nanak.
Analyzing redistribution policies.
Includes index.
1. Income distribution – Government policy – Australia.
2. Taxation, Progressive – Australia.   3. Transfer
payments – Australia.   4. Australia – Social conditions.
I. Title.
HC610.I5K35   1986   339.5′2   85–31342

ISBN 978-0-521-30838-0 Hardback
ISBN 978-0-521-12631-1 Paperback

Contents

v

Part II   Measures of income inequality, redistribution, and equity

Part III   Distribution and redistribution of income

Preface

In any welfare state, an important objective of the government is to have an equitable distribution of national resources. Toward that end, the fiscal policies of many governments have been directed to the redistribution of income and welfare. In order to judge the impact of such policies, one needs to measure their redistributive effects. The measurement of such effects depends on the resolution of certain conceptual and empirical issues as well as the availability of appropriate tools and techniques. This book carefully examines the issues, both conceptual and empirical, and develops the techniques to analyze the redistributive effects of government policies.

In Australia our knowledge and understanding of the distribution of income and welfare are inadequate and must be improved to evaluate government policies that affect the economic welfare of people. This book adds to our store of knowledge in the area of distribution of income and welfare in Australia. Although analytical techniques developed in the study are exclusively applied to Australia, they are widely applicable and should be valuable to researchers in other countries interested in these issues.

This study represents the past four years of my research on income distribution, and some of the analysis contained in it has been drawn from a number of articles published in *Advances in Econometrics, Journal of Development Economics,* and *The Economic Record.* The study was carried out with the support of a grant from the Reserve Bank of Australia. The views expressed in it are not necessarily those of the Reserve Bank.

I wish to express my gratitude to Professor John Nevile for giving me help and encouragement at various stages of this work. Robert Horn and Nripesh Podder read some chapters of the first version of the manuscript and offered many critical comments which proved quite useful. The study could not have been completed without the expert computational assistance given by Michael Mekhitarian, to whom I am greatly indebted.

Silvana Tomaseillo typed the draft manuscript with great care and patience, for which I am grateful.

N.K.

CHAPTER 1

Introduction

Since the introduction of progressive income tax, the fiscal policies of many governments have included the redistribution of income as a major goal and, with the recent emergence of welfare states, redistributive policies have been accepted as a social norm. Increasingly, it is being realized that the government could play an important role in reducing, if not eliminating, poverty by appropriate redistributive policies.

The government can alter the pattern of income distribution in many ways and at different stages of income generation. The various redistributive policies of government may be classified into two broad categories. The first category relates to those policies that have direct impact on the working of markets generating incomes for households or individuals. These policies change the distribution of factor incomes by altering the prices and supply of goods and factors. Minimum-wage legislation, subsidized interest rates for home buyers, and wage indexation are some of the examples of such policies either followed, or advocated, by many governments.

The second category includes fiscal policies that redistribute factor incomes received by individuals through market operations. The redistribution of income is achieved by direct and indirect taxes, collected by federal, state, and local governments; and by various income support programs designed to help low-income families. Fiscal policies have relatively little direct effect on the process of price and income formation. Indirectly, however, such effects cannot be avoided. In principle, any transfer of income will influence the demand for goods and services, the supply of labor, and the levels and patterns of savings and investments which, in turn, affect the prices of goods and factors. A full analysis of these indirect effects requires an elaborate general equilibrium approach that accounts for all possible changes induced by an income transfer.

1.1   Aims of the study and major contributions

The main objective of government redistributive policies is to increase the welfare of people. In order to evaluate the effects of such policies, it is essential to understand the extent and nature of income inequality and

1

welfare in the society. The study develops appropriate techniques to analyze these problems and to measure the direct impact of taxes and government cash transfers on the distribution of income and welfare by size of income and other household characteristics. The study is concerned with questions like: What is the extent of the inequality of income and which way is it moving? Is the burden of taxation evenly distributed across the population? Do the rich pay proportionately more or less taxes than the poor? What are the effects of current government programs on the welfare of particular groups in the community? Techniques are developed to answer these and other related questions. The techniques are shown in practical use on Australian data obtained from the Household Expenditure Survey, 1975-6.

The Household Expenditure Survey of 1975-6, which is used for the empirical work in the present study, covers the whole of Australia except remote and sparsely settled areas.[1] It provides a detailed breakdown of households according to various socioeconomic and demographic characteristics. It is thus an exceptionally appropriate set of data to use in the present study, which utilizes all this information and provides considerable insight into issues concerning the impact of the government tax-transfer policies on specific groups in the community.

The level of economic welfare enjoyed by individuals in a household cannot be adequately measured without taking into account the needs of households. Two households enjoying the same income are equally well off only if they have the same needs. Since households differ in size and age composition, it is expected that they will have different needs. Clearly, then, the measurement of economic welfare should take into account the differing needs of the households. The present study analyzes how the magnitudes of distribution and redistribution of income and welfare vary when income is adjusted for varying household size and composition.

The principles of horizontal and vertical equity play a fundamental role in any debate on taxation. The principle of horizontal equity means that individuals in equal positions should be treated equally. The principle of vertical equity, on the other hand, requires that the tax burden on individuals should increase in line with capacity to pay. It is widely believed that a tax system should conform with both these principles (Musgrave 1959: 160). The study provides quantitative measurements of both types of equity and also discusses their relationship to measures of tax progressivity and income redistribution.

Indirect taxes are usually regressive and hit the poor harder than the rich. But the government could avoid the worst of regressive effects by carefully selecting the goods and services to be taxed. This study provides a quantitative basis for formulating a comprehensive indirect tax scheme with least regressive impact.

This study also considers an alternative approach to measuring welfare that captures the sense of envy felt by individuals when they compare their incomes with each other. This approach is utilized to measure the impact of personal income tax and government cash transfers on the distribution of economic welfare by the size of income and by other household characteristics.

The main objective of any income-support policy is to reduce, if not eliminate, poverty. The extent to which this objective is achieved should be an issue of utmost importance to the policy makers. This study attempts to measure the aggregate level of poverty and to what extent it is affected by personal income tax and government cash transfers. The results of a breakdown of aggregate poverty according to several socioeconomic and demographic characteristics of households are also examined.

While the analytical techniques introduced in this study could be applied to many countries, we intend to ensure the applicability and reality of analysis by tying it carefully into an ongoing empirical study of the Australian situation. And that requires some brief description of the Australian tax and social security systems, which is provided in the next two sections. Although the Australian institutions are reasonably similar to those in other developed countries, some of the special features brought out in these sections would be of general interest to researchers and policy makers in many other countries.

1.2 An overview of the Australian tax system

Federal, state, and local governments are the three taxation authorities in Australia. The tax revenue of the federal government far exceeds that of other governments. It has been collecting about 80 percent of total tax revenue in the postwar period.

An overall picture of the Australian tax system during the years 1970-1 and 1979-80 is represented by Table 1.1. It can be seen that of all the taxes, personal income tax represents the largest source of tax revenue. Among all the OECD (Organization for Economic Co-operation and Development) countries, Australia ranks fourth in terms of the percentage of personal income tax in total tax receipts. By comparison with taxes on goods and services, its ranking is eighteenth.[2]

Due to a high rate of inflation and insignificant tax indexation,[3] the share of personal income tax in taxation revenue increased from 36.88 percent to 43.96 percent for the period 1970-1 to 1979-80. During the same period, the share of indirect taxes went from 30.37 percent to 29.97 percent, despite the fact that the government has been levying an increasingly heavy excise duty on crude oil since 1975-6. In the financial year 1979-80, the excise due to crude oil alone was as much as 27 percent of

Table 1.1. *Australian taxation by type of tax as a percentage of total tax revenue*

Type of tax	1970–1	1979–80
Personal income tax	36.88	43.96
Company tax	16.58	10.23
Total income taxes	53.46	54.12
Custom and excise duty	17.65	19.27
Sales tax	7.35	5.45
Other indirect taxes[1]	5.37	5.25
Total indirect taxes	30.37	29.97
Taxes on property[2]	8.50	5.54
All other taxes[3]	7.67	10.30
Total tax	100.00	100.00

[1] Other indirect taxes include primary production taxes, liquor taxes, taxes on gambling, and taxes on ownership and operation of motor vehicles.
[2] Taxes on property include estate, gift, probate and succession duties, and property taxes.
[3] All other taxes include payroll tax, stamp duties and taxes, fees, fines, etc.

the total tax on goods and services. It can be seen, therefore, that sales tax plays a minor role in the overall tax system. During the 1970s, the share of sales tax declined from 7.35 percent to 5.45 percent.

The rate structure of Australian personal income tax is progressive in the sense that the marginal tax rate increases with income. Prior to 1973–4, the income tax schedule had 29 tax steps (or marginal tax rates) at different income levels. But in recent years the structure of taxation has undergone considerable changes which have reduced the number of tax steps to 15 in November of 1974, to 7 in 1975, and to 3 since 1977. This reduction in the number of tax steps generally favors high-income earners.[4]

In Australia personal income tax is levied on individuals to whom income accrues. It means that a husband and wife have to submit separate tax returns. Individuals with dependent spouse and dependent children are granted some tax concessions that reduce income-tax liabilities. Until 1975–6, these tax concessions were given in the form of concessional deductions from assessable income. This meant that the value of these concessional deductions in absolute amount rose with income because of the progressive tax structure. For this reason, the system was criticized by both the Taxation Review and the Poverty Inquiry Commission.

The Poverty Inquiry Commission recommended that concessional deductions from assessable income be replaced by tax credits or rebates of equal value to all taxpayers. These proposals were adopted by the government during the 1975-6 financial year. The 1976-7 budget introduced yet another major tax reform which replaced the tax rebate for dependent children by the family allowance, paid directly to the mothers of the children. This change was designed to benefit, in particular, large families with low incomes who would normally not receive any benefits from tax rebates. From an equity point of view these were the most significant tax reforms favoring low-income earners.[5]

Personal income tax in Australia is assessed on net income, which is defined as gross income from all sources: wages and salaries, interest, dividend, business activities, and rent; less any expense directly incurred in the production of such incomes. The imputed rent of an owner-occupied house is tax exempt.[6] Capital gains on the sale of real estate and other assets, if declared speculative by the Tax Commissioner, are taxed as ordinary income only if they have been held for less than one year. In other circumstances there is absolutely no tax on capital gains. Thus, the Australian tax structure provides considerable incentive to taxpayers to convert income into capital gains.

Because of the heavy reliance on income tax, the Australian tax system would probably be the most progressive among all the developed countries. This increasing personal income tax burden has been the cause of considerable dissatisfaction for quite some time among tax payers, particularly those subject to PAYE taxation.[7] Several political and economic journalists involved with tax policy have expressed concern over the possible disincentive effects of high tax rates.[8] It has been suggested that tax avoidance and evasion due to high tax rates may have drastically reduced the progressivity of the overall system.[9]

For these reasons, the Australian Taxation Review Committee recommended that the taxation system should place greater reliance on goods and services by the inclusion of a broad-based tax. The major drawback of the present system of indirect taxation is that it has a very narrow tax base and is restricted only to a few goods and services; about 80 percent of the total revenue from the taxation of goods and services comes from the taxes on liquor, tobacco, petroleum products, and motor vehicles and parts. Therefore, a significant increase in revenue cannot be achieved even with a large increase in tax rates. This aspect of taxation has been subjected to strong criticisms, particularly from Head (1983: 12).

In general I think it is fair to say that the Australian system of taxing goods and services is a rare old mess based on a mind-boggling and contradictory mixture of cynical revenue-maximizing motives (in the case of excises) and a possibly well-intended but totally misconceived attempt to "humanise" the wholesale sales tax. As a result the pattern of resource allocation is arbitrarily distorted and horizontal equity is grossly violated with any significant amelioration of the inherent regressive tendencies of indirect consumption taxes.

In the past, the government has resisted the temptation to introduce a broad-based indirect tax such as a retail turnover tax and a value added tax because of its potential inflationary effect. Due to a recent decline in inflation rate, it will be easier for the government to introduce such a tax in line with comparable tax systems in other countries. Thus it seems that, in future, the government will rely more on indirect taxes and less on direct taxes.

The taxation of wealth has an important effect on income distribution. It provides one means through which a government can ensure greater equality of opportunity without, at the same time, causing major disincentive effects. However, Australia is one of the few developed countries in the world where wealth attracts hardly any tax. The only form of wealth tax in Australia is the property tax; the importance of that too has declined from 8.50 percent to 5.54 percent during the period from 1970-1 to 1979-80. This decline occurred largely due to the abolition of death duties at the federal level and in most states. It is now fair to say that Australia has virtually no tax on wealth. This may be the most undesirable feature of Australian taxation because, in the absence of a capital-gains tax, people can avoid paying tax on the income that generated the wealth. The rich are more likely to benefit from this than the poor.[10]

Although the Australian Tax Review Committee rejected the introduction of such a tax, due to administrative difficulties involved in its collection, it did recommend certain other measures that can achieve broadly the same objectives as a wealth tax. These proposals would have involved widening the base of the estate and gift duty at the federal level and introducing a capital-gains tax. Instead of adopting these tax reforms, the Commonwealth government as well as the governments of most states chose to abolish the estate and gift duty.

1.3   An overview of the Australian social security system[11]

In Australia the federal government plays the dominant role in providing social security. Transfer programs, administered by the Department of Social Security, provide direct financial assistance to those who are not expected to work, have some kind of disability to work, or are unable to find work. These payments are made to persons from general government revenues in return for which no services are rendered or goods supplied.

Table 1.2. *Classification of transfer payments to persons by the Commonwealth government 1975–6 and 1979–80*

Type of transfer payments	1975–6 Total amount paid ($ millions)	1975–6 % of total government outlay	1979–80 Total amount paid ($ millions)	1979–80 % of total government outlay
Age pension	2150.7	10.03	3541.3	11.12
Invalid pension	438.1	2.04	858.4	2.70
Ex-servicemen	563.7	2.63	959.6	3.01
Widows and single parents	452.5	2.11	821.0	2.58
Total pensions	3605.0	16.81	6180.3	19.41
Unemployment benefits	506.0	2.36	925.2	2.91
Sickness and special benefits	116.6	.54	179.2	.56
Family allowances	265.5	1.24	1012.7	3.18
Other social security benefits	13.5	.06	91.1	.29
Total social security	4506.6	21.02	8388.5	26.08

Table 1.2 gives the classification of transfer payments during years 1975–6 and 1979–80. It can be seen that in 1975–6 these payments accounted for just more than 21 percent of the total Commonwealth budget outlays. In four years this percentage increased from 21.02 percent to 26.08 percent in 1979–80.

These payments may be classified into two broad categories. The first category includes payments that are made over long periods, such as pensions and family allowances. Unemployment and sickness benefits are regarded as short-term payments and therefore fall into the second category. Short-term payments as the percentage of the total budget outlay have increased only slightly during the period 1975–6 to 1979–80, whereas long-term payments show a considerable increase during the same period. It is interesting to note that, despite the increase in the level of unemployment during this four-year period, the unemployment benefits as the percentage of the total government outlays show only a marginal increase. This may be explained by the substantial fall in the real value of the unemployment benefits over the period.

The substantial increase in the outlay on pensions may be attributed to an increase both in the number of beneficiaries and in the pension rates. The number of beneficiaries increased because of several relaxed eligibility criteria introduced during this period. For instance, the age at which the means test for age pensioners ceased to apply was reduced in 1975 from 75 to 70 years. Pension rates increased substantially due to the introduction of automatic six-monthly indexation of standard and married rates of pensions and benefits. Automatic indexation did not, however, apply to unemployment and sickness benefits for single people under 18.

During the period 1975-6 to 1979-80, family allowances as the percentage of total government outlays increased from 1.24 to 3.18 percent. This increase may be attributed to a major policy change in 1976 when the child endowment and consequent deductions for dependent children were replaced by the family allowance, with substantially higher benefits for families with multiple children. One of the main objectives of this change was to provide financial assistance directly to mothers, whereas previously the major part of assistance for children was provided via reduced taxes paid by the fathers.

1.4   Scope and limitations

As this study is based on the Household Expenditure Survey of 1975-6, the data are already eight years old. Since 1976, the Australian economy has undergone considerable changes, the most significant being the increased levels of unemployment and inflation, which may have altered patterns of income distribution as well as the structure of the tax-transfer system. Since the main emphasis of the present study is on the methods of analyzing the redistribution policies, this limitation is not of serious consequence.

For the purpose of measuring economic welfare, the definition of income should be as comprehensive as possible. It should include all its components that affect the economic well-being of the recipient units both directly and indirectly. Although the income concept used in the present study is fairly comprehensive, it is still deficient from a welfare point of view. For example, it excludes several in-kind transfers, imputed rent, the value of home production, capital gains, and voluntary leisure. Exclusion of these factors can alter the true economic status of the household and, as a consequence, biased estimates of the distribution of economic welfare may emerge. Available data are insufficient to take account of these factors. Nonetheless, the present study provides a thorough discussion of the direction of such biases, which may occur when using Australian data.

The major limitation of the present study is that it measures only the direct impact of taxes and government cash transfers on the levels of income and welfare inequality and poverty in Australia. It assumes that the indirect effects of taxes and government transfers on the market operations that generate factor incomes are either negligible or neutral in the sense of opposing effects canceling one another out. The proper estimation of indirect effects is a gigantic task which cannot yet be attempted.

A variety of services and assistance-in-kind has long been supplied to individuals and families by local, state, and federal governments. Most notable among them are medical treatment of pensioners, accommodation and personal services for the aged, and child-care centers. Although these in-kind benefits may have considerable impact on the distribution of economic welfare, it is outside the scope of the present study to take account of them, mainly due to lack of the extensive information required for this purpose.

The discussion in the present study is confined to three major types of taxes: personal income tax, indirect taxes, and property taxes. In 1979–80, the contribution of these taxes was 79.47 percent of the total tax revenue. The remaining taxes are excluded from the analysis because of serious difficulties of allocating them to the households.

Despite the above limitations, the present study provides the most detailed investigation of the Australian tax-transfer system so far attempted. This is the first study that attempts to quantify the effects of horizontal and vertical equity on income redistribution. In measuring the magnitudes of income distribution and redistribution, it takes into account the differing sizes and composition of households, an aspect completely ignored by other studies carried out in Australia.

1.5   Framework for analysis

This study is divided into four parts. The first part is focused on some methodological and conceptual problems in measuring the distribution of income and welfare. The second part deals with some of the basic issues in the measurement of income inequality, redistribution, and equity. The third part presents the empirical results on the distribution and redistribution of income in Australia and discusses policy conclusions emerging from them. The last part considers issues concerning the measurement of welfare and poverty and presents the empirical evidence for Australia relating to these areas.

The measurement of economic welfare of individuals involves a number of conceptual and practical difficulties. One major problem that arises in this connection is the selection of an appropriate income-recipient unit: whether the individual, the family, the household, or some other entity is most appropriate as the unit whose income is to be measured. This problem is discussed in Chapter 2, which also provides an appraisal of equivalent-income scales estimated for Australia. These scales play an important role in comparing the welfare levels of households that differ in size and composition.

Chapter 3 discusses the shortcomings of the income concept employed in the Household Expenditure Surveys. In this chapter, an attempt has been made to determine the direction of the bias that is introduced, in the Australian case, by the use of a less-than-ideal income concept.

Chapter 4 is concerned with problems of the measurement of inequality of income distribution. The first issue is concerned with the definition of the degree of inequality from the welfare point of view. It is argued that welfare economics does not provide much help in resolving this issue. Further, a brief review of alternative inequality measures is provided.

Chapter 5 is concerned with some methodological issues in the measurement of the progressivity and redistributive effect of taxation and public expenditure. Measures of horizontal and vertical equity are derived from the notion of concentration curves. These methods are applied to the Australian data in the subsequent chapters.

Chapter 6 discusses several aspects of the size distribution of income from the viewpoint of public policy. Because the economic welfare of households depends, in addition to income, on household size and composition, the latter is an essential consideration in an accurate measurement of income inequality. This chapter analyzes how the magnitudes of income inequality vary with respect to alternative income scales used to adjust the income for household size and composition. An international comparison of income inequality is also given in this chapter.

Chapter 7 examines how taxes and government benefits are distributed across income ranges. These indices of relative tax burdens and relative benefits received are computed for various income quintiles and several policy implications are discussed.

In Chapter 8, the measures of progressivity and horizontal and vertical equity are used to analyze the distributional effects of taxes and government cash benefits. A comparison of these estimates with those of an earlier study by Podder and Kakwani (1975) is also provided, along with a discussion of several policy conclusions.

Chapter 9 is concerned with the distribution and redistribution of income between and within income groups classified according to several socioeconomic and demographic characteristics of households. This chapter provides insight into issues concerning the impact of government tax-transfer policies on particular groups in the community.

Chapter 10 deals with taxation on goods and services. It provides estimates of the degree of progressivity (or regressivity) of the sales or excise tax on more than 350 consumption items. The usefulness of considering such a fine classification of goods and services is demonstrated along with a discussion of several policy implications.

Chapter 11 analyzes the extent and nature of welfare in Australia. An alternative approach to measuring welfare is developed and many useful applications of it are discussed.

Chapter 12 is concerned with the problem of determining the optimal negative income tax structure, one that is associated with maximum social welfare. The main objective of this chapter is to explore how the sense of envy felt by individuals affects the optimal tax structure. The social welfare measures developed in Chapter 11 form the basis for this exercise.

Finally, Chapter 13 discusses issues in the measurement of poverty. Numerical estimates of poverty for Australia are presented along with a discussion of many policy implications that emerge from them.

PART I

Conceptual issues in the measurement of income distribution

Income-recipient units and their differing needs

There is a vast literature on distribution theory that seeks to explain factor income distribution, that is, proportion of national income accruing to labor, capital, and land. But it is the size distribution of income that is most relevant for the purpose of analyzing the distribution of economic welfare among individuals. This objective can be achieved only if we can find an appropriate measure of economic welfare for each individual in the society.

The measurement of economic welfare of individuals is not an easy task. It involves a number of conceptual and practical difficulties. The first problem that arises in this connection is the selection of an appropriate income recipient unit. The three main types of income recipients which have been used in studies of the size distribution of income are (a) the individual, (b) the family, and (c) the household.

Since income is earned largely by individuals, it seems natural to use individuals as the basic unit for analyzing income distribution. Moreover, if the purpose is to explain the generation of income by means of economic and institutional factors (such as sex, age, occupation, education, and even family status), the individual income earner seems to be the logical choice. But from the welfare point of view, the use of the individual as the recipient unit raises a number of conceptual problems which will be discussed in this chapter.

The income unit used in the present study is the household. Although the household is the central unit within which production and consumption decisions are taken, it is not certain whether it can be considered to be the most appropriate income-recipient unit. This chapter brings out both the limitations and strong points of using the household as an income unit.

The level of economic welfare enjoyed by a household cannot be measured without taking into account the needs of the household. Since households differ in size, and in age and sex composition, it is expected that they will have different needs. Clearly, then, the measurement of economic welfare should take into account the differing needs of the households. To this end attempts have been made to construct equivalent-income scales that would facilitate the comparison of different kinds of households.

15

Equivalent-income scales play a very important role in providing the rationale for government policies. For example, in Australia, the Department of Social Security gives cash benefits to families in the form of pensions, unemployment benefits, family allowance, and maternity allowance. The amount of these benefits depends on the size and composition of households and can be determined appropriately only if equivalent income scales are available to the policy makers. Further, these income scales can be useful in designing the tax schedule which maintains horizontal equity in personal income taxation. Finally, these scales are important in defining the poverty line, since minimum-consumption needs certainly vary with household consumption.

The construction of equivalent-income scales presents serious methodological and empirical difficulties and as a consequence several methods have been tried. This chapter discusses theoretical problems and limitations of various methods and provides an appraisal of equivalent-income scales estimated for Australia.

2.1   Individual as the income unit

Kuznets (1974, 1976) has proposed three criteria that must be satisfied by the income-recipient unit. The first criterion is that the income unit must be easily identifiable. In the case of wage and salary income, the problem of identification of an individual as the income earner is not serious. On the other hand, the problem becomes almost unsolvable with respect to income from small-scale family enterprises or property that are jointly owned by the family members. The allocation of income among husband, wife, and other members of the family in these situations is almost arbitrary. The problem becomes even more severe if we attempt to allocate nonmoney income among the family members.

The second criterion proposed by Kuznets relates to independence of income unit. It implies that the decisions made by recipient unit A on income gaining and income spending are not dependent on unit B. This assumption of independence among individual income units is hard to justify given the fact that a considerable sharing or pooling of income takes place within families and households. Although a large number of married women and children have either very low or zero income, they enjoy a standard of living that would be impossible if they depended only on their own incomes. The individual as recipient unit is, therefore, too narrow a concept primarily because it ignores customary dependency relationships (Epstein 1969: 158). These dependency relationships can also affect directly the individual decisions whether or not to earn money income. For instance, the choice between income-earning and other (e.g., education) activity for the young, as Kuznets points out, is largely determined by a family decision. Similarly, the decision of a married woman on whether to join the workforce depends in part on her husband's income and the number of children and their ages within the family.

One method of ensuring independence among individual recipients is to exclude from the analysis those persons who are largely dependent on others. This would mean excluding the younger, largely nonworking individuals, retired old people, and a large proportion of women who are not engaged in money-earning activities. It is obvious that the more we omit from the population of individual income recipients, the greater the independence among them. Unfortunately, this method of achieving independence violates Kuznets's inclusion criterion which states that income-recipient units must include total population, in order to link income flow (and disposition) to the totals of earners and users. Since we are interested in the economic welfare of the total population, the exclusion of a large proportion of the population from our analysis would clearly lead to misleading conclusions. Moreover, which individuals should be included or excluded is not at all easy to decide due to the identification problem already discussed.

2.2   The family

For welfare purposes, the family has been considered to be a more appropriate income-recipient unit than the individual. In this context a family refers to a nuclear family consisting either of single person or a married couple with or without minor children. "The members of the family," as Brady (1958) points out, "share the goods and services owned or acquired for consumption and pay for their purchases from their joint receipts from earnings or other sources of income." The income of the family as a whole is clearly more identifiable than that of particular individuals belonging to it. Do these characteristics of the family make it a particularly appropriate income-recipient unit? The answer to this question depends on how the income or other resources possessed by the family are actually shared by the family members. There is hardly any literature that deals with the family's allocation mechanism. The best we can do is to clarify the assumptions about the family decision process under which the family will be the suitable income-recipient unit.

One obvious assumption is that the family members share their income equally. Since the family members differ with respect to age, sex, and role within the family, their needs will also be different. Therefore, equal income (or resources) allocated to each family member with different needs will automatically lead to unequal distribution of economic welfare among them. As a consequence, we will get a misleading picture of the distribution of economic welfare of individuals in the population.

The family will be an appropriate recipient unit only if we can assume that the sharing of income is such that every member within the family derives exactly the same welfare. This assumption implies that the family head, who is the main earner in the family, enjoys the same economic welfare as the spouse and children, who may have either low or zero income. The validity of this assumption is again difficult to assess because of the limited knowledge of the internal structure of the family.[1] If, however, we can assume that the family members care about each other,[2] then it may be reasonable to say that the family will allocate its resources so that each family member enjoys the same level of economic welfare.

The question which then arises is whether there exists a welfare criterion that ensures that each family member derives exactly the same level of welfare. If each family member has the same utility function (which is an increasing function of income and is also concave), the utilitarian welfare function of the family,[3] when maximized subject to a given total family income, leads to a perfectly equal distribution of income between family members. Since each family member has exactly the same utility function, the perfectly equal distribution of income will, automatically, imply equal utility for each family member. If, however, each family member has a different utility function as a result of different needs, the maximization of utilitarian family welfare must give more income to a less needy person and, therefore, the resulting distribution of welfare between family members will be very uneven. Thus, the utilitarian criterion, although popular among economists, is not useful in achieving an egalitarian distribution of welfare among family members.

The equal distribution of welfare among family members with different needs can be achieved, however, if the family welfare function is based on Rawls's (1958) *max–min rule,* whereby the objective of the family is to maximize the welfare level of the worst-off individual within the family. For instance, consider a family consisting of two persons. If one person has a uniformly lower welfare function than the other, then the Rawls criterion would require that the person with the lower welfare function should have that much more income, which would make his or her actual level of welfare equal that of the other. And this procedure can be extended to families with three or more members. Note that this requirement cannot be satisfied if the person with lower welfare function remains more disadvantaged than the other despite having all the income of the family.[4]

2.3   The household

Since the surveys used in the present study are based on households instead of families, the difference between these two concepts should be explored. A household is defined as a group of people who live together as a single unit in the sense that they have common housekeeping arrangements; that is, they have some common provision for food and other essentials of living. Persons living in the same dwelling but having separate catering arrangements constitute separate households.[5] The family is a subset of the household, which may consist of a family plus other persons, or contain only unrelated persons. In the Australian Household Expenditure Surveys, families and households were the same in approximately two-thirds of the cases.

Kuznets argues that if the recipient is to be the decision unit with respect to long-term income plans and goals of its members and of the disposition of such incomes, household is not fully appropriate. Since all the members of a household may not have long-term ties, it will be difficult to assume that they pool their incomes and dispose of it in such a way that the economic welfare of each of them will be the same. For example, adult children sharing the parental home before marriage may contribute only a proportion of their income to the household expenditure. Their decisions in spending the remaining income depend on their long-term aspirations, which may be different from the other members of the household. Similarly, married children, lodgers, and families sharing accommodation are likely to see their present situation as a temporary one and may keep their income separate except for making a contribution toward household expenditure. Older parents living with a child's family may have a standard of living lower than that of other family members, even if they contribute all their income to the household budgeting.

For welfare purposes it seems that the family is a more appropriate recipient unit than the household. But if we collect information on families only, then all the households which are not families by definition have to be excluded from the analysis. This will violate Kuznets's inclusion criterion. An alternative will be to treat all the families contained in households as independent units as if they were living separately. To clarify it, consider the following example of a household consisting of

> Head of household;
> Wife of head;
> Daughter, 22 years;
> Father of head;
> Unrelated person.

Table 2.1. *Income recipients and total population of males and females in Australia 1973–4*

	Income recipients based on 1973–4 survey ('000)	Population estimates based on census ('000)	Income recipients as percentage of populants (%)
Males	4466.8	6778.5	65.9
Females	4265.6	6711.2	63.5
Persons	8732.4	13489.7	64.7

Source: The data on income recipients in column 1 are from *Income Distribution, 1973–1974 Part 1, Australian Bureau of Statistics,* No. 17.6; and, in column 2, are from *Estimated Age Distribution of the Population, States, and Territories of Australia,* June 1981 to June 1976, Australian Bureau of Statistics Catalogue No. 3201.0.

Using the definition of a family, this household consists of four families. This alternative implies that we must use four family units instead of one household unit in our analysis. The difficulty with this procedure is that these four families would have an entirely different standard of living if they had the same income but were living separately. These differences in living standards when the families live together or separately will almost certainly bias our conclusions about the actual disparity of economic welfare. This problem becomes more severe if any one of these families has zero or very low income; in which case such a family cannot survive on its own. But living together with other household members, it may even have a reasonable standard of living. Moreover, families living together in the same household cannot be assumed to be completely independent of each other. The income sharing which in fact takes place among families within same households should be taken into account. Thus, the families living in the same household cannot be treated as independent units.

2.4   Population coverage by different income-recipient units

Tables 2.1, 2.2, and 2.3 provide estimates of the population coverage by individual income recipients, full-time workers, and Australian taxpayers, respectively.

The estimates in column 1 of Table 2.1 relate to all income recipients 15 years of age and over, except members of the permanent armed forces, certain diplomatic personnel, patients in institutions such as hospitals and sanatoria, and inmates of jails. This table shows that the individual income

Table 2.2. *Age distribution of full-time workers as the percentage of all persons in Australia 1975*

	Males			Females		
Age	Full-time workers ('000)	All persons ('000)	Full-time workers as percentage of all persons	Full-time workers ('000)	All persons ('000)	Full-time workers as percentage of all persons
15–19	268.4	625.0	42.9	231.9	599.9	38.6
20–24	426.4	585.6	72.8	283.3	574.0	49.3
25–34	805.1	1067.5	75.4	254.1	1014.4	25.0
35–44	580.8	805.1	72.1	194.3	758.0	25.6
45–54	567.2	793.8	71.4	182.9	755.8	24.2
55–59	205.3	308.6	66.5	47.3	314.7	15.0
60 and over	163.1	779.5	20.9	27.3	993.1	2.7
Total	3016.3	4965.1	60.7	122.1	5009.9	24.4

Source: Figures in columns 3 and 6 are from *Estimated Age Distribution of the Population, States, and Territories of Australia,* June 1971 to June 1976, Australian Bureau of Statistics, Canberra Catalogue No. 3201.0; and those in columns 2 and 5 are from *Income Distribution* 1975, Australian Bureau of Statistics, Canberra.

recipients cover about 65 percent of the total Australian population. Among males, the percentage coverage is slightly higher than females. It should be noted that a large number of individual income recipients reported in the table are not primary earners and have incomes too low to be independent units. If we exclude such persons, the population coverage would be much lower.

Table 2.2 gives estimates of population coverage by full-time workers. It can be seen that male full-time workers cover 60.7 percent of the total male population, but for females this percentage is only 24.4. If we use full-time workers as income-recipient units, a large proportion of population has to be omitted from the analysis of income distribution. The full-time worker would be the appropriate income-recipient unit only if our main concern was with the way in which the income derived from production is distributed among the people engaged in production. Since our concern is with the welfare of the total population, it is important to select the income unit that covers the largest proportion of population.

Until the first household expenditure survey was carried out in 1966, income-tax statistics were the only source of data on size distribution of income in Australia (Lydal 1965). The use of income-tax statistics as a

Table 2.3. *Number of taxpayers and total population of
males and females in Australia – June 1971*

	Taxpayers ('000)	Population ('000)	% of taxpayers to population
Males	3588.8	6506.2	55.1
Females	1981.9	6431.0	30.8
Total	5570.7	12937.2	43.0

Source: Number of taxpayers are from *Taxation Statistics,* 1971–1972,
The Parliament of Australia 1973 – Parliamentary Paper No. 10. Popu-
lation figures are from *Estimated Age Distribution of the Population,
States, and Territories of Australia,* June 1971 to June 1976, Australian
Bureau of Statistics, Canberra, Catalogue No. 3201.0.

basis for size distribution of income raises a number of problems, which
have been discussed by Brown (1957). Here we wish to comment only on
the population coverage by taxpayers as contrasted with that for other
income recipients.

It can be seen from Table 2.3 that, in June 1971, the population coverage by all taxpayers was only 43 percent. The percentages for males and
females separately were 55.1 and 30.8, respectively. This low population
coverage by taxpayers makes the income-tax statistics unsuitable for analyzing the size distribution of income, at least from the welfare point of
view.

Table 2.4 shows that the population coverage by household units is
almost 93 percent and it is marginally higher for females than males. For
persons under 18 years, this percentage is as high as 98.1. Although we
would have liked to see a higher percentage of population coverage for
elderly persons aged 65 years and more, we consider the figure 85.4 to be
reasonable. If we use family as the basic income-recipient unit, the population coverage would be only 61 percent. It can, therefore, be concluded
that the household is superior to all other income-recipient units on the
basis of population coverage.

2.5   Differing needs of recipient units

The economic welfare of households is determined not only by their income but also by their needs as well. Two households enjoying the same
income are equally well off only if they have the same needs. Since households differ in size, age composition, and other characteristics, it is ex-

Table 2.4. *Comparison of population distribution according to age and sex as estimated from the Household Expenditure Survey, 1975–6 and the census*

	1975–6 survey ('000)	Estimated population from the census 1975–6 ('000)	Column 1 as the percentage of column 2
All persons	12852.8	13843.5	92.8
Males	6405.6	6946.3	92.2
Females	6447.2	6897.2	93.5
Persons under 18 years	4450.6	4537.4	98.1
18 and under 65 years	7362.3	8088.0	91.3
65 years and over	1039.9	1218.1	85.4

Source: Population figures in column 2 are from *Estimated Age Distribution of the Population, States, and Territories of Australia,* June 1971 to June 1976, Australian Bureau of Statistics, Canberra, Catalogue No. 3201.0.

pected that they will have differing needs. Clearly, then, the measurement of economic welfare should take into account the differing needs of the households.

The problem of assessing relative needs is indeed a very serious one. The needs of a person depend on several factors including health, age, sex, occupation, environment, tastes, and several other characteristics and it will, indeed, be a hopeless task to quantify all these factors. Moreover, for several of these factors quantification would require normative judgments on the part of the person attempting it, which could lead to unending controversies.

In order to assess the needs of one household relative to another, it has been a common practice to consider only a few quantifiable variables that affect the needs of a household. One such variable is household size. Clearly, a larger household has greater needs than a smaller one. It has, therefore, been suggested that per capita household income be used as a measure of economic welfare of the household.

Although per capita household income has been widely used as a basis of welfare comparisons between households, it has two serious drawbacks which must be pointed out. First, this procedure assumes that all persons within the household have exactly the same needs, irrespective of age and sex. It will be difficult to justify the assumption that both adults and children have the same needs. Therefore, per capita income as a measure of welfare would be biased in favor of households with children.

Secondly, the per capita measure overlooks the economies of scale that operate for many items of consumption. It assumes that a household of four persons needs twice as much income as a household of two persons in order that both the households enjoy the same standard of living, which clearly does not hold. The larger households can economize, for instance on buying and cooking in bulk or by sharing several of the household durable goods like washing machine, car, and even clothing and footwear. This measure will, therefore, tend to underestimate the true economic welfare of the large household.

In order to cope with these problems, attempts have been made to construct equivalent-income scales that would facilitate the comparison of households of different sizes and age composition.

The equivalent-income scale, which is also referred to as the *equivalent-adult scale,* measures the relative income required by families of different composition to maintain the same level of satisfaction. Such a scale is designed to answer questions of the type, What income level would make a family of husband, wife, and two children as well off as a family of husband and wife only with income of, say, $10,000 per year. In 1955, Prais and Houthakker introduced the concept of the specific consumer-unit scale, which measures the relative consumption expenditures on specific items of consumption required by different household-composition groups. Both scales may be called consumer-unit scales.

The problem of estimating equivalent-income scales (or consumer-unit scales) has been considered by several authors, and there are at least three approaches used for this purpose. Prais and Houthakker (1955) used a method based on the Engel curve, which attracted considerable attention.[6] They employed an iterative procedure to estimate the specific scales for food items using family budget data collected by the United Kingdom Ministry of Labour in 1938. Their method is, however, based on the assumption that if an estimate can be made of the income scale, it should be possible to obtain estimates of the specific scales. Forsyth (1960) continued the work of Prais and Houthakker and concluded that separate specific and income scales cannot be estimated from the cross-section data on expenditures alone. Singh and Nagar (1973) proposed a new iterative procedure that yields the estimates of both specific and income scales independently of any such restrictions and assumptions. Although their procedure provides numerical estimates of both scales, it suffers from "a crucial identification problem," as pointed out by Muellbauer (1975).[7]

In order to avoid the identification problem, it is necessary to have some restrictions on certain coefficients of the Engel curve.[8] For example, if one assumes that the income elasticity of a commodity is zero, or approximately so, then the specific scale can be estimated by regressing the consumption of that particular commodity on household consumption, ignoring entirely the effects of income. This procedure will, of course, be applicable only to necessities. It can be shown that if the income elasticity is positive, this method will tend to underestimate the scale, the degree of underestimation being proportional to the income elasticity for the commodity (Prais and Houthakker 1955: 133).

Another approach, which was suggested by Rothbarth (1943) and subsequently considered by Nicholson (1949) and Henderson (1949), is based on the assumption that the consumption of some standard commodities (such as tobacco), which are consumed only by adults, is unaffected by any variation in the number of children, so that the number of children affects the household expenditure on such commodities only via a general income effect. This approach, which depends heavily on the choice of the standard commodity, suffers from two serious drawbacks. First, the consumption-expenditure information generally available for the kind of commodities that can be used as "standard" commodities is highly unreliable. Second, the assumption that the children's coefficient in the Engel curve is zero may not hold true (the adults may be driven to drink or smoke because of the children, for example) (Prais and Houthakker 1955: 132).

Barten (1964) analyzed the family composition effect, using basic consumption theory. His model assumes that the family or household is the basic decision-making unit and has the utility function of the form[9]

$$u = u\left(\frac{q_1}{m_1}, \frac{q_2}{m_2}, \dots, \frac{q_n}{m_n}\right)$$

where q_i is the quantitity consumed of commodity i, m_i is a function of household composition that measures the effect of household composition on utility. Note that m_i is independent of the amounts of commodities consumed. Under the assumption of maximization behavior, the household utility function is maximized subject to the budget constraint

$$\sum_{i=1}^{n} p_i q_i = y$$

where p_i is the price of commodity i and y is the total household expenditure.

This maximization behavior conditional upon a given household composition yields the cost function

$$y = c(u, p_1 m_1, p_2 m_2, \dots, p_n m_n)$$

which is interpreted as the minimum income (or total expenditure) that will be required to buy u amount of utility at prices $p_1, p_2, \dots, p_n$ by a household with household composition parameters $m_1, m_2, \dots, m_n$. Suppose that for a standard household $m_i = 1$ for all i, the cost function of such a household then becomes

$$y^* = C(u, p_1, p_2, \ldots, p_n)$$

and, therefore, the equivalent income at constant prices of a household with composition parameters $m_1, m_2, \ldots, m_n$ relative to that of a standard household will be given by y/y^*, which converts the income of a nonstandard household into the equivalent income of a standard household while the two households remain at the same level of utility.

Barten's analysis of the household composition effect is intuitively appealing because it determines the equivalent income scale by explicitly comparing the utilities of households of different composition.[10] Prais and Houthakker, on the other hand, do not base their analysis on such utility comparisons, although there may exist a link between their model and the utility theory. Muellbauer (1974· 80) has in fact demonstrated that such a link indeed exists, and that the Prais–Houthakker model is a special case of the Barten model when the compensated price elasticities are all zero. Thus, the Prais–Houthakker model does not permit price substitution, which is a rather extreme requirement.

Like the Prais-Houthakker model, the Barten model also suffers from an identification problem that does not permit the estimation of family composition parameters (Muellbauer 1977). Kakwani (1977c), however, estimated the Barten model using Australian data by imposing an identifying restriction, which will be discussed in the next section.

2.6   Household-equivalence scales

In order to measure poverty in Australia, the Commission of Inquiry into Poverty headed by Professor Henderson used an equivalent-income scale that was produced in 1954 by the Budget Standard Service of New York. This scale is presented in Table 2.5 in the form of minimum cost of families of different size and composition. It is mentioned that the commission adopted the New York equivalent scale because of the "almost complete lack of material in Australia on which to base judgments of this kind" (Henderson, Harcourt, and Harper 1970).[11]

The Henderson scale is based on the cost of prescribed quantities of goods and services consumed in New York in October 1954. Therefore, it has been subjected to considerable criticism on the grounds that it is hardly relevant to the Australian lifestyle (see, for instance, Sebel 1976; Richardson 1979; Stanton 1980; Saunders 1980). Clearly, this scale is appropriate only if contemporary Australian lifestyles are similar to those of New York a generation ago, which, as Sebel (1976) points out, is too heroic an assumption. Even if the two lifestyles were exactly identical, the scale would be inappropriate because it is constructed on the basis of physical needs of individuals. The acceptability of such an approach

Table 2.5. *The Henderson equivalent-income scale based on the New York Survey*

Type of household	Minimum cost in Australia 1973	Scale
Single adult	33.40	1.0
Married couple	44.70	1.34
Couple plus 1 child	53.70	1.61
Couple plus 2 children	62.70	1.88
Couple plus 3 children	71.70	2.15
Couple plus 4 children	80.70	2.42
Couple plus 5 children	89.30	2.67
Couple plus 6 children	97.90	2.93
Couple plus 7 children	106.50	3.19
Single parent plus 1 child	42.90	1.28
Single parent plus 2 children	51.90	1.55
Single parent plus 3 children	60.90	1.82
Single parent plus 4 children	69.90	2.09
Single parent plus 5 children	78.90	2.36

Table 2.6. *Podder's equivalent-income scale*

Type of household	Equivalent-income scale
Family with household head only	.488
Household head and wife	1.000
Household head, wife, and 1 child	1.250
Head, wife, and 2 children	1.481
Head, wife, and 3 children	1.675
Head, wife, and 4 children	1.972
Head, wife, and 5 children	2.381
Head, wife, and 6 children	2.731

obviously depends on the criterion adopted for assessing the physical needs. It is also doubtful if all the families adopt the same criterion of assessing the needs of their members when they are allocating their resources. Such an approach also ignores the possibility of complementarity among the various nutritional elements (Prais and Houthakker 1955: 133).

The first attempt to estimate the equivalent-income scale for Australia was made by Podder (1971) using the Survey of Consumer Finances and Expenditures. His scale is presented in Table 2.6.

Note that the scale in the table is presented for eight different family compositions. All families that are of different composition from those mentioned in the table are excluded. In measuring the distribution of economic welfare, this scale is not helpful because it excludes the one-adult household with children as well as all the three-or-more-adult households with or without children. The proportion of such households is fairly large in Australia and their exclusion will certainly lead to biased estimates of the size distribution of economic welfare.

The estimation procedure adopted by Podder is based on the assumption that the level of welfare or the standard of living attained by a family is determined by percentage of income, or by total expenditure, spent on food. It implies that the households that spend the same proportion of total expenditure on food enjoy the same level of welfare. This assumption of equivalence is rather arbitrary, although Podder asserts that it has found wide acceptance. Friedman (1952) – whose reference is given by Podder to support his assertion – has, in fact, demonstrated that there is no logical defense for any such assumption. The choice of the food base or any similar expenditure component as the basis for determining equivalence indices is arbitrary and in fact comes very close to assuming the result.[12] It can be argued that the proportion of income spent on housing may be as good a measure of welfare but it leads to quite different equivalence scales.

It is generally believed that there exist economies of scale even on items such as food. There is also a common saying that two persons can live as cheaply as one person. But Podder's scale seems to suggest diseconomies of scale. From Table 2.6, it is seen that the cost of the one-member family is less than half of that of the family consisting of husband and wife only. The justification given by Podder – that the two-member family has to buy proportionally more food to entertain guests than the one-member family – is not convincing. Food is only one item of expenditure and Australian families spend, on average, only 20 percent of their total expenditure on food. Although the information on the food expenditure that is used for entertaining guests is not available, it is unlikely to be more than a negligible fraction of the total expenditure. This item of expenditure cannot, therefore, offset the effect of the other expenditures, which are known to display economies of scale. Thus, the diseconomies of scale as shown by Podder's equivalent scale are more likely to be due to the faulty procedure adopted by him.

Kakwani (1977a) estimated the equivalent-income scale using the same data as Podder but a different method. The scale is presented in Table 2.7. Kakwani's equivalent scale differs considerably from both the Henderson scale and the Podder scale. His scale shows considerable economies of

Table 2.7. *Kakwani's equivalent-income scales*

Type of household	Income scale at different level of per capita income			
	≤ $1220	$2000	$3000	$4000
Family with household head only	.438	.444	.447	.449
Head and wife	.725	.729	.731	.732
Head, wife, and 1 child	.877	.879	.880	.880
Head, wife, and 2 children	1.000	1.000	1.000	1.000
Head, wife, and 3 children	1.075	1.072	1.070	1.070
Head, wife, and 4 children	1.114	1.102	1.096	1.092
Head, wife, and 5 children	1.151	1.128	1.116	1.110
Head, wife, and 6 children	1.187	1.144	1.122	1.111

scale in household size, which are not apparent in either the Henderson or the Podder scales. An important feature of Kakwani's scale is that it varies with the level of income (i.e., rich and poor households have different income scales). It is, however, seen from Table 2.7 that the variation in income scale is negligible over a wide range of per capita income. Kakwani concluded from this table that if the size of a family is more than four, additional children with a given income do not diminish the living standard as much as if the family existed at a lower level of income. If, however, the family size is less than four, the reduction in the standard of living with additional children will be higher than at a higher level of income.

The estimation procedure adopted by Kakwani was based on the Barten model, which requires the specification of a utility function in order to compare the welfare levels of households of different composition. He assumed the Stone–Geary type of utility function (Geary 1950-1; Stone 1954).

$$u = \sum_{i=1}^{n} \beta_i \log\left(\frac{q_i}{m_i} + \gamma_i\right)$$

where q_i is the quantity consumed of the ith commodity, m_i is a function of household composition, and β_i and γ_i are the parameters that satisfy the restrictions

$$0 < \beta_i < 1, \quad \gamma_i \geq 0 \quad \text{and} \quad \sum_{i=1}^{n} \beta_i = 1$$

This utility function leads to the linear expenditure system, modified for the household composition:

$$p_i q_i = p_i \gamma_i m_i + \beta\left(y - \sum_{i=1}^{n} p_i \gamma_i m_i\right) \tag{2.1}$$

where p_i is the price of the ith commodity and $y = \sum_{i=1}^{n} p_i q_i$ is the total expenditure.

In order to identify the household composition parameters, Kakwani introduced the aggregated consumption function

$$y = \alpha x + (1 - \alpha)\left(\sum_{i=1}^{n} p_i \gamma_i m_i\right) \tag{2.2}$$

where x is the household income and α is the marginal propensity to consume. The system of $(n+1)$ equations given in (2.1) and (2.2) leads to Lluch's (1973) extended linear expenditure system, when all the parameters m_i are unity.

The utility function used by Kakwani can be considered to be highly restrictive because it is additive separable and rules out the possibility of having complementary goods. It can, therefore, be estimated only for a broad category of consumption goods such as food, clothing, housing, and so forth. This may result in the biased estimates of the equivalent-income scale and the magnitude of this bias cannot be assessed.

Another criticism of Kakwani's procedure has been made by Muellbauer (1977), who considers the identifying restrictions to be rather implausible. He does not give any reason for such a criticism. The only other plausible method of identifying the model using constant price data is to estimate it with two years of expenditure data (Howe 1974). Since the comparable data for two years are not available in Australia, such a procedure cannot be applied.

The equivalent-income scales estimated by Kakwani and Podder are based on the Survey of Consumer Finances and Expenditures 1966–8 carried out jointly by the Macquarie and Queensland Universities. These data are now fifteen years old and may be of questionable relevance to present Australian lifestyles. Moreover, the doubts expressed about these data by several writers (see, for instance, Richardson 1979: 32) surely diminish confidence in these scales.

The alternative source of data – namely, the Household Expenditure Survey of 1975–6 – is more reliable, but these data are available only in grouped form, which makes it difficult to estimate the equivalent-income scales using sophisticated procedures. In fact, several alternative estimation procedures were applied on these data by the present author, but no sensible income scale emerged from these attempts, mainly due to the use of grouped data. The only solution to these uncertainties seems to be to estimate the distribution of economic welfare using several alternative income scales.

2.7 Summary of conclusions

The main purpose of this chapter has been to assess the suitability of various income-recipient units that have been used for the purpose of analyzing the size distribution of income. Following Kuznets, three criteria are identified as being relevant to the choice of income-recipient unit: identifiability, independence, and inclusivity. The individual as the recipient-income unit is judged to be deficient by all three criteria. For welfare purposes, the family is considered to be the most appropriate income-recipient unit, mainly because of the high degree of income sharing occurring within the family. But it is argued that the family will be an appropriate recipient unit only if we can assume that the sharing of income is such that every member within the family derives exactly the same welfare. The validity of this assumption is difficult to assess because of the limited knowledge available on the internal structure of the family.

On the basis of independence (or income-sharing) criterion, the household is even less appropriate than the family. But it was demonstrated that the household is superior to all income-recipient units on the basis of Kuznets's inclusive criterion, which states that the income-recipient units must include total population. This criterion is particularly relevant since we are interested in economic welfare of the total population.

The income-recipient unit used in the present study is the household. Since households differ in size and composition, they need a different amount of available income to reach the same level of economic welfare. To cope with this problem, the common practice is to construct equivalent-income scales that would facilitate the comparison of different kinds of households. It is concluded that the various methods that have been used to estimate equivalence in Australia raise difficulties of one kind or another and the only solution to this seems to be to estimate the distribution of economic welfare using several alternative equivalent-income scales.

CHAPTER 3

Income concept in the analysis of income distribution

In order to analyze the distribution of personal economic welfare, we need to measure the economic welfare of each individual in the society. Although money income is widely used to measure economic welfare, it has many serious drawbacks.

An ideal welfare measure should incorporate all factors that contribute to welfare directly as well as indirectly. Income, as conventionally measured, excludes many factors that contribute to economic welfare. The Household Expenditure Surveys which form the basis of most income-distribution studies do not provide enough information to take into account all the relevant factors affecting economic welfare. Moreover, as Sen (1973b) points out, "to aspire for an ideal welfare measure which takes into account all the factors is a hopeless task because typical concepts of welfare tend to be extremely complicated when made operational." But even if all the factors cannot be incorporated, due to data limitations, it is important to specify them and evaluate their effects on the distribution of economic welfare.

In this chapter, we advocate a broader definition of income than that employed in the Household Expenditure Surveys, and discuss a number of items that should be incorporated into the definition of income. In each case, attempts are made to gain some idea of the effects of including each item into the income definition on income inequality. In discussing these issues, reference is made, when possible, to Australian data, and indication given of the bias that is introduced, in the Australian case, through using a less than ideal income concept.

3.1 Problems associated with the income concept used in the present study

The income concept adopted for both Household Expenditure Surveys (1974–5 and 1975–6) was gross weekly income from all sources current at the time of the interview. In most cases income information was obtained on a last-pay-period basis and converted to a weekly income equivalent. In the case of income from investment and self-employment, it was usually only possible to obtain details related to the previous 12-month period or to the last financial year. This figure was then converted to a weekly equivalent.

The total household income was derived by adding the weekly income equivalent of all household members aged 15 years and over. If any income was reported for persons under the age of 15 years, this was included with the income of the head of the household. The following are the components of income:[1] wages and salaries, business income, government cash benefits, and other income.

Wages and salaries include all gross earnings (including overtime, bonus, commission, tips, etc.) received by each member of the household from the main and additional jobs. However, if the amount received was not considered by the respondent to be the usual pay, the amount usually received was recorded. The value of any goods and services provided free and on a regular basis by a person's employer was also included under wages and salaries.

Business income, the income of a person working in his or her business or in a partnership, was his or her share of trading profit after deduction of business expenses but before deduction of personal tax. Such income included any wages and income-in-kind taken from the business. If the business made a loss over the period, a negative figure was recorded.

Government cash benefits include regular income received from Australia or state government social security and other benefits. The following are the components of government cash benefits:

a. *pensions:* there are six types of pensions – age, invalid, widow, war service, and war widow;
b. *family allowance,* which includes child and student–child endowment;
c. *unemployment benefits*;
d. *sickness and special benefits*;
e. *other government benefits,* which include government home-saving grants, maternity allowances, T.B. allowance, state pensions, and other miscellaneous benefits.

Other income includes the following items:

a. income from investment, bank, and other interests, dividends, royalties, and rent;
b. educational grants and scholarships received in cash;
c. any benefits received from an overseas government;
d. income received for professional advice outside the normal job situation;
e. earnings from odd jobs;

f. superannuation, worker's compensation, alimony or mainte-
    nance allowances, and any other allowances regularly received.

In general, income was regarded as all receipts that were received regularly and were of a recurring nature. Certain receipts were not considered
to conform to this criterion and were therefore treated as being outside
the scope of the survey. Such receipts included the following:

a. maturity payments on insurance policies, superannuation, etc.
    These lump-sum receipts were regarded as maturity of an invest-
    ment rather than income;
b. lump-sum compensation for injury, legal damages received;
c   windfall gains (e.g., such as gambling and lottery winnings);
d. lump-sum inheritances and other lump-sum receipts;
e. withdrawals from savings, loans obtained, loan repayments re-
    ceived;
f. profit from buying and selling of stocks and shares, unless as a
    business;
g. value of home-produced goods where the economic activity of
    the household was not associated with the production of these
    goods; and
h. monetary gifts if not regularly received, and the value of non-
    monetary gifts from another household.

Although the income concept used in the present study is fairly comprehensive, it is still deficient from the welfare point of view. For instance, it excludes several in-kind transfers, imputed rent, capital gains,
home production, voluntary leisure, and net worth or wealth. Exclusion
of these factors can substantially alter the true economic status of the individuals living in the household and, as a consequence, biased estimates
of the distribution of economic welfare may emerge. The available data
are insufficient to determine the size of these biases. We shall discuss the
direction of some of these biases using Australian data in the subsequent
sections.

3.2   Value of home production

The Australian Bureau of Statistics (ABS) income definition does not include the value of home production, the contribution of which to the
household's economic welfare can be substantial. For instance, with increasing home ownership in Australia, many people do a considerable
amount of renovation work on their houses. This activity increases the

value of the house which, if sold after renovation, can lead to considerable monetary gains. Even if the householder does not sell the house after renovation, it still amounts to an increased standard of living of the household members. Since, on average, the nonrenter (the owners') households are likely to have higher income than the renter households, the failure to include the value of home renovation activity in the income is likely to understate the level of inequality. On the other hand, among the nonrenter households, it is likely that only the poorer households engage in renovation activities. Hence, omitting renovation activity could have the effect of overstating the level of inequality. It is, therefore, difficult to assess the exact nature of this bias because of the limited information.

Next, we consider the contribution of a large number of married women who are not in the labor force. These women are engaged in various productive activities at home, the product of which is not included in the conventional definition of income. The effect of including the intrafamily services of the household in the income definition has been investigated by Kuznets (1976), who makes the observation that "it is likely that in the poorer families [i.e., those in which the income of the husband does not meet the family's requirements] the greater engagement of the wife in money or other types of income-earning activity limits the intrafamily services of making a home and providing training and guidance to the children, limits them more than in the case of the more affluent families." Thus, he concludes that "while the engagement of the wife in money-earning activities outside the family may narrow the differentials in family income shown in the conventional size distribution of income, the inclusion of the intrafamily activities of the wife in a wider income concept would tend to widen the differentials in the size distribution of this wider income total."

Examining 1971 U.S. data on 4,840 households, Benus and Morgan (1975) arrived at a conclusion similar to that of Kuznets's. They concluded that the addition of the spouse's labor income (the income earned outside the household) to that of the head's labor income reduces the inequality of labor income by approximately 2 percent.

Table 3.1, relating to the Australian Income Distribution 1973–4, gives the percentage of married couples with wife not working and the mean earned income of wives, classified according to the earned income of husbands. Several interesting findings emerge from this table.

First, Kuznets's hypothesis that the lower income of the husband induces the wife to engage in money-earning activities in order to meet the family's requirements seems to be supported by the Australian data only for incomes from $2,000 per annum upwards. The hypothesis is refuted

Table 3.1. *Married couple income units: husbands' earned income and wives' earned income in Australia 1973-4*

Earned income of husband ($)	Percentage of married couples with wife not working to the total number of married couples	Mean earned income of the working wife ($)
under 1,000	84.7	400
1,000-2,000	47.0	1,000
2,000-3,000	40.8	1,500
3,000-4,000	42.0	1,620
4,000-5,000	44.7	1,560
5,000-6,000	44.4	1,710
6,000-7,000	47.0	1,650
7,000-8,000	46.7	1,710
8,000-9,000	48.6	1,810
9,000-10,000	53.2	1,470
10,000-11,000	49.0	1,840
11,000-13,000	53.8	1,720
13,000 and over	52.6	2,510
Total	51.1	1,550

Source: Income Distribution 1973-1974, Part 3, Australian Bureau of Statistics, Canberra, Catalogue No. 6504.0.

at low incomes of the husband, probably due to the fact that these low-income groups consist of a large proportion of retired married couples who do not participate in the work force because of their age.

Secondly, the table reveals that the wife's income is positively correlated with the husband's income (i.e., the higher the husband's income, the higher the wife's income is likely to be). This observation suggests that the addition of the wife's labor income to that of the head's labor income may increase rather than decrease the inequality of the family labor income, although a more definitive statement on this issue will require a further investigation of the data.[2]

Table 3.2 gives the percentage of married couples with wife not working to the total number of married couples by the total income of the married couples. Total income includes earned as well as unearned income such as government social service benefits, superannuation or annuity, interest, dividends, rents, etc. This table reveals that the labor force participation of wives increases monotonically with the total family income in the range from $2,000 to $15,000. For income $15,000 upwards, there is a small decrease in the labor force participation of wives. This suggests

Table 3.2. *Married couple income units: total income and percentage of married couples with wife not in workforce in Australia 1973–4*

Total income ($)	Percentage of married couples with wife not working to the total number of married couples
Under 2,000	77.8
2,000–4,000	85.8
4,000–6,000	74.1
6,000–7,000	60.2
7,000–8,000	48.5
8,000–9,000	39.2
9,000–10,000	30.8
10,000–12,000	25.9
12,000–15,000	23.8
15,000–21,000	27.7
21,000 and over	30.4
Total	51.1

Source: Income Distribution 1973–1974, Part 3, Australian Bureau of Statistics, Canberra, Catalogue No. 6504.0.

that the differentials in the size distribution of money income may be narrowed by giving monetary benefits to the families in which the wife is not engaged in money-earning activities. These monetary benefits to the families can be given in either of two forms: higher tax rebates for the dependent wife, or direct payments to the families, like child or family allowance. However, greater disaggregation of data is necessary in order to assess the influence of age and the household composition on the wife's decision to enter the work force. Furthermore, such payments are likely to influence the decision regarding labor force participation of wives and, therefore, the net impact of such a policy on income inequality must be evaluated.

The nonmoney income among the rural households engaged in farming is relatively more important than among the total population. The consumption of home-produced output by farmers can be substantial and should be taken into account. Since the average income of rural households is generally lower than that of nonrural households, the effect of excluding this kind of income will be to overstate income inequality. In Australia, only 8.7 percent of the total number of households live in rural areas, and the percentage of households engaged in farming will be even lower. Therefore, the magnitude of overstatement of income inequality due to exclusion of home-produced consumption of the farm households is likely to be small.

3.3   Fringe benefits

It has become customary for many employers to provide several fringe benefits in the form of free or subsidized goods and services to their employees. Many of these benefits are not marketable, and therefore their value to individuals cannot be easily assessed. Nevertheless, these benefits do contribute additional economic welfare and should be incorporated in the analysis of economic welfare.

The effect of fringe benefits on income distribution has been analyzed by Lampman (1954) as

The new age of welfare capitalism has given rise to a host of business-supplied substitutes for immediate money income, including various types of deferred payment plans which spread income over a longer period, paid vacations, recreational opportunities, health and old-age security benefits, and numerous other guarantees and services. The tax laws have encouraged the increasing of personal expense accounts rather than increasing salaries or "take home" compensation whenever discretion is allowed. While some of these benefits are distributed in such a way as to narrow inequalities among those receiving them, the fact that they are not distributed throughout the whole population, and exclude most of the very low income groups, would indicate that their full counting would increase rather than decrease the inequality of income when income is defined as consumer-power income.

Although it is difficult, if not impossible, to assess accurately the value of fringe benefits to the individual, the ABS income definition includes the value of any goods and services provided free on a regular basis by a person's employer. In the income questionnaire, the following two questions were asked to gather information on benefits in kind:

1. Do you regularly receive any of these goods and services free from your employer?
2. In the last 2 weeks what was the value of these regular goods and services?

> Food
> Clothing
> Fuel
> Use of vehicle
> Other transport
> Housing
> Other (specify)

The valuation of these free goods and services supplied by the employer was largely done by the respondents, with only minimal checks. This could have resulted in an underestimation of the actual benefits received by the individual. The goods and services provided at highly subsidized prices were not included as benefits. Similarly, benefits in the form of old-age security and paid holiday under the guise of business trips were not assessed for inclusion of the income definition. Since these business holidays and handsome old-age security benefits are the privileges generally given to highly paid executives, their full counting would increase the income inequality.

3.4 Imputed rent

The ABS income definition does not include the imputed rent of an owner-occupied house. Although owning a house does not provide a cash income, the services of the dwelling nevertheless do have a value equivalent to the net income that could be obtained by letting the dwelling to a tenant.

There are several difficulties associated with the imputation of net income from an owner-occupied dwelling. The main difficulty is the estimation of cost incurred in owning a house. For instance, if there are two persons A and B living in two different houses of the same rental value, A may be paying considerably higher mortgage repayments than B because of the difference in their repayment period, or the time when they bought the house, or even for the difference in interest rates. Even if A and B have exactly the same money income and enjoy the same quality of house, A will have less money to spend on other goods and services than B. Since the interest on housing loans is on a reducible basis, A pays less interest than B in the current period, which means that the net imputed income adjusted for the interest cost for A will be higher than for B, despite the fact that A has less resources to command than B in the current period. This suggests that if our purpose is to measure the distribution of economic welfare in the current period, the imputed rent should be adjusted for the actual mortgage payment rather than the actual interest paid on the housing loan. But then it can be argued that every individual generally saves a proportion of current income for future security and the non-interest component of the mortgage payment clearly adds to equity in the house and is, in effect, savings. Consequently, the owner can afford to spend a larger proportion of current income on consumption, which gives a higher current economic welfare. It is, therefore, important to separate the current cost of maintaining the house from the saving component in the total expenditure on owner-occupied dwelling, which is not easy to do. This problem is further complicated by the fact that houses depreciate or appreciate at different rates.

The estimation of the rental value of the owner-occupied dwelling itself presents several conceptual difficulties. One method is to leave the imputation of the rent to the discretion of the owner. But it is known that the owners have their personal biases about the value of their houses and may provide exaggerated estimates of the true rental value. In the United Kingdom, the rateable value of the property is used to provide the estimate of the national rental equivalent to the dwelling occupied.[3] This procedure may be appropriate for the United Kingdom where the rateable value is assessed on the basis of the letting value. In Australia, however, the rates are assessed on the basis of the unimproved capital value of the property, and therefore the rateable value has little or no relationship to the letting value.

Home ownership depends on the age of the family head as well as on income. Therefore, a relatively high proportion of owners is found among high-income groups and those low-income groups where there is a high concentration of older families. Hence, it is not possible to evaluate on a priori grounds whether inclusion of imputed rent will narrow or widen the income differences among households. Since there is a high concentration of older people in the lower-income brackets, the exclusion of imputed rent will lead to an overestimation of the poverty level.

Podder (1978) has studied the effect of imputed rent on the Australian income distribution based on the Survey of Consumer Finances and Expenditures 1966–8. He observed that when rent from owner-occupied houses is added to actual money income of the household, the distribution of income becomes more equal. From this he concludes that there is a more than proportionate ownership of homes among the families belonging to lower-income ranges, which has important implications for welfare provision. This conclusion, however, does not seem to be supported by the Household Expenditure Survey 1974–5 data. This can be seen from Table 3.3, which shows that the home ownership increases monotonically with household income; hence, Podder's conclusion of disproportionately high home ownership among the families in the lower income ranges is refuted by the 1974–5 survey data.[4]

The imputed rent used in Podder's study is not net of all costs. It does not make allowance for such costs as depreciation of the house, interest paid on loans, and land and water rates. This would clearly exaggerate the incomes of home owners.

3.5   Capital gains

Stark (1972) defines capital gains as the net increase in the value of personal wealth during a year, irrespective of whether it has been realized or

Table 3.3. *Percentage of house ownership by income classes in capital cities of Australia 1974-5*

Weekly income ($)	Sydney	Melbourne	Brisbane	Adelaide	Perth	Hobart	Canberra	All capital cities
0–40	55.2	66.0	68.4	71.4	51.3	62.8	24.6	61.3
40–80	72.5	71.6	73.0	75.3	57.0	69.3	55.0	70.6
80–110	49.7	63.5	57.4	61.7	58.0	56.5	55.6	57.3
110–140	59.2	58.9	60.6	69.4	65.5	64.9	56.9	61.2
140–170	63.4	66.1	78.0	67.9	69.5	68.7	49.2	67.0
170–200	63.7	73.0	75.3	76.7	71.3	76.1	63.0	70.3
200–230	66.4	72.6	74.3	75.0	70.2	75.3	44.0	70.1
230–260	68.5	69.5	69.6	73.9	77.1	78.7	42.2	69.9
260–300	66.1	70.8	77.1	80.8	74.9	76.1	61.5	70.8
300–340	73.3	71.7	69.5	85.5	86.1	83.8	63.1	74.4
340–400	77.9	82.3	79.6	88.2	87.5	78.9	58.6	80.6
400 and over	80.3	84.6	86.0	89.1	91.6	82.2	74.1	83.4
Total	66.0	70.5	71.9	74.7	69.9	71.5	57.6	69.2

not. Most of the studies on income distribution do not include accrued capital gains. Nevertheless, there is a strong case for including them in the personal income because they enhance the purchasing power of an individual. They can be spent or saved like any other type of income. Hence, their inclusion in the income definition will lead to an improved measure of economic welfare. The Australian tax structure is such that it provides considerable incentive to taxpayers to convert money income into capital gains. Although the actual magnitude of these gains is not known, it appears that they are a significant factor in the distribution pattern of economic welfare.

Since the capital gains are likely to be confined to upper-income recipients, their effect on income distribution will be to increase the income inequality. The general validity of this conclusion is difficult to establish because of the limited number of studies undertaken in this area. Nevertheless, the available evidence tends to support this conclusion. On the basis of the United States data, McElroy (1970) concluded that in most years when there were accrued gains, the expanded concept of income (i.e., personal income plus capital gains) was more unequally distributed than personal income. This conclusion, however, was not supported during the year 1962 when there were large amounts of accrued losses.

A more detailed study on the U.S. data was conducted by Bhatia (1974) who allocated the aggregate estimates of capital gains on corporate stock, nonfarm real estate, and farm assets, according to value of assets owned by income units in various income groups. He arrived at a conclusion similar to McElroy (1970); when gains are included in income, the income inequality is increased during the 1960–4 period but the reverse was true for the year 1962. However, these studies are based on some restrictive assumptions which tend to bias the results toward equality.

Stark (1972), working with United Kingdom data, concluded that capital gains are a significant factor in the distribution pattern and would appear to reduce considerably the number of low incomes and increase the number of high incomes. He points out that it is not possible to draw a more detailed conclusion because of data imperfections. Even this broad conclusion may be rendered useless by virtue of numerous sources of error in any estimate of capital gains.

The existing data base in Australia does not permit a detailed study of capital gains as they affect income distribution. The direct estimation of this effect is not possible because the ABS income definition does not include any form of capital gains. The second-best solution to this problem is to assume that such gains will be distributed more or less like the assets on which they accrue. If we had a breakdown of all assets holdings of households, it would have been possible to form some judgment about the income distribution of accrued gains. Unfortunately, the ABS Household Expenditure Surveys were not designed to collect any information on the asset holdings of the households. The Survey of Consumer Finances and Expenditures 1966–8 does provide the information on assets and liabilities of households along with their incomes and expenditures, which will be used here to examine the effect of capital gains on income distribution.

Table 3.4 presents the percentage and cumulative percentage shares of income and assets accruing to different household income ranges. The table shows that among low-income families, the percentage share of assets is higher than the percentage share of income. For instance, the income share of the families with income less than $4,000 per year is 43.3 percent whereas the percentage share of assets is 47.3. If we assume that the capital gains are proportional to assets, these figures clearly show that the inclusion of capital gains in income will make the resulting distribution more equal. This conclusion casts doubt on the common belief that the capital gains are confined to upper-income families and, therefore, they tend to make the distribution more unequal. Note that the average assets holding of a household increases with the household income, but this condition alone does not imply that the capital gains will have an unequalizing effect on income distribution. They will have an unequalizing

Table 3.4. *Percentage and cumulative percentage shares of income and assets according to household income ranges*

Income ranges ($)	Percentage share of income	Cumulative percentage share of income	Percentage share of assets	Cumulative percentage share of assets
≤ 1,000	1.0	1.0	3.4	3.4
1,000–1,999	4.7	5.7	7.4	10.8
2,000–2,999	14.9	20.6	15.0	25.8
3,000–3,999	22.7	43.3	21.5	47.3
4,000–4,999	19.3	62.6	17.5	64.8
5,000–5,999	13.0	75.6	11.4	76.2
6,000–6,999	7.6	83.2	6.7	82.9
7,000–7,999	5.0	88.2	4.3	87.2
8,000–8,999	2.9	91.1	3.8	91.0
9,000–10,999	3.8	94.9	4.2	95.2
11,000 and over	5.1	100.0	4.8	100.0
Total	100.0	–	100.0	–

Source: The Survey of Consumer Finances and Expenditures 1966–8.

effect only if the cumulative share of assets is lower than the cumulative share of income for all income classes, which is not suggested by the data in Table 3.4.

Our conclusion that the capital gains have equalizing effects on income distribution depends on the assumption that the capital gains are roughly proportional to the asset holdings. This assumption may not be valid because the rates of capital appreciation are different for different types of assets. Moreover, given that Australia, by and large, does not have a capital gains tax, it would appear that higher-income recipients have a greater tax incentive to convert other (taxable) income into capital gains, whilst at the same time being most able to arrange their financial affairs this way. This suggests the opposite conclusion to the one reached, although the picture is further complicated when home ownership is included. In order to establish the validity of our conclusion, it is necessary to analyze more detailed disaggregated data on asset holdings. Unfortunately, lack of appropriate data makes it impossible for us to investigate this problem adequately.

3.6   Household net-worth adjustment

The economic welfare of households depends not only on income but on wealth as well. Many aged people, for example, receive quite low income and yet they may have sufficient wealth to fall back on in case of emergency. If current income alone is used as a measure of economic welfare, it would imply that consumption financed out of capital rather than income yields zero welfare (Taussig 1973: 32). Since wealth adds to the potential consumption of individuals, it may be said that both income and wealth together determine the economic position of a household to which individuals belong.

The word *wealth* is used in the sense of *net worth,* net worth being defined as the total value of assets held by the household minus total debt. One way of combining income and wealth is to add net worth, positive or negative, to current-year income and use the resulting variable as a measure of economic welfare (David 1959). This approach seems extreme because households are unwilling to dispose of their entire assets to finance consumption in the current period unless there is extreme emergency. A less extreme alternative, as Taussig (1973) points out, would impute some potential consumption value to positive net worth, with the exact amount of the contribution of net worth to economic welfare depending on assumptions about the extent to which families dispose of their assets to finance consumption over their lifetime.

In order to impute the potential consumption value of the current net worth, we may assume that a household liquidates and consumes all its net worth (or repays all its net liabilities) evenly over its expected lifetime. This procedure was followed by Weisbrod and Hansen (1968), whose measure of economic welfare is defined as the sum of (1) current annual household income and (2) the annual lifetime annuity value of current household net worth:

$$X_t^* = X_t + W_t A_n$$

where X_t is the current income minus interest earned on the net worth W_t and X_t^* is interpreted as the income obtainable in period t if the household's net worth were converted so as to yield an equal lifetime income flow.

The annuity value, $W_t A_n$, is clearly an increasing function of W_t (i.e., the greater the net worth of the household, the greater will be the net worth component of the welfare measure). To determine A_n, which is a function of the life expectancy of the household as denoted by n and the interest rate r, suppose that a household liquidates Y amount every year for the current consumption; then the present discounted value of these lifetime amounts must be equal to its current net worth. Thus

$$W_t = Y \sum_{i=1}^{n} \frac{1}{(1+r)^i}$$

which on summation gives the annual lifetime annuity value of the current net worth as

$$Y = W_t A_n$$

where

$$A_n = \frac{r(1+r)^n}{(1+r)^n - 1}$$

We can now discuss how the annuity value varies with the life expectancy and the interest rate. For any given interest rate, A_n decreases monotonically with n (i.e., the shorter the life expectancy, the greater is the annuity value). This suggests that older people, who tend to have a higher proportion of net worth to current income and lower life expectancies, will be most affected by inclusion of net worth in the income definition.

As n approaches infinity, A_n approaches r, the annuity value will be equal to rW_t, which is the interest income and will be included in the current income. Hence, if the net worth was annuitized over an infinite period, the economic welfare of a household would then be determined by its current income. Alternatively, if the net worth is annuitized entirely during the current period, A_n will be equal to $(1+r)$, which gives

$$X_t^* = X_t + rW_t + W_t$$

where $(X_t + rW_t)$ is the current income of the household. Thus the economic position of a household is determined by the sum of current income and the net worth.

Because of the limited data available on wealth in Australia, it is not possible to provide a detailed investigation of the net-worth effect on income distribution. We will, however, make some observations on this issue on the basis of the Survey of Consumer Finances and Expenditures 1966–8 data.[5]

Table 3.5 presents the percentage and cumulative percentage shares of income and net worth according to income ranges. The last column in the table is the ratio of net worth to income. If we assume that the net worth is annuitized entirely during the current period, the distribution of net worth across the income ranges will enable us to draw inferences about the relationship between the distributions of income and income–net-worth combination measure.

Overseas evidence suggests that the additional net worth component has an unequalizing effect on income distribution (see, for instance, Weisbrod and Hansen 1968, and Taussig 1973). This inference will be valid if the cumulative shares of net worth are smaller than the corresponding cumulative shares of income for all income ranges, which is not supported by

Table 3.5. *Percentage and cumulative percentage shares of income and net worth according to income ranges*

Income ranges	Percentage share of income	Cumulative percentage share of income	Percentage of net worth	Cumulative percentage share of net worth	Ratio of net worth to income
≤1,000	1.0	1.0	3.8	3.8	11.2
1,000–1,999	4.7	5.7	8.2	12.0	5.5
2,000–2,999	14.9	20.6	14.7	26.7	3.1
3,000–3,999	22.7	43.3	20.0	46.7	2.7
4,000–4,999	19.3	62.6	16.7	63.4	2.7
5,000–5,999	13.0	75.6	11.2	74.6	2.7
6,000–6,999	7.6	83.2	6.9	81.5	2.8
7,000–7,999	5.0	88.2	4.6	86.1	2.8
8,000–8,999	2.9	91.1	4.3	90.4	4.5
9,000–10,999	3.8	94.9	4.4	94.8	3.7
11,000 and over	5.1	100.0	5.2	100.0	3.2
Total	100.0	–	100.0	–	–

Data Source: Survey of Consumer Finances and Expenditures, 1966–8.

the data given in the table. In fact, the cumulative shares of net worth are higher than the corresponding income shares, up to the income level of $5,000; beyond this income level, shares are almost equal. These data, therefore, tend to suggest that the inclusion of net worth in income equalizes the income distribution. This conclusion is further supported by the ratio of net worth to income, which seems to be decreasing with income up to the income level of $8,000, and then it increases slightly.

Table 3.6 presents the calculations of annual lifetime annuity value of current net worth. The interest rate is assumed to be 6 percent. The net worth is annuitized over n years of life expectancies assigned to the household according to the formula $n = 75 - a$, where a is the age of the household head. This assumption may be questioned on two accounts: (1) all individuals expect to live exactly 75 years and (2) no account is taken of the life expectancies of household members other than the head.

Taussig (1973) defined the

$$n = n_m + \tfrac{2}{3}(n_f - n_m)$$

where n_m and n_f are the life expectancies of a male and female of a given age, respectively. This procedure assumes that the full annuity is received while the husband is alive but that a surviving wife would receive only two-thirds of the full amount during her widowhood. He did not take

Table 3.6. *Annual lifetime annuity value of current net worth as percentage of current disposable income: disposable income range by age of household head*

Disposable income range (%)	Age				
	Under 30	30–39	40–49	50–59	60 and over
≤1,000	19	65	47	130	157
1,000–1,999	6	19	22	36	99
2,000–2,999	9	15	23	34	64
3,000–3,999	8	13	21	32	77
4,000–4,999	9	16	20	28	53
5,000–5,999	6	15	19	31	51
6,000–6,999	5	15	17	32	72
7,000–7,999	7	14	20	27	72
8,000–8,999	–	39	18	29	120
9,000–10,999	3	16	33	27	51
11,000 and over	4	9	28	35	49
Total	8	15	21	31	75
Mean disposable income	3490	3914	4347	4158	2608
Mean disposable income adjusted for the annuity value	3769	4501	5260	5447	4564
Percentage households in each age group	11.7	23.1	25.1	17.8	22.3

Data Source: Survey of Consumer Finances and Expenditures, 1966–8.

account of the life expectancies of the other members of the family. We did not consider it worthwhile to adopt this procedure because of the arbitrariness involved in weighing the life expectancies of different family members.

A number of interesting findings emerge from the numerical results given in Table 3.6. First, the annuity value as a percentage of disposable income increases monotonically with the age of the household head. This percentage for the age group 60 and over is as high as 75, against only 8 for the age group under 30. These differences are wide and have significant implications for the extent of poverty and overall inequality. The age group 60 and over, although the poorest on the basis of disposable income, appears to be enjoying relatively high economic welfare. Looking at the figures in the last column, it is clear that the extent of poverty will be much less among the older households when net worth is taken into account than is the case when current income alone is the criterion for measuring poverty. This conclusion is similar to the one arrived at by Weisbrod and Hansen (1968) for the United States.

Secondly, the income–net-worth approach seems to narrow the income differences between the age groups, which will have the effect of reducing the overall welfare inequality. Within each income range, the ratio of the annuity value to disposable income is highest in the lowest income range and it decreases somewhat as income increases. It can, therefore, be concluded that the net-worth adjustment tends to narrow the differentials in the size distribution of this wider income combination.

Thirdly, if we arrange the households according to disposable income adjusted for net worth, it seems that the maximum number of households falling into the bottom end of the distribution will be from the under-30 years age group.

It can be concluded that the inclusion of the net-worth components of income has considerable impact on poverty as well as overall inequality. Its effect on the economic position of the aged is particularly striking. Although the income–net-worth measure of welfare has many useful attributes, it is not free of faults. One major problem with this measure is that it does not distinguish between the marketable and nonmarketable wealth. If the wealth is not easily marketable, the ability of wealth holdings to satisfy current consumption needs is less than that of income. Unless the distinction is made between the two types of wealth, the income–net-worth measure will lead to misleading conclusions about the extent of poverty and income inequality. Projector and Weiss (1969) have criticized the measure on the grounds that the constant annuity calculation implies that other sources of well-being will tend to remain stable over time. Since families of different ages are likely to have different expectations for the future, particularly for earned incomes, a more complicated allocation model needs to be considered.

3.7   The time period of measurement

The next conceptual problem that concerns us in this chapter is the time period over which income should be measured. This is a highly controversial issue and has attracted the attention of several economists.[6] In the short run, income is likely to have substantial fluctuations which are averaged out in the longer run. Friedman (1957) emphasized the importance of long-run and short-run variations, by introducing the concept of *permanent income* as against the measured (or observed) income, the difference between them being the transitory income.

The observed income, measured over a short period, is subject to transitory fluctuations and, therefore, shows greater inequality than the permanent income. The influence of the transitory component diminishes, however, as the time period over which income is measured is enlarged.

Thus, the shorter the time period of measurement, the greater will be the income inequality.

The choice of measurement period depends on the particular aspect of economic welfare in which a researcher is most interested. Taussig (1976) clarifies the various aspects of economic welfare as

For the ordinary individuals, say, suffering from hunger, the relevant accounting period is a single day; for the starving graduate student, however, the period stretches far beyond the current year past the completion of the dissertation. The calendar year is long enough to average out most temporary fluctuations in income and short enough to reflect pressing consumption needs in a world in which capital markets do not accept future earnings as collateral for loans.

According to Taussig (1976), annual income does give a reasonable measure of economic welfare. But some economists may argue that the current-year income grossly neglects the long-run aspects of the distribution of economic resources. The lifetime income averages out all the short-term transitory fluctuations and may provide a better indicator of the actual economic position of an individual than his or her current income. The shortcomings of the current income become particularly pronounced when we consider the fact that many individuals forgo their current earnings to invest in human capital, in order to have higher income in the future. If our concern is with measuring poverty, the lifetime income is not very relevant, but it has many attractions when we are measuring the degree of overall inequality. Several difficulties arise in the measurement of lifetime income distribution. The main difficulty lies in obtaining the required data to measure the lifetime income. The collection of income data on a lifetime basis through the survey method is *not* feasible on two accounts: (1) people do not know how long they will live and what will be their future income and (2) the information on income obtained during the past several years will be based on memory, which will obviously be unreliable to the extent of being useless.[7] Nordhaus (1973) has, however, suggested a model to analyze the distribution of lifetime income that does not require lifetime income streams of individuals. He demonstrates that on the assumption that individuals maximize utility, which is a function of lifetime consumption, the level of economic welfare is approximately equal to the lifetime wealth divided by the life expectancy. In order to make this model operational, we need joint observations on income, wealth, and life expectancy for each income unit. Such data do exist in Australia for a single year, 1966-7 (Survey of Consumer Finances and Expenditure), but it is outside the scope of the present study to estimate the model. Moreover, this model is based on highly restrictive assumptions which make the model unattractive to estimate.

Another serious problem with the lifetime income concept is concerned with the income-recipient unit. If the household is the income-recipient unit, we do not know how the size and composition of the household will change over the lifetime. In this connection, Taussig (1976) points out that the incomes of individuals vary more or less systematically over their lifetime but their living arrangements change less systematically. The data problems involved in following large samples of individuals through their lifetimes, and estimating their changing equivalent incomes or consumption over time as members of different family or household groupings, are beyond the capability of available research resources.

In a conference on income distribution (an overview of which is given by Danziger 1976), Thurow and others who opposed the lifetime income concept asserted that only individuals have lifetime incomes and that an acceptance of the lifetime income concept implies a rejection of consuming units or families as the recipient unit. It has been argued in the previous chapter that if the purpose is to measure the distribution of economic welfare, the individual is the most inappropriate income unit. Thus, the lifetime income concept, although it averages out short-term income fluctuations, creates serious problems in choosing the most appropriate income-recipient unit, which are not easy to resolve.

A still more serious problem with the lifetime income concept concerns the uncertainty and capital-market imperfections that make it difficult for individuals to borrow against their future incomes. If individuals cannot average their incomes over time by borrowing or lending, the disutility suffered during the low-income periods may be far greater than the utility enjoyed during the high-income periods. Kuznets (1974) makes this point forcefully as

When the average income per person or per consumer is low, the negative impact of short-term failures may be far greater than the positive impact of quantitatively compensating short-term successes. Moreover, short-term breakdowns have often been the cause of major economic and social displacements that have had major long-term effects. Concentration on long-term or lifetime incomes may lead to a neglect of short-term income differentials and changes that may have lasting effects.

Despite several conceptual problems involved in the measurement of lifetime income, it is relevant to know the relationship between the current and lifetime income distributions. Since the lifetime income concept is closely related to the age of the household head, we may make some deductions about the lifetime income distribution and its relationship with the current income distribution from the degree of inequality within age groups. This was attempted by Paglin (1975), who showed remarkably large effects of age-adjusting the data on the measurement of earnings inequality in the United States.

There has been considerable controversy over whether the Paglin–Gini index is an appropriate alternative to the conventional Gini index (e.g., see Danziger and Smolensky 1977; Johnson 1977; Kurien 1977; Minarek 1977; and Nelson 1977). It has been implied that the Paglin–Gini index does not measure what Paglin said it measured.[8] It is futile to review this debate here. Nevertheless, it will be useful to make the following point, not mentioned in the debate (Kakwani 1984c).

Since the Paglin–Gini index is defined as the difference between the Lorenz–Gini and the Age–Gini indexes, fewer age groups will imply a smaller value for the Paglin–Gini index. This is a significant result, and it casts doubt on Paglin's conclusion that the Gini ratio overstates income concentration in the United States by a third. If the U.S. population were divided into a sufficiently large number of age groups, Paglin's measure would show considerably smaller deviation from the Gini ratio. Alternatively, if the population were divided into only two age groups, the Gini ratio could overstate income inequality by more than 90 percent. Clearly, Paglin's measure is arbitrary and depends on the number of age groups as well as on how these age groups are formed.

3.8 Voluntary leisure

The total household income consists of the earned income of the head, spouse, and other adult household members, and the unearned income from capital and transfers. The earned-income component depends on the hourly earnings received by the adult members of the household and the number of hours each adult within the household works in the labor market.

If the time period over which income is measured is short – say, one year or less – then the hourly earnings of individuals (which are largely determined by their education, skills, knowledge, and experience) can be assumed to be fixed. The variation in the earned income of a household would then be explained by the amount of time adults in the household devote to paid market work. Work hours, which are a measure of productive effort, vary from household to household. How the differing work hours of households affect the distribution of economic welfare will now be discussed. Time not spent in market work may be called leisure which, depending on its nature, can give enjoyment to individuals. If people have the choice between the amount of leisure time they consume and the income they earn, then the marginal utility of their leisure time must be equal to the marginal utility of their income. This suggests that leisure (which, depending on its nature, is voluntary) gives enjoyment to individuals, and its value must be included in the economic welfare of the household. If, however, the leisure is involuntary and is forced upon the people because of unemployment, disability, or unwanted retirement, then it may even lead to unhappiness or disutility. Thus, it is necesary to know two things in order to include the use of leisure time in a measure of economic welfare: (1) the relationship between income and leisure and (2) the extent to which leisure is a desired and appreciated commodity or an involuntary and unwanted necessity (Morgan, et al. 1962: 327).

In a study based on U.S. data on hourly earnings of spending-unit heads, Morgan et al. (1962) observed a negative relationship between the head's wage rate and the number of hours worked, which implies that the higher wage rate induces the head to enjoy the higher level of voluntary leisure. But, on the other hand, wives tend to work more when the other family income is higher. The net effect of these two opposite tendencies tends to give positive correlation between the family income and the combined work hours of the family members. This positive correlation suggests that families with higher (lower) income tend to enjoy lower (higher) level of leisure. Thus, the inclusion of leisure in a welfare measure would tend to narrow the differentials in the size distribution of welfare, although a more definite statement on this issue would require a further investigation of the techniques as well as data.

In order to arrive at an indicator of economic welfare that takes into account the value of leisure, Becker (1965) has introduced the concept of *full-time income,* which is defined as the maximum potential money income a consumer unit could enjoy if all available time is devoted to producing money income. The essential feature of this measure is that the leisure enjoyed by an individual is valued at his or her market wage rate, which implies that each individual is in equilibrium in the allocation of his or her time between market work and leisure. This is a strong assumption because it values even the involuntary leisure, which is forced upon individuals, at the same rate as their wages.

Despite this strong assumption, Taussig (1973) has attempted to estimate the value of full income for families, using the 1966 U.S. Bureau of Census data. He produced two sets of estimates of full income, of which the first set includes the value of the leisure of wives and of heads of families, but not the leisure of other adults in the family unit. Regarding the value of leisure, he made two alternative assumptions:

1. Each hour of leisure is valued for both husband and wife at $1.60 an hour (which was the minimum federal wage rate in the United States during 1966).

2. Each hour of leisure is valued according to the individual's own actual or imputed market wage rate.

A comparison of these two alternative distributions showed that the full income obtained by valuing both spouses' leisure at a common $1.60 an hour is somewhat more equally distributed than the corresponding money income, but the distribution of full income computed under the second assumption, which takes into account the differences in individual wage rates in valuing leisure, is not very different from the distribution of money income.

The second set of estimates of full income that includes the value of leisure of all the adults within the household also leads to a conclusion similar to that of the first set, that the distributions of money income and full income are not strikingly dissimilar.

It should be pointed out that the small differences in the inequality of money income and full income were not merely due to the fact that the value of leisure time was small relative to the value of money income. As a matter of fact, the mean value of spouses' leisure was observed to be 21.3 percent of mean money income, after tax; the mean value of heads' leisure was 33.2 percent of mean money income; and the mean value of all other adults' leisure was about 9.9 percent of mean money income.

An alternative measure of economic welfare that takes into account the value of leisure has been proposed by Morgan (1968), who assumes that the economic welfare of families can be approximated by a rectangular hyperbola between the consumption of market goods and leisure. His measure is, therefore, given by the algebraic product of the family's money income adjusted for the family's needs and leisure enjoyed per adult within the family.

This measure, although it appears intuitively appealing, has been criticized by Taussig (1973) on two counts. First, it treats every hour of leisure as if it were of equal value regardless of the wage rate of an individual and, therefore, it is at variance with the static theory of consumer choice, which suggests strongly that the opportunity cost of leisure is greater for an individual with a relatively high rate of transformation between time and market goods than for an individual with a relatively low rate. Second, Morgan's measure is not compatible with the standard assumption of diminishing marginal productivity. For instance, doubling income while holding leisure constant results in a doubling of economic welfare, which is inconsistent with the diminishing marginal productivity postulate. On the basis of these two criticisms, Taussig (1973) concluded that Morgan's technique is an inappropriate means of including the value of leisure in a comprehensive measure of economic welfare.

It is interesting to note that Morgan and Smith (1969), using Morgan's technique, concluded that the distribution of money income and the comprehensive welfare measure that takes account of the value of leisure are almost similar. This finding is identical to that of Taussig (1973), despite the fact that the two studies differ greatly both in data source and in the procedure used.

Since the Australian Household Expenditure Surveys do not provide information on the work hours of the household members, it would not be possible to investigate the effect of the value of leisure on the distribution of economic welfare. However, we have requested the Australian Bureau of Statistics to collect the information on work hours in the survey to be conducted during the financial year 1981–2. Until such information is available, this issue cannot be pursued further.

3.9   Some comments

In order to analyze the distribution of economic welfare, we need to employ a broader income concept than that employed in the Household Expenditure Surveys. In this chapter, an attempt has been made to determine the direction of the bias that is introduced, in the Australian case, through using a less-than-ideal income concept.

It can be seen that the conclusions emerging from this chapter are heavily loaded with qualifications. Nonetheless, they provide considerable insight into the issues of income distribution and poverty in Australia. The main contribution of this chapter has been to highlight several difficulties of a conceptual nature that arise in analyzing the distribution of economic welfare.

PART II

Measures of income inequality, redistribution, and equity

CHAPTER 4

On the measurement of income inequality

In Chapter 3, "Income Concept in the Analysis of Income Distribution," we discussed various issues concerning the measurement of economic welfare of individuals or households. It was argued that the income concept should include all the factors that contribute to welfare directly as well as indirectly. Once such an income concept is decided, after taking into account the practical difficulties of the measurability of several factors, an adjustment should be made to allow for diversity of needs based on household size and composition. An index of economic welfare so obtained measures the potential consumption per equivalent household unit over a specified period of time and will be referred to as *income* in this chapter.

The main focus of this chapter will be the problem of measurement of inequality of income distributions. Inequality measures have been devised to answer a wide range of questions: How great is income inequality and which way is it moving? What are the effects of current government programs on income inequality? Which of the taxes or government transfers lead to greater or less equality in the distribution?

An inequality measure is supposed to display the deviation of a given distribution of income from the "ideal distribution." What do economists have to say about the ideal distribution of income? It is argued that welfare economics does not provide much help in resolving this issue. Therefore, the perfectly equal distribution of income is assumed to be the ideal distribution, even though its justification from the welfare point of view is based on highly restrictive assumptions.

It is now widely recognized that alternative inequality measures lead to conflicting rankings of income distributions (see, for instance, Yntema 1933; Ranadive 1965; Weisskoff 1970; and Atkinson 1970). This raises the difficult problem of choice among these measures and has aroused much discussion in the literature about the social welfare function that should be adopted in making a choice among the measures or the types of social welfare function implied by various measures of income inequality (see Atkinson 1970; Dasgupta, Sen, and Starrett 1973; Newbery 1970; Sheshinski 1972b; and Rothschild and Stiglitz 1973). In this chapter, after a brief review of various inequality measures, a new class of measures has been derived which will be extensively used in analyzing the income distribution in the subsequent chapters.

4.1   Equity and welfare economics

As has already been pointed out, an inequality measure reflects the deviation of a given distribution of income from the "ideal" distribution. All the existing measures of inequality represent deviation from perfect equality. The question then arises whether there exists a reasonable welfare criterion that justifies the perfect equality of income as the ultimate bliss.

In an attempt to answer this question, let us first consider the Pareto optimality criterion, which implies that *a change is a Pareto improvement if it makes no one worse off and someone better off.* A situation will be Pareto optimal if there exists no change that is a Pareto improvement. It means that an economy can be optimal in this sense, even when there is a considerable disparity between the rich and the poor, as long as nobody can be made better off without making anybody else worse off. Obviously, any given income distribution with fixed total income is Pareto optimal, because any redistribution of income that makes someone better off is going to make someone else worse off. Thus, the Pareto optimality criterion says nothing as to what is the most desirable income distribution.

Alternatively, one may attempt to arrive at an ideal distribution from the individual preferences. This analysis requires that each individual ranks all possible alternative states of the society. The question then arises whether these individual orderings can be combined together to arrive at a collective social ordering. Arrow (1963) has shown with his impossibility theorem that a set of extremely mild-looking but desirable conditions completely eliminates the possibility of arriving at a collective-decision rule. Sen (1973) has presented a theorem that rules out all decision rules that express any distributional judgment whatsoever. Thus, the theory of collective choice based on individual preferences only fails to provide a framework for distributional discussion without any use of interpersonal comparisons (Sen 1973: 23).

Next we consider the utilitarian approach, which is most widely used for policy making. With this approach, the objective of a society is to maximize the sum of individual utilities. It can be demonstrated that the maximization of utilitarian social welfare from a given total income leads to an egalitarian distribution only if everyone has the same utility function with diminishing marginal utility. If each individual has a different utility function, the maximization of social welfare may lead to a highly unequal distribution of income (Sen 1972, 1973a).

Since people's tastes do differ, the assumption of identical utility function for each person cannot be defended. When the utility functions differ, the utilitarian approach may well be in direct conflict with the equalization of utilities. Consider, for example, two individuals. *A* is an unfortunate individual who, because of his disability, enjoys uniformly less utility than *B*. It can be seen that the utilitarian approach, which equates the marginal utilities of the two individuals in order to arrive at an optimum distribution, gives more income to *B* than to *A* because of his superior enjoyment power. This example demonstrates that a utilitarian approach can lead to a highly inegalitarian distribution of utilities. The utilitarian approach, which developed an egalitarian reputation, is in fact far from egalitarian. Sen (1973a) has rightly called it "a blunt approach to measuring and judging different extents of inequality." In search of an ideal distribution of income, he has explored several welfare criteria, including the ones discussed here, and concluded that "for the problem of inequality evaluation, the royal roads of welfare economics do look a trifle bleak."

4.2   The Lorenz curve and social welfare

The Lorenz curve is widely used to represent and analyze the size distribution of income and wealth. It is defined as the relationship between the cumulative proportion of income units and the cumulative proportion of income received when units are arranged in ascending order of their income.

The Lorenz curve is represented by a function $L(p)$, which is interpreted as the fraction of total income received by the lowest pth fraction of income units. It satisfies the following conditions (Kakwani 1980a):

a. if $p = 0$, $L(p) = 0$

b. if $p = 1$, $L(p) = 1$

c. $L'(p) = \dfrac{x}{\mu} \geq 0$ and $L''(p) = \dfrac{1}{\mu f(x)} > 0$

d. $L(p) \leq p$ (4.1)

where income x of a unit is a random variable with the probability density function $f(x)$ with mean μ, and $L'(p)$ and $L''(p)$ are the first and second derivatives of $L(p)$ with respect to p, respectively.

These conditions imply that for income $x \geq 0$ for all income units, the Lorenz curve is represented in a unit square (Figure 4.1). The ordinate and abscissa of the curve are $L(p)$ and p, respectively. Condition (c) further implies that the slope of the Lorenz curve is positive and increases monotonically; in other words, the curve is convex to the p-axis. From

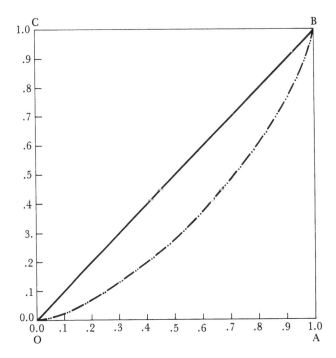

Figure 4.1   The Lorenz curve.

this it follows that $L(p) \leq p$. The straight line represented by the equation, $L(p) = p$, is called the egalitarian line.

In Figure 4.1, the egalitarian line is the diagonal OB through the origin of the unit square. The Lorenz curve lies below this line. If the curve coincides with the egalitarian line, it means that each unit receives the same income, which is the case of perfect equality of incomes. In the case of perfect inequality of incomes, the Lorenz curve coincides with OA and AB, which implies that all the income is received by only one unit.

Because the Lorenz curve displays the deviation of each individual from perfect equality, it captures, in a sense, the essence of inequality. The nearer the Lorenz curve is to the egalitarian line, the more equal will be the distribution of income. Consequently, the Lorenz curve could be used as a criterion for ranking income distributions. However, the ranking provided by the curve is only partial. When the Lorenz curve of one distribution is strictly inside that of another, it can be safely concluded that the first distribution is more equal than the second. But when two Lorenz curves intersect, neither distribution can be said to be more equal than the other. This partial ranking need not, however, be considered a weakness of the Lorenz curve. In fact, Sen (1973a) criticized complete ranking on the grounds that "the concept of inequality has different facets which may point in different directions, and sometimes a total ranking cannot be expected to emerge." The concept of inequality is, therefore, essentially a question of partial ranking and the Lorenz curve is consistent with such a notion of inequality.

We now turn to the welfare interpretation of the Lorenz curve. Atkinson (1970) proved a theorem that shows that if social welfare is the sum of the individual utilities and every individual has an identical utility function that is concave, the ranking of distributions according to the Lorenz curve criterion is identical to the ranking implied by the social welfare function, provided the distributions have the same mean income and their Lorenz curves do not intersect. This indeed is a remarkable theorem in the sense that one can judge between the distributions without knowing the form of the utility function, except that it is increasing and concave. If the Lorenz curves do intersect, however, two utility functions that will rank the distributions differently can always be found.

Atkinson's theorem relies on the assumption that the social welfare function is equal to the sum of individual utilities, and that every individual has the same utility function. These assumptions have been criticized by Dasgupta et al. (1973) as well as by Rothschild and Stiglitz (1973), who have demonstrated that the result is, in fact, more general and would hold for any symmetric welfare function that is quasiconcave.

Despite the fact that the Lorenz curve provides only a partial ranking of the distributions, it is a powerful device to judge the distributions from the welfare point of view, provided the distributions have the same mean income. If the distributions have different means, however, the Lorenz curve criterion may fail to provide a welfare ranking of the distributions. Consider an example of two distributions X and Y, which have means μ_x and μ_y, respectively. If X has the higher Lorenz curve than Y, then it can be unambiguously inferred that if $\mu_x \geq \mu_y$, X is a better distribution than Y. On the other hand, if $\mu_x < \mu_y$, the Lorenz curve alone does not allow us to make any normative statement about the two distributions.

The Lorenz curve makes the distributional judgments independently of the size of income, which, as Sen (1973a) points out, "will make sense only if the relative ordering of welfare levels of distributions were strictly neutral to the operation of multiplying everybody's income by a given number." This is rather an extreme requirement because social welfare depends on both the size and the distribution of income. Sen, recognizing this limitation, concluded that "the problem of extending the Lorenz ordering to cases of variable mean income is quite a serious one, and this –

naturally enough – restricts severely the usefulness of this approach." He argued that in order to make Lorenz curve comparisons of income distribution with different mean income one would have to bring in some symmetry axiom for income, which may not be particularly justifiable.

Working independently on extensions of the Lorenz partial ordering, Shorrocks (1983) and Kakwani (1984b) arrived at a criterion that would rank any two distributions with different mean incomes without requiring a symmetry axiom for income. The new ranking criterion developed by them is given by $L(\mu, p)$, which is the product of the mean income μ and the Lorenz curve $L(p)$, whereas the Lorenz ranking is based only on $L(p)$. Ranking the distributions according to $L(\mu, p)$ will be identical to the Lorenz ranking if the distributions have the same mean income. This criterion of ranking can be justified from the welfare point of view in terms of several alternative classes of social welfare functions.

The following implications emerging from this new criterion are discussed in Kakwani (1984a).

1. If the two distributions have the same Lorenz curve, the distribution with larger mean income will be welfare-superior.
2. Even if the Lorenz curves of two distributions intersect, it may still be possible to infer that one distribution is welfare-superior to another. For example, consider the two distributions

   X: $(2, 3, 5, 6)$

   Y: $(1, 4, 4, 5)$,

   the Lorenz curves of which intersect; but the above criterion implies that the distribution X is welfare-superior to the distribution Y.
3. Even if one distribution has a higher Lorenz curve than another at all points, it may still be welfare-inferior. Consider the two distributions

   X: $(3, 3, 5, 13)$

   Y: $(2, 4, 4, 4)$,

   where X has a lower Lorenz curve than Y but still is welfare-superior according to the above criterion.

These implications suggest that the Lorenz ranking when applied to cases of differing mean incomes may not be very useful in making distributional judgments from the welfare point of view. Despite these limitations the Lorenz curve is a powerful device to measure relative inequality. In the present study, the measurement of relative inequality is important because it enables one to make distinctions between the equity and efficiency aspects of social welfare.

Income shares of deciles or quintiles are frequently used to describe income inequality and can be readily obtained from the Lorenz curve. These measures provide a useful description of distributions and will be extensively used in the present study to analyze the distribution and redistribution of income in Australia.

4.3   The Gini index and its variants

Whereas the Lorenz curve provides only a partial ordering of distributions, measures of inequality have been devised to provide complete orderings. If $x_1 < x_2 < \cdots < x_n$ is an ordered income distribution among n persons denoted by a vector

$$\mathbf{x} = (x_1, x_2, ..., x_n),$$

the inequality measure $\theta(\mathbf{x}, n)$ is defined as a unique function of $x_1, x_2, ..., x_n$ and n, satisfying certain desirable properties. If the function $\theta(\mathbf{x}, n)$ is homogeneous of degree zero in incomes, the measure is said to be mean independent. This requirement implies that the value of inequality remains unchanged if each income is altered by the same proportion. Such measures are called the relative or rightist measures of inequality.[1] Alternatively, Kolm (1976) has proposed the absolute or leftist measures of inequality which do not show any change in inequality when each income is increased or decreased by the same amount. There is still a third kind of measure, called centrist measures, again suggested by Kolm (1976), which satisfies Dalton's (1920) principle of equiproportional additions to income (i.e., an equiproportional increase in all incomes must increase the inequality). An argument against the leftist and centrist measures is that the inequality of income can be diminished or increased simply by calculating all incomes in cents instead of in dollars. Therefore, "if we study variation of inequality over time in an inflationary country," as Kolm pointed out, "we must call x_i the real incomes discounted for inflation; or if we make international comparisons of inequality, we must use the correct exchange rates." This need not be done if we use the studies on relative or so-called rightist measures of inequality. The present study is confined to relative measures only.

Of all the relative measures, the Gini index is the most widely used. The index is equal to one minus twice the area under the Lorenz curve.

Since the Gini index is a linear function of income levels, the group welfare function implied by it is not strictly concave. This property has come under attack recently. Dasgupta, Sen, and Starrett (1973), as well as Rothschild and Stiglitz (1973), demonstrated that there exists no strictly quasiconcave welfare function that would give the same ranking of the distributions as the Gini index would give. Sen (1973a: 34), however, does not consider this criticism particularly serious: "The implied group welfare function may not be strictly concave but it is concave all right, and furthermore any transfer from the poor to the rich or vice versa is strictly recorded in the Gini measure in the appropriate direction." In fact, non-strict quasiconcavity of incomes is a useful attribute of a measure because it allows one to analyze the contribution of each of the various factor incomes to the inequality of total income (see Section 6.3).

A general class of inequality measures that are linear in income levels may be defined as

$$\theta = A(n) \sum_{i=1}^{n} g_i v_i(\mathbf{x})$$

where $A(n)$ is a function of n only and $g_i = (\mu - x_i)/\mu$ is the proportional income short-fall of the ith individual and $v_i(\mathbf{x})$ is the weight attached to his or her income short-fall given the income distribution $\mathbf{x}$ with mean income μ. It should be understood that $v_i(\mathbf{x})$ has been defined as a function of the whole income-distribution vector $\mathbf{x}$ and not of x_i alone, which implies a more general social welfare function than the one that is additive-separable. An additive-separable welfare function is obtained by adding up the individual welfare components which are independent of the welfare (or income) of others. If the concept of inequality is based on the relative deprivation as defined by Runciman (1966),[2] then the assumption of additive separability will obviously be too restrictive.

Sen (1974) proposed to capture the relative deprivation aspect of inequality by making the weights $v_i(\mathbf{x})$ to depend on the ranking of all individuals.[3] The lower a person is on the welfare scale, the greater the sense of deprivation with respect to others in the society. Therefore, according to Sen's (1974) rank-order axiom, the weight $v_i(\mathbf{x})$ on the income short-fall of person i depends on the number of people compared to whom i is relatively deprived. Kakwani (1980a), on the other hand, proposed an axiom that makes the ith person's sense of relative deprivation depend on the actual income enjoyed by those who are at least as rich as person i. In another contribution in connection with the derivation of welfare measures, Kakwani (1981a) suggested capturing the relative deprivation by combining both the factors, viz., the actual income enjoyed by those who are richer, and the number of such persons who enjoy these incomes. It can be demonstrated that all these characterizations of the relative deprivation lead to the same measure of inequality, the well-known Gini index.

A generalization of Sen's rank-order axiom may be introduced as

$$v_i(\mathbf{x}) = (n+1-i)^k$$

which makes the weight $v_i(\mathbf{x})$ on the income short-fall of person i equal to the kth power of the number of persons who are at least as well off as person i. This generalization was proposed by Kakwani (1980a) in connection with the derivation of a class of poverty measures, where he considered the income ranking of the poor only, whereas here it relates to the income ranking of the whole population. This leads to a class of inequality measures

$$G(k) = \frac{(n-1)}{n[\phi_n(k)-n]} \frac{1}{\mu} \sum_{i=1}^{n} (\mu-x_i)(n+1-i)^k$$

where $\phi_n(k) = \sum_{i=1}^{n} i^k$, which will be referred to as the generalized Gini index.[4]

Substituting $k = 1$ and using the fact that $\phi_n(1) = n(n+1)/2$, $G(k)$ is reduced to

$$G = 1 + \frac{1}{n} - \frac{2}{\mu n^2} \sum_{i=1}^{n} (n+1-i)x_i$$

which is a well-known Gini index. Thus, the Gini index is a particular member of the generalized Gini index when $k = 1$.

The recent literature on income inequality provides a considerable discussion of the relative sensitivity to transfers at different income levels (see Atkinson 1970; Sen 1973a; and Kolm 1976). If the society is particularly averse to inequality among its members, the inequality measure must give maximum weight to the poorest member and the weight should decrease with the level of income. The Gini index attaches more weight to transfers near the mode of the distribution than at the tails. It is not clear whether such weighting is desirable.

The relative sensitivity of the generalized Gini index depends on the value of k. If $k = 0$, $G(k)$ is zero for all income distributions, implying an inequality-neutral attitude of the society. It can be demonstrated that the larger the value of k, the more and more weight is attached to the lower end of the distribution, and less weight to transfer at the top. The value of k should be chosen according to the society's preference for the sensitivity of the measure to an income transfer at different income positions.

4.4   Additive-separable inequality measures: a brief review

With the exception of the Gini index (now the generalized Gini index), all the measures proposed in the literature take the form of an additive function of incomes or income shares. Of all these measures, the relative mean deviation proposed by Bresciani-Turroni in 1910 and rediscovered by Schutz (1951) and Kuznets (1957) is widely mentioned.[5] If the population is divided into two groups, (a) those who receive less than or equal to the mean income and (b) those who receive more than the mean income, then the relative mean deviation represents the percentage of total income that should be transferred from the second group to the first so that both groups have exactly the same mean income. This definition of the relative mean deviation reveals that the measure is completely insensitive to transfers of income among individuals on one side of the mean. If a poor person is made poorer by transferring income from him to someone richer, the measure may remain completely insensitive. This feature casts the relative mean deviation in an unattractive light.

The coefficient of variation as a measure of dispersion, suggested by Pearson, is defined as the ratio of the standard deviation of the distribution and the mean income. It can be demonstrated that this measure is equally sensitive to transfers at all levels of income (Kakwani 1980a). Sen (1973a) criticized the measure because of this property. Although he agreed that our intuitive ideas of inequality are relatively vague, he expressed preference for the measures that attach greater importance to income transfers at the lower end of the distribution. One such measure is the standard deviation of the income power or the logarithm of income. The main drawback with this measure is that any transfer of income from rich to poor at income levels greater than ge (g being the geometric mean of the distribution and e the well-known mathematical constant) would increase the inequality rather than decrease it. As Kakwani (1980a) points out, that may constitute a strong objection to this inequality measure.

Another measure that attached greater importance to income transfer at the lower end of the distribution is the one proposed recently by Kakwani (1980a). It is given by

$$L = \frac{l - \sqrt{2}}{(2 - \sqrt{2})}$$

where

$$l = \frac{1}{\mu} \sum_{i=1}^{n} \sqrt{\mu^2 + x_i^2}$$

is the length of the Lorenz curve. The new measure is sensitive to changes at the low tail, making it particularly applicable to problems such as measuring the intensity of poverty. Moreover, the measure is closely associated with the Lorenz curve. The computation of this measure from grouped data may be somewhat more difficult than the other measures.

Finally, we must mention Theil (1967), whose two inequality measures are based on the notion of entropy in information theory. These measures have gained popularity because of their decomposability property.[6] If a population is divided into a number of groups according to certain socioeconomic characteristics of individuals, these measures can be decomposed into *between-group* and *within-group* income inequality. Shorrocks

(1980) has derived the entire class of measures that are decomposable under relatively weak restrictions on the form of the index. The subclass of mean independent measures is given by the single-parameter generalized-entropy family

$$I_c = \frac{1}{nc(c-1)} \sum_{i=1}^{n} [\lambda_i^c - 1], \qquad c \neq 0, 1$$

$$I_0 = \frac{1}{n} \sum_{i=1}^{n} \log(1/\lambda_i)$$

$$I_1 = \frac{1}{n} \sum_{i=1}^{n} \lambda_i \log \lambda_i$$

where $\lambda_i = x_i/\mu$. I_0 and I_1 are two inequality measures proposed by Theil (1967). The square of the coefficient of variation is a member of this class when $c = 2$. The parameter c can be interpreted as a measure of the degree of equality-aversion. As c decreases, the index becomes more sensitive to transfers at the lower end of the distribution and less weight is attached to transfers at the top; when $c = 2$, the index attaches the same weight to transfers at all income levels.[7]

Suppose the population is divided into k mutually exclusive groups. Then the decomposition equations for the generalized-entropy measures are[8]

$$I_c = \sum_{j=1}^{k} f_j \lambda_j^c I_c^j + \frac{1}{c(c-1)} \sum_{j=1}^{k} f_j [\lambda_j^c - 1], \qquad c \neq 0, 1$$

$$I_0 = \sum_{j=1}^{k} f_j I_0^j + \sum_{j=1}^{k} f_j \log(1/\lambda_j)$$

$$I_1 = \sum_{j=1}^{k} \lambda_j f_j I_1^j + \sum_{k=1}^{k} \lambda_j f_j \log \lambda_j$$

The first term in these equations (the within-group component) is a simple weighted sum of the subgroup inequality values. The second term is the between-group component, measuring the inequality contribution due solely to differences in the group means.

It should be mentioned that the nonadditive measures discussed in the previous section are generally not decomposable in the above sense and have been criticized on this account by Mookherjee and Shorrocks (1982). They point out that the nondecomposability of these measures may lead to perverse results. For instance, an increase in inequality in one group, keeping group means and population sizes constant, may result in decrease in inequality in the population overall, or – putting it differently – inequality can go up in New South Wales, say, but down in Australia as a whole, even though nothing changes in the distribution of income elsewhere in Australia. This may sound to be a serious criticism against measures such as the Gini index, but this is not so because of the nature of these measures.

Since these measures imply the individual welfare components to be dependent on the welfare (or income) of others, it makes little sense to measure inequality in a subgroup of the population without taking into account incomes of individuals elsewhere. The assumption that the satisfaction an individual derives is independent of the consumption of others is highly restrictive, because people do compare themselves with others and feel deprived when they see others having higher consumption. But this is an essential requirement for any decomposable measure. Even if we accept the additive-separable framework, the individual welfare functions implied by decomposable measures are not the ones that are overflowing with intuitive sense (Sen 1973a: 36).

4.5   Normative measures of income inequality

In the preceding sections of this chapter, only the positive measures of income inequality were discussed, and their welfare implications examined. These conventional measures of inequality have been subjected to criticism on the ground that these are statistical devices that measure the relative dispersion of a frequency distribution without reference to the normative notion of social welfare. Dalton (1920), who pioneered an attack on these measures, argued that the economist is primarily interested not in the distribution of income as such, but in the effect of the distribution of income upon the distribution and total amount of economic welfare that may be derived from incomes, and therefore any inequality measure must incorporate society's preferences. He proposed a measure based on the idea of proportional welfare loss resulting from income inequality. It is assumed that social welfare is the sum of individual utilities that are functions of their respective incomes, and each individual has the same utility function, which is concave. Then total utility will be maximized if income is equally distributed. Any movement from a completely equal to an unequal distribution will result in welfare loss. Dalton's measure is thus given by the proportional loss of utility caused by having the actual, rather than a completely equal, distribution of the given total income.

Atkinson (1970) criticized Dalton's measure on the ground that "it is not invariant with respect to linear transformation of the utility function"[9] and proposed an alternative class of inequality measures that are based on the concept of "the equally distributed equivalent level of income." Instead of measuring the actual proportional loss of welfare caused by income inequality, he measured the proportional loss of income that would result by having the actual, rather than a completely equal, distribution of the given income.

Let x^* be the equally distributed equivalent level of income, the level which, if received by every individual, would result in the same level of social welfare as the present distribution. Atkinson assumed that the social welfare function is utilitarian and every individual has exactly the same utility function. Under these restricted assumptions, the social welfare function will be

$$W = \sum_{i=1}^{n} u(x_i)$$

where $u(x_i)$ is the utility derived by an individual with income x_i.

The inequality measure proposed by Atkinson is

$$A = 1 - \frac{x^*}{\mu}$$

where the equally distributed equivalent level of income x^* is given by

$$u(x^*) = \frac{1}{n} \sum_{i=1}^{n} u(x_i)$$

If Atkinson's measure is to be scale-independent (i.e., the relative or rightist measure of inequality under Kolm's (1976) terminology) further restrictions on the form of the utility must be considered. It can be shown that the measure will be scale-independent if and only if the utility is of the form

$$u(x) = A + \frac{Bx^{1-\epsilon}}{(1-\epsilon)}, \quad \epsilon \neq 1$$

$$= \log_e(x), \quad \epsilon = 1$$

where $\epsilon > 0$ is the measure of relative risk-aversion, which is constant for this utility function.[10] Under this utility function, which is homothetic, Atkinson's index is equal to

$$A(\epsilon) = 1 - \frac{1}{\mu} \left(\sum_{i=1}^{n} x_i^{1-\epsilon} \right)^{1/(1-\epsilon)}$$

where ϵ is a measure of the degree of inequality-aversion – or the relative sensitivity to income transfers at different income levels. As ϵ rises, more and more weight is attached to transfers at the lower end of the distribution and less weight to transfers at the top. If $\epsilon = 0$, it reflects an inequality-neutral attitude, in which case the society does not care about the inequality at all.

Both Dalton's and Atkinson's measures rely heavily on the value judgments represented by the individual utility function chosen and therefore are called normative measures. They in fact measure, in two alternative ways, the loss of welfare caused through maldistribution. Meade (1976), calling this welfare loss "distributional waste," demonstrated that a measure of distributional waste is not really in any fundamental sense a measure of inequality at all. It is a measure of inefficiency or of the loss of utility from a less-than-optimal distribution of the available income. Thus, a strong case is made for rejecting these so-called normative measures for the purpose of measuring inequality.

It should be pointed out that these alternative measures of inequality do not provide the same ranking of distributions. Yntema (1933) was the first to demonstrate such conflicting ranking. Weisskoff (1970) and Kanadive (1965) also arrived at the same conclusion that the differences in ranking are highly contradictory. Choice of the measure then is quite a serious problem; much of the literature has been concerned with it. On the basis of a simulation study conducted in 1974, Champernowne concluded "that there can be no single 'best' measure; that the choice of a measure should depend on the particular aspect of inequality in which one is interested; and that some measures are more suited to reflect particular aspects of distribution than others."

4.6   Estimation of inequality measures from grouped data

Data on the distribution of personal (or household) incomes are provided in the group form, giving (a) the number of persons with incomes in each income range, and (b) the total (for each range) of their incomes. From these basic data we derive the data on ps and $L(p)$s for each income range. The following equation of the Lorenz curve was estimated by the ordinary least-squares method after applying the logarithmic transformation:

$$L(p) = p - ap^{\alpha}(1-p)^{\beta}$$

where a, α, and β are the parameters and are assumed to be greater than zero. Note that $L(p) = 0$ for both $p = 0$ and $p = 1$. The sufficient conditions for $L(p)$ to be convex to the p axis are $0 < \alpha \le 1$ and $0 < \beta \le 1$. This new functional form of the Lorenz curve was introduced by Kakwani (1981a) in connection with the estimation of a class of welfare measures. His empirical results on 62 countries indicated that the density function underlying this Lorenz curve provides an extremely good fit to the entire income range of the observed income distributions. In the present study, this new functional form has proved to be extremely useful in estimating the quintile shares of income and the various inequality measures for comparing alternative distributions of economic welfare.

4.7   Conclusion

This chapter has been concerned with the problem of measuring inequality of income distribution. A brief review of alternative measures of inequality that have been proposed in the literature suggests that no single set of statistics can give a full and satisfactory description of a whole distribution.

Of all the inequality measures, whether positive or normative, the Gini index is the most widely used. This measure has been subjected to several criticisms, the most serious among them being that it is extremely insensitive to redistribution of income at the lower end of the distribution. In order to meet this deficiency, this chapter proposes a generalization of the Gini index, which permits various alternative assumptions about transfer sensitivity. This class of inequality measure should provide a reasonably full description of any distribution of economic welfare and enable us to make reasonable comparisons of various government policies affecting the distribution of economic welfare.

Since the inequality measures are estimated on the basis of sample observations, we need to test whether the observed differences in their values are statistically significant. No significant test has yet been devised for inequality measures such as the Gini index because of their complex nature. Moreover, the derivation of these tests will require highly restrictive assumptions about the underlying population distribution. In this study we shall simply assume that all differences in the observed values of inequality measures are statistically significant. This assumption may be justified on the grounds that the sample sizes used are fairly large, leading to very small standard errors.

CHAPTER 5

Measures of redistribution and equity

This chapter focuses on the problem of measuring progressivity and the redistributive effect of taxation and public expenditure.[1] This problem has attracted the attention of several writers. Among the important contributions in this field are those of Dalton (1955), Slitor (1948), Musgrave and Thin (1948), and, more recently, Jakobsson (1976), Kakwani (1977a, 1979), and Suits (1977). These studies indicate that a considerable disagreement exists among economists with respect to measuring the degree of progressivity.

There is, however, little disagreement among economists about the definition of progressivity, which is generally given in terms of the average tax rate along the income range. A tax system is said to be (a) progressive when the average rate of tax rises with income, (b) proportional when the average tax is constant, and (c) regressive when it decreases with rising income. A local measure of progression indicates the extent to which a given tax system deviates from proportionality at a given income level. On the other hand, an overall single measure of progressivity (or regressivity) indicates the extent of the overall deviation of a tax system from proportionality.

While defining the degree of progression (or progressivity), we must distinguish between observed and causal tax schedules. A progressivity index may refer to observed tax schedules, and measures the degree of progression of taxes actually paid and government benefits received by income units or households. This measure depends on both the distribution of taxes paid (or benefits received) and the distribution of income. Alternatively, a measure of tax progressivity may refer to the degree of progression of the causal tax schedule as legislated by the government. Such an index does not measure the progressivity of the incidence of taxes but only indicates the progressivity of graduation of the tax scale. In this study, we will be concerned with the progressivity of the actual incidence of taxes (including indirect taxes) and public expenditures.

Since a number of different measures of tax progression (or progressivity) have been proposed, some criteria are needed to evaluate their relative merits. This chapter develops and applies such criteria. The major contribution of this chapter, however, is the establishment of the conceptual distinction between measures of progressivity and those of income redistribution. It has been demonstrated that the concept of progressivity defined in terms of the deviation of a tax system from proportionality is not compatible with the redistributive effects of taxation. Clearly, then, a distinction must be made between the two concepts. Much of the empirical literature seems to have ignored such a distinction.

The principles of horizontal and vertical equity play a fundamental role in any debate on taxation. The principle of horizontal equity means that people in equal positions should be treated equally.[2] The principle of vertical equity, on the other hand, requires that the tax burden on individuals should increase in accordance with their capacity to pay. It is widely believed that a tax system should conform with both these principles (Musgrave 1959: 160).

In order to see the extent to which a given tax system conforms with these principles, it is essential to develop tools for quantitative measurements.[3] In this chapter, an attempt is made to develop the measures of horizontal and vertical equity and to derive their relationship with the measures of progressivity and income redistribution. In the subsequent chapters, these methods are applied on the Australian data to analyze the effects of taxes and government cash benefits on equity.

5.1 Axioms of tax progressivity and the redistributive effect of taxes

The following two basic axioms are proposed, which conform to the intuitive notion of tax progressivity.

Axiom 5.1: *The degree of progressivity is unaffected if the share of tax liability of every individual remains the same irrespective of total tax yield.*

Any observed tax schedule incorporates two distinct factors: the average tax and the distribution of tax liability over the income ranges. The concept of progressivity is concerned with the second factor (i.e., the distribution of tax liability). If the tax liability is distributed among individuals in proportion to their income, the tax is said to be proportional. The tax system is said to be progressive (regressive) if the richer (poorer) individual pays a higher proportion of his or her income as taxes. Therefore a measure of progressivity (regressivity) shows the extent of the deviation of a tax system from proportionality in favor of the poorer (richer). This interpretation of progressivity implies that a measure of progressivity should not be affected by increasing or decreasing tax by the same rates at all income levels.

Table 5.1. *An example of two taxpayers*

Pre-tax income	Tax liability	Average tax rate	% tax liability
Tax system I			
$100	$ 20	20%	10
$500	$180	36%	90
Total	$200	33.3%	100
Tax system II			
$100	$ 28	28%	11.67
$500	$212	42.4%	88.33
Total	$240	40%	100
Tax system III			
$100	−$400	−400%	
$500	$400	80%	
Total	$ 0.0	−	

Axiom 5.2: *If the share in the total tax liability of a person with income x is increased (decreased) and that of a person with lower income ($x - h$) is decreased (increased), then progressivity must increase (decrease).*

This axiom conforms to the intuitive idea that if the poor person is penalized more heavily than the rich person, the progressivity must decrease.

Musgrave and Thin (1948) proposed a measure of progressivity based on the comparison of the inequality indexes of the pre-tax and post-tax income distributions. Their measure indicates the extent to which a given tax system results in a shift in the distribution of income toward equality: A progressive tax system is associated with a decrease in income inequality, whereas the regressive tax structure leads to an increase in income inequality.[4] The measure implies that the degree of progressivity remains constant when post-tax income is changed equiproportionately, rather than when tax burden is changed equiproportionately.

It will now be demonstrated, with the help of an example of two taxpayers given in Table 5.1, that Musgrave and Thin's measure violates both axioms of progressivity stated above.

Tax system II is obtained by reducing the after-tax income of both individuals by 10 percent. According to the Musgrave and Thin measure, both these tax schedules are equally progressive despite the fact that the shares of tax liability of two individuals differ under the two tax systems. Further, note that under tax system I, the poorer person pays only 10 percent of the total tax, whereas under tax system II, the poorer person pays 11.6 percent of the total tax. Therefore, Schedule II should be less progressive than Schedule I, but this measure would indicate that both tax systems are equally progressive. Thus, Musgrave and Thin's measure violates Axioms 5.1 and 5.2.

This implies that Musgrave and Thin are in fact measuring the redistributive effect of taxation rather than progressivity. Although these two concepts are closely related, their distinction can be seen by comparing tax systems I and III. As we move from tax system I to III, we find that the average tax rate of the poorer person is reduced from 20 percent to −400 percent, whereas that of the richer person increases from 36 percent to 80 percent. Obviously, system III should be considerably more progressive than system I, but according to the Musgrave and Thin measure, tax system III is in fact proportional (i.e., has zero progressivity), whereas tax system I is progressive. This suggests that the concept of progressivity (or regressivity) defined in terms of deviation of a tax system from proportionality is not compatible with the redistributive effect of taxes. Clearly, then, the distinction must be made between "progressivity" and redistributive effects; but the empirical literature seems to have ignored such a distinction.

This distinction is important because it shows how the distributive effects of taxation are influenced by changes in the average tax rate while progressivity remains constant and vice versa. For instance, moving from tax system I to tax system II, we note that the progressivity decreases (because the proportion of total tax liability of the poor has increased and that of the rich decreased) which should increase the after-tax income inequality, but this effect was offset by the increase in the average tax rate.

Further, note that tax system III is highly progressive (due to the fact that the average tax of the poorer person is −400 percent while that of the richer person is 80 percent) which should increase the redistributive effect of the tax, but this effect was offset by the change in the ranking of individuals in the post-tax distribution of income. Thus, the pre- and post-tax income distributions are identical despite the highly progressive tax structure.

One might argue that, from the equity point of view, we should care only about the redistributive effects of taxation and public expenditure. Since changes in the ranking of individuals, tax progressivity, and average tax rate are all important policy instruments that influence the redistributive power of a tax system, it is important to distinguish these concepts in order to measure their effects on the redistribution of economic welfare. In the subsequent sections of this chapter we develop the tools that can be used to measure their effects.

5.2   Ranking of tax systems

Four alternative local measures of progression proposed by Musgrave and Thin (1948) are

1. *Average rate progression,* defined as the ratio of change in average tax rate to change in income
2. *Liability progression,* defined as the percentage change in tax liability to percentage change in income
3. *Residual income progression,* defined as the ratio of percentage change in after-tax income to percentage change in before-tax income
4. *Marginal rate progression,* defined as the ratio of change in marginal tax rate to change in income

All these measures of progression belong to the same family. They relate to progression at a given point in the income scale and, therefore, do not give a single index of overall tax progressivity.

Kakwani (1980a) has demonstrated that the various measures of progression applied to the same distribution of income and taxes give different degrees of change in progression when moving up the income scale. Musgrave and Thin were aware of these conflicting results, and therefore suggested that statements about changes in the pattern of progression should be made strictly in the context of specific measures.

It can easily be demonstrated that among the four measures of progression discussed above, the *liability progression* is the only one that satisfies the two basic Axioms 5.1 and 5.2. This measure is equal to the tax elasticity, which is defined as the elasticity of the tax function $T(x)$ with respect to pre-tax income x. Since the tax elasticity is unity for a proportional tax system, the magnitude of the difference of tax elasticity from unity provides the local measure of tax progression.

Let $L(p)$ be the Lorenz curve of income, which is interpreted as the fraction of total income received by the lowest pth fraction of income units. Kakwani (1977b) generalized the concept of the Lorenz curve, which was later used to develop a measure of progressivity of a tax system. He introduced the idea of the concentration curve of taxes, $C(p)$, which is interpreted as the proportion of tax paid by the lowest pth fraction of income units when income units are arranged in ascending order of their income.

The vertical distance between the Lorenz curve of income and the concentration curve of tax depends only on the tax elasticity. If this elasticity is unity at all income levels, the two curves coincide. It follows from Theorem 8.1 of Kakwani (1980a) that the larger the deviation of tax elasticity from unity, the greater is the distance between the two curves. This suggests that, for a given before-tax income distribution, the concentration curve can be used as a criterion for ranking alternative tax systems. If the concentration curve of one tax system is strictly inside that of another, one can conclude from the liability progression measure that the second tax system is more progressive than the first. If, however, the two concentration curves intersect, neither tax system can be said to be more progressive than the other. Therefore, the ranking of the tax systems provided by the concentration curve is only partial, and one has to consider a single measure of progressivity to arrive at complete ranking. Since a number of single measures of progressivity have been proposed, some criteria are needed to evaluate them. These criteria are developed in the next section.

5.3 A criterion for evaluating alternative measures of tax progressivity

The basic axioms of progressivity proposed in Section 5.1 will be used to evaluate the relative merits of alternative measures of tax progressivity.

Suppose the pre-tax income x is a random variable with probability density function $f(x)$. If $T(x)$ is the tax paid by a unit with income x and Q is the total tax revenue collected, then $t(x) = T(x)/Q$ will be the proportion of tax liability borne by the unit with income x.

All the progressivity measures proposed so far are of the general form

$$\theta = \int_0^\infty V[t(x), x] f(x) \, dx, \tag{5.1}$$

where $V[t(x), x]$ is some function of $t(x)$ and x. It is obvious that a measure of this form will always satisfy Axiom 5.1. The following lemma, which is proved in the appendix, gives the condition under which Axiom 5.2 will also be satisfied.

Lemma 5.1: *Any progressivity index that is written in the form* 5.1 *will satisfy Axiom* 5.2 *if and only if* $K(x)$, *defined as*

$$K(x) = V'[t(x), x] - V'[t(x-h), x-h], \tag{5.2}$$

is positive for all x and $h > 0$, where $V'[t(x), x]$ is the first derivative of $V[t(x), x]$ with respect to $t(x)$.

Lemma 5.2: *If the share of tax liability of a unit with income x is increased (decreased) and that of a person with lower income $(x - h)$ is decreased (increased), then the magnitude of change in the tax progressivity depends on the magnitude of $K(x)$.*

Proof follows immediately from Lemma 5.1.

This lemma enables us to examine the relative sensitivity of progressivity to a change in the share of tax liability at different levels of income. For instance, if the function $K(x)$ is constant, it implies that the effect of changes in the share of tax liabilities would be independent of the income levels at which the changes take place. Further, if $K(x)$ is a monotonically decreasing function of x, then the progressivity index gives higher weight to changes in the tax share at the lower end of the distribution, and the weight decreases monotonically as income increases. Similarly, if $K(x)$ is a monotonically increasing function of x, then the weight increases with income. There can be a situation when $K(x)$ increases initially and then decreases. This situation implies that the progressivity index attaches more weight to changes in the share of tax liability at the middle of the distribution than at the tails.

5.4   Evaluation of measures of tax progressivity

We are now in a position to examine the relative merits of alternative measures of tax progressivity.

The concentration measure of tax progressivity

Kakwani (1977a) has derived a measure of progressivity by comparing the Lorenz curve of pre-tax income and the concentration curve of taxes. This measure, which will be referred to as the concentration measure, is given by

$$P = C - G \tag{5.3}$$

where G is the Gini index of pre-tax income and C is the concentration index of tax, which is defined as one minus twice the area under the concentration curve. It is obvious that P is equal to twice the area between the Lorenz curve of pre-tax income and the concentration curve of taxes. P is positive (negative) if the tax elasticity is greater (less) than unity for all x and assumes value zero when the tax elasticity is unity for all incomes. Thus, the positive value of P implies a progressive tax and the negative value implies a regressive tax.[5]

The measure can be written as

$$P = 2 \int_0^1 [L(p) - C(p)] \, dp$$

which on integration by parts becomes

$$P = 2 \int_0^\infty \left[t(x) - \frac{x}{m} \right] F(x) f(x) \, dx$$

where $f(x)$ is the probability density function of x, $F(x)$ is the distribution function which is interpreted as the proportion of units having income less than or equal to x, and m is the total income of the society. This equation gives

$$K(x) = 2[F(x) - F(x-h)]$$

which is always greater than zero for $h > 0$. Thus, Axiom 5.2 is always satisfied by the concentration measure of tax progressivity. Since $dF(x)/dx = f(x)$, the first derivative of $K(x)$ is given by

$$K'(x) = 2[f(x) - f(x-h)]$$

For a typical unimodal income distribution, $f(x)$ increases up to the mode and then it decreases. This means that $K(x)$ is an increasing function of x up to the modal income, and then it becomes a monotonically decreasing function of x. Thus, the following conclusion immediately follows from Lemma 5.2: *The concentration measure of tax progressivity attaches maximum weight to a transfer of the share of tax liability at the mode of the income distribution.*

The measure proposed by Suits

D. B. Suits (1977) proposed a measure of progressivity that is equal to one minus twice the area under the relative concentration curve of $T(x)$ with respect to x:[6]

$$S = 1 - 2\int_0^1 C(p)\, dL(p)$$

which after integrating by parts can be written as:

$$S = 2\int_0^\infty [F_1(x) - \tfrac{1}{2}]\, t(x) f(x)\, dx$$

where $F_1(x)$ is the cumulative proportion of income of units having income less than or equal to x. This equation gives

$$K(x) = 2[F_1(x) - F_1(x-h)]$$

which is always greater than zero for $h > 0$. Thus, Suits's measure satisfies Axiom 5.2.

The first derivative of $K(x)$ with respect to x is

$$K'(x) = \frac{2}{\mu}[xf(x) - (x-h)f(x-h)]$$

where μ is the mean income of the society. Let x^* be an income level such that

$$f(x^*) + x^* f'(x^*) = 0 \qquad (5.4)$$

It can be seen that $xf(x)$ is an increasing function of x up to the income level x^*, and then decreases monotonically. Obviously, then, $K(x)$ increases monotonically with x up to the income level x^*, and then decreases.

Equation (5.4) shows that for a typical unimodal income distribution, x^* exceeds the modal income. This leads to the following conclusion: *Suits's measure of tax progressivity attaches maximum weight to a transfer of the share of tax liability at an income level higher than the mode.*

5.5   Derivation of a new measure of tax progressivity

Let us consider a family of tax progressivity measures

$$\theta = \int_0 (x/m - t(x)) w(x) f(x) \, dx \qquad (5.5)$$

where $w(x)$ is the weight attached to a unit with income x with the density function $f(x)$. Note that θ is equal to the weighted sum of the difference between income shares and tax shares of the units at different income levels.

It can be seen that Axiom 5.1 is always satisfied by θ for all $w(x)$.

It is obvious that θ will be zero if the tax system is proportional at all income levels. If the tax system is progressive (regressive) in the entire income range, θ must be positive (negative). This condition requires that the weight $w(x)$ must be positive for all x.

$K(x)$ defined in (5.2) is, in this case, given by

$$K(x) = -[w(x) - w(x - h)] \qquad (5.6)$$

which, on using Lemma 5.1, shows that Axiom 5.2 will be satisfied if $w(x)$ is a monotonically decreasing function of x.

If we substitute

$$w(x) = 2[1 - F(x)]$$

into (5.5), we obtain Kakwani's concentration measure of tax progressivity. Similarly, Suits's measure is obtained by substituting

$$w(x) = 2[1 - F_1(x)]$$

Thus, we have demonstrated that the two recent measures of tax progressivity belong to the same class of progressivity measures (5.5). The two measures differ, however, in one respect: In the case of Kakwani's measure, the weight $w(x)$ depends on the number of persons or units who have income greater than x, whereas in the case of Suits's measure this weight is proportional to the total income of units with income greater than x. Because of this differing weighting scheme, the two measures may lead to quite different results about the degree of progressivity, particularly when the pre-tax income distribution is not fixed over time.

The problem of choosing between the two measures is a difficult one and cannot be resolved here. Nevertheless, it should be mentioned that Kakwani's measure has an advantage over that of Suits in one respect: It provides the relationship between measures of progressivity and that of the redistributive effect of taxation. This problem is the subject matter of the next section.

As regards the relative sensitivity of progressivity to a transfer of tax share, both Kakwani's and Suits's measures are almost similar in the sense that the sensitivity increases first and then decreases, or (in other words) the measures are most sensitive at the middle of the income distribution. If the society is more concerned with the increase in tax share of the poor than that of the rich, the progressivity measure must be most sensitive at the bottom end of the distribution and the sensitivity must decrease monotonically with income. In order for a progressivity index to possess such a property, $K(x)$ must be a monotonically decreasing function of x, which in turn implies that the first derivative of $K(x)$, given by

$$K'(x) = -[w'(x) - w'(x-h)]$$

has to be negative for all values of x. Thus, a measure of progressivity that is most sensitive at the bottom end of the distribution must satisfy the following restrictions.

$$w(x) > 0$$
$$w'(x) < 0$$
$$w''(x) > 0$$

where $w''(x)$ is the second derivative of $w(x)$. A simplest function that satisfies all these restrictions is[7]

$$w(x) = m/x$$

which on substituting (5.5) leads to a new measure of progressivity:

$$\theta = 1 - \frac{1}{e} \int_{J}^{\infty} \frac{T(x)}{x} f(x)\, dx$$

where $e = Q/m$ is the average tax rate of the society. In the discrete case, this measure can be written as

$$\theta = 1 - \frac{1}{ne} \sum_{i=1}^{n} e_i$$

where e_i is the average tax rate of the ith income unit.

5.6   Measures of horizontal and vertical equity

The principle of horizontal equity means that people in equal positions should be treated equally. In other words, two persons with identical incomes and needs must pay the same tax or receive the same government benefits. This principle can be violated under various circumstances. For instance, it is alleged that people earning income from business pay less tax than those earning wages. These inequalities in taxation may alter the ranking of individuals in the pre- and post-tax distributions of income. This led Feldstein (1976) to propose an alternative definition of horizontal equity which requires that taxes should not alter the utility ordering of individuals.

Feldstein (1976) and Rosen (1978), therefore, have proposed measures of horizontal equity in terms of the rank correlation coefficient between the pre- and post-tax orderings of utilities. Their approach requires the specification of the individual or the family utility function, which has a number of well-known limitations. Moreover, the relationship between their measures of horizontal equity and the measures of income redistribution is not that obvious, although the two concepts are closely related.[8]

The change in the ranking between the pre- and post-tax distributions will affect the after-tax income inequality. This effect has been examined by Atkinson (1980), who proved that the Gini index of the after-tax income is reduced as a result of the re-ranking of individuals according to the after-tax income. This result will form the basis of our measure of horizontal equity.

The principle of vertical equity requires that people with different income (adjusted for their needs) should pay different tax. In fact, the concept of progressivity – defined in terms of the distribution of tax liability among persons with different income – measures the extent to which different people pay different rates of taxation. Thus, the two concepts are closely related.

Suppose that income units are arranged in ascending order of their pre-tax income; if $T(x)$ is the tax paid by a unit with income x, then the after-tax income of the individual is given by

$$d(x) = x - T(x)$$

which on applying Theorem 8.2 of Kakwani (1980) yields

$$(m - Q)C_d(p) = mL(p) - QC(p)$$

where $C_d(p)$ is the concentration curve of the after-tax income, $L(p)$ is the Lorenz curve of the pre-tax income, $C(p)$ is the concentration curve of taxes, and m and Q are the total pre-tax income and the total tax revenue, respectively. This equation can also be rearranged as

$$L(p) = C_d(p) - \frac{e}{(1-e)}[L(p) - C(p)] \tag{5.7}$$

where $e = m/Q$ is the average tax rate of the entire society.

If we denote by $L^*(p)$ the Lorenz curve of the post-tax income distribution, then the index of the redistributive effect of taxes will be obtained by comparing the differences between the curves $L^*(p)$ and $L(p)$ for all values of p in the interval $0 \le p \le 1$. Subtracting quantities in both sides of (5.7) from $L^*(p)$, we obtain

$$[L^*(p) - L(p)] = [L^*(p) - C_d(p)] + \frac{e}{(1-e)}[L(p) - C(p)] \tag{5.8}$$

which shows that the redistributive effect of taxes is equal to the sum of two components, each of which has the following interpretations.

Note that $C_d(p)$ is the proportion of the post-tax income of the lowest pth fraction of units arranged in ascending order of their pre-tax income, while $L^*(p)$ is the proportion of the post-tax income of units arranged in ascending order of their post-tax income. Obviously, if the ranking of all units is unaltered between the pre- and post-tax distributions of income then $L^*(p) = C_d(p)$ for all p, which suggests that an appropriate summary measure of differences between $L^*(p)$ and $C_d(p)$ will lead to an index that measures the effect of horizontal inequity on income redistribution.

In Section 5.2 it was argued that an appropriate index of tax progressivity is obtained by comparing the differences between the Lorenz curve of the pre-tax income and the concentration curve of taxes. It follows that the second component in (5.8) depends on the average tax rate and the progressivity, which is measured by the differences between the curves $L(p)$ and $C(p)$ and is equal to the redistributive effect of taxes when the horizontal inequity is zero. Thus, the second component represents the redistributive impact of taxation induced purely by taxing different individuals differently, and should therefore provide an index measuring the effect of vertical equity on income redistribution.

Integrating (5.8) on both sides in the range $0 \le p \le 1$, we obtain

$$(G - G^*) = (C_d - G^*) + \frac{pe}{(1-e)}$$

where G and G^* are the Gini indices of the pre- and post-tax income distributions respectively; C_d is the concentration index of the post-tax income distribution and P the concentration measure of tax progressivity. Therefore, the index of redistributive effect of taxes R, measured by the percentage change in the Gini index of the pre- and post-tax distribution of income, is given[9]

Table 5.2. *An example of four tax systems*

Pre-tax income	Tax liability	After-tax income
Tax system I		
$100	$ 20	$ 80
$500	$180	$320
Tax system II		
$100	$ 20	$ 80
$500	$430	$ 70
Tax system III		
$100	$ 10	$ 90
$500	$440	$ 60
Tax system IV		
$100	$ 11	$ 89
$500	$484	$ 16

$$R = H + V \tag{5.9}$$

where

$$H = \frac{C_d - G^*}{G}$$

$$V = \frac{ep}{(1-e)G}$$

are the proposed indices measuring the effects of horizontal and vertical equity (or inequity) on income redistribution, respectively.[10]

Kakwani's (1980a) Corollary 8.7 shows that $C_d \leq G^*$ which implies $H \leq 0$; $H = 0$, when the ranking remains the same between the pre- and post-tax distribution of income, otherwise it will be negative. Thus, the violation of horizontal equity in the Feldstein sense will have the effect of reducing the redistributive effect of taxation.

It can be seen that V is greater (less) than zero if the tax system is progressive (regressive), and that V assumes value zero when the tax system is proportional.

5.7   An example

Let us consider an example of four tax systems, given in Table 5.2, to illustrate the methods developed in the previous section. The numerical

Table 5.3. *Measures of progressivity and equity*

Tax system	I	II	III	IV
Average tax rate e	.333	.750	.750	.825
Progressivity index P	.134	.245	.289	.289
Horizontal equity				
H (%)	0.0	−20.25	−60.04	−208.62
Vertical equity				
V (%)	10.00	110.24	130.04	204.35
Redistributive effect of the tax system				
R (%)	10.00	89.99	70.00	−4.27

results of measures of progressivity and equity based on this example are presented in Table 5.3. The conclusions are summarized below.

Tax system I is progressive and results in a 10-percent decrease in income inequality. It does not violate the principle of horizontal equity and, as a result, the index of vertical equity is equal to the index of redistributive effect of tax.

Tax system II is made more progressive than tax system I and it also has a higher average tax rate. As a result, the index of vertical equity increases substantially from 10 percent to 110.24 percent, but at the same time horizontal inequity is also introduced, which has the effect of increasing income inequality by 20.25 percent. This example shows that there can be a clash between horizontal and vertical equity. Increasing vertical equity may lead to horizontal inequity.

Tax system III is made even more progressive than tax system II while keeping the same average tax rate. The index of vertical equity is further increased from 110.24 percent to 130.04 percent; this should have increased the index of tax redistribution, but its effect was offset by a substantial increase in horizontal inequity. As a result, the index of redistribution decreased from 89.99 percent to 70 percent. It should be noted that although the two tax systems give exactly the same post-tax ranking of individuals, the magnitude of the index of horizontal inequity happens to be substantially different in the two systems. This observation demonstrates that the index of horizontal inequity is sensitive not only to changes in rankings but also to the magnitude of income differences produced by taxation.

Tax systems III and IV have exactly the same progressivity but differ with respect to the average tax rate. It can be seen that increasing the average tax rate while keeping the same progressivity increases substantially the index of vertical equity from 130.04 percent to 204.35 percent.

This increase in vertical equity is accompanied by an even greater increase in horizontal inequity. As a result, the index of tax redistribution decreases from 70 percent to -4.27 percent. Thus, a change in average tax rate can substantially alter the vertical and horizontal equity even if the progressivity of taxation has been kept constant.

The above conclusions are based on an artificial example designed to illustrate the methodology developed in this chapter. A detailed analysis of the actual data based on this methodology is presented in the subsequent chapters.

Appendix: proof of Lemma 5.1

Proof: Equation (5.1) in the discrete case is equivalent to

$$\theta = \sum_{i=1}^{n} V(t_i, x_i) \tag{A.1}$$

where n is the total number of income units and t_i is the share of tax liability of the ith person.

Suppose the share of the tax liability of the ith person is increased and that of the jth person decreased by the same amount δ. If δ is sufficiently small, we have

$$d\theta = \frac{\partial \theta}{\partial t_i} \delta + \frac{\partial \theta}{\partial t_j}(-\delta)$$

which on using (A.1) gives

$$\frac{\partial V(t_i, x_i)}{\partial t_i} - \frac{\partial V(t_j, x_j)}{\partial t_j} > 0$$

for all $x_i > x_j$. Substituting $x_i = x$ and $x_j = x - h$ proves the necessary condition of the lemma. The sufficient condition follows immediately from the above proof.

PART III

Distribution and redistribution of income

CHAPTER 6

Distribution of income in Australia

Much of the economic literature on the distribution of income is devoted to the functional distribution of income (i.e., the way in which income is shared by various factors of production). However, from the welfare point of view, it is the personal distribution by size of income that is most relevant. While the data describing the functional distribution of income are interesting and informative, their relationship to the size distribution of income may not be obvious. This chapter discusses several aspects of the size distribution of income from the viewpoint of public policy.

While our primary interest is in the degree of inequality in the personal distribution of income, an attempt will be made to analyze the relationship between the functional and size distributions of income. Total household income consists of wages and salaries, business income, government transfers, and other miscellaneous components of income; the contribution of each of these factor components to the inequality of total household income is of utmost interest for public policy.

The Gini index is widely used to measure the degree of inequality in the distribution of income. However, no single statistical measure can describe the whole of income distribution adequately. Therefore, we compute alternative inequality measures (discussed in Chapter 4) and quintile shares for the distribution of each definition of income.

This chapter also attempts to make an international comparison of income distributions, although there are considerable problems with such comparisons. Consequently, we have been careful in drawing only broad conclusions because of certain severe limitations. In order to avoid some of the pitfalls, the comparison was restricted to a few developed countries that were similar in political and socioeconomic structure and provided income-distribution data with definitions of income and the income-recipient unit closest to the Australian definitions.

Most of the income-distribution studies carried out in Australia, based on household income, make no adjustment for household size and composition. Since the number of children and adults varies from household to household, it is essential that inequality be measured with respect to adjusted household income. This adjustment is done by dividing the income of each household by a certain number of *equivalent-adults* obtained by the use of certain equivalent-income scales. This chapter analyzes how the magnitudes of income inequality vary with respect to alternative income scales used to adjust household income.

The major contribution of this chapter, however, is that it makes a distinction between the distribution of the individual's income as against that of the household's. In the conventional studies on income distributions of households, each household is given an equal weight, irrespective of size. This leads to giving greater weights to individuals belonging to smaller households, and smaller weight to those belonging to larger households, which is difficult to justify from the welfare point of view. In this study we construct size distributions of income that give equal weight to each individual's welfare, irrespective of the size and composition of the household to which they belong. The empirical results show that differences in inequality between the two types of distributions are significant and vary with respect to the income concept used.

6.1   Household income in Australia

According to Australian National Accounts, household income is the total income, whether in cash or kind, received by persons normally resident in Australia. Various components of income are

1. *Wages and salaries* – consist of payments by employers in the nature of wages and salaries, including allowances for income in kind (board and quarters, etc.).
2. *Supplements to wages and salaries* – consist of employers' contributions to pension and superannuation funds, direct payments of pensions and retiring allowances by employers, and amounts paid as workers' compensation for injuries.
3. *Business and professional income* – consists of unincorporated enterprise income from farm and other business and professional activities. It is equal to gross product at factor cost less estimated production costs other than wages and depreciation.
4. *Rents, dividends, and interest* – includes net income from dwellings, imputed interest on life and superannuation funds, other interests and dividends. However, it excludes any income that might be said to accrue to persons in the form of undistributed company income. It includes any property income received by nonprofit organizations such as private schools, churches, etc.
5. *Government transfers* – include cash transfers from general government for health, social security and welfare, education, and other payments.
6. *Other income* – includes third-party insurance transfers and transfers from overseas.

Table 6.1. *Household income by types of income in Australia for 1969–70, 1975–6, and 1979–80*

	1969–70		1975–6		1979–80	
Source of income	($) million	(%) c'bution	($) million	(%) c'bution	($) million	(%) c'bution
Wages and salaries	15527	65.4	39541	64.1	58546	60.4
Supplements to wages and salaries	552	2.3	2039	3.3	3220	3.3
Business and professional income	3129	13.2	6476	10.5	11295	11.7
Rents, dividends, and interest	2589	10.9	6717	10.9	12632	13.0
Government transfers	1659	7.0	6400	10.4	10332	10.7
Other income	273	1.2	524	0.8	876	0.9
Total household income	23729	100.0	61697	100.0	96901	100.0
Household disposable income	20205	85.1	50916	82.5	79701	82.2

Source: Australian National Accounts: National Income and Expenditure 1979–80, Australian Bureau of Statistics, Catalogue No. 5204.0.

Table 6.1 presents household income, by types of income in Australia for 1969–70, 1975–6, and 1979–80. The total household income amounted to $61,697 million in 1975–6. Wage and salary payments amounted to $39,541 million or about 64 percent of the total household income. Various supplements to wages and salaries came to $2,039 million, contributing 3.3 percent of the total household income. Business income accounted for 10.5 percent of household income; rents, dividends, and net interest including imputed interest on life and superannuation funds, 10.9 percent; government transfers, 10.4 percent; and other incomes, 0.8 percent.

The household disposable income – which is defined as household income less direct taxes, fees, fines, etc. charged to persons by general government, consumer debt interest, and transfers overseas – amounted to $50,916 million in 1975–6. Thus, the disposable income is computed to be 82.5 percent of the total household income.

Income from wages and salaries as a percentage of total income has declined from 65.4 percent to 60.4 percent during the period 1969–70 to 1979–80, whereas supplements to wages and salaries showed a slight increase from 2.3 percent to 3.3 percent during the same period. Business and professional income showed a sharp decline from 13.2 percent to 10.5 percent during the period 1969–70 to 1975–6, but then it increased to 11.7 percent in 1979–80. Income from rents, dividends, and interest remained rather constant at 10.9 percent of total income in 1969–70 and 1975–6, but then it increased markedly to 13.0 percent in 1979–80. The greatest relative gain was made by transfer payments, which amounted to 7 percent of total income in 1969–70 compared to 10.4 percent in 1975–6 and 10.7 percent in 1979–80.

Household disposable income as a percentage of household income showed a marked decline during the period 1969–70 to 1975–6 – 85.1 percent for 1969–70 as compared to 82.5 percent for 1975–6. This decline continued during 1975–6 to 1979–80 period but at a considerably slower rate. This suggests that direct taxes, fees, and fines charged to persons by government have been increasing at a faster rate than the total household income.

Although these broad figures have some use in understanding the process of income generation, they tell little as to how the incomes are distributed among individuals, households, and other units. For instance, it is commonly believed that the larger the family's average income, the smaller the proportion derived from employment. From this proposition one may conclude that any policy that increases the labor share of the functional distribution may decrease the inequality of the size distribution of total income. Both these propositions are half true as can be seen from the empirical evidence presented in the next section.

6.2   Functional distribution of income by income ranges

This section is intended to give some insight into the relationship between the functional and size distribution of income. The data used for this purpose are obtained from the Household Expenditure Survey, 1975–6.

Table 6.2 presents the percentage shares of various income components according to the ranges of household income. The definitions of various income components used in the table have already been given in Chapter 3. It should be pointed out that these definitions are somewhat different from those employed by Australian National Accounts.

Income from wages and salaries is the major functional component, contributing 75.43 percent of total household income. Income from business forms the second major functional component and has a share of 10.62 percent in total income. The third major component is the income received from the government in the form of cash benefits. Other income, including investment income such as interest, dividends, and rents, has a share of only 6.78 percent in total income.[1]

Shares of various income components vary widely over the income ranges. The proposition that the share of employment income decreases with income is not supported by the data. In fact the relationship appears to be rather the reverse, due to the high concentration of poorer house-

Table 6.2. *Factor distribution of income by gross household income brackets: Australia 1975-6*

Range of weekly household income	Wages and salaries	Business income	Total gov't cash benefits	Other income
Under $40	25.45	−85.27	135.94	23.89
$40–$80	4.21	7.96	70.73	17.09
$80–$110	21.58	14.81	41.74	21.88
$110–$140	65.65	9.77	12.61	11.97
$140–$170	74.15	8.50	8.83	8.52
$170–$200	79.18	8.60	6.15	6.06
$200–$230	79.74	8.78	5.00	6.48
$230–$260	84.00	7.96	2.58	5.45
$260–$300	85.01	7.55	2.49	4.90
$300–$340	83.85	9.52	2.26	4.37
$340–$400	87.32	5.88	2.03	4.77
$400 and over	73.96	18.74	1.58	5.74
All households	75.43	10.62	7.11	6.78

holds who are largely dependent on government transfers, and retired people with property income. It would appear, then, that any policy that increases the labor share of the functional distribution may increase rather than decrease the inequality of total household income. This could be an important finding and will be considered further in the next section.

Government cash transfers account for 7.16 percent of total household income. This percentage is 135.94 for the lowest income group and decreases monotonically to only 1.58 for the highest income group. Thus, it may be concluded that government cash transfers are highly progressive and will have equalizing effects on the income distribution.

It was noted in the previous section that the wage share declined and the share of government cash benefits increased during the period 1969-70 to 1979-80. Since both these factors have equalizing effect on the income distribution, it could be expected that the inequality of household income in Australia would have decreased during the 1970s.

6.3   Income inequality by factor components

After the total household income is broken down into income from various sources such as wage income, capital income, and transfer income, the question is: Of the total inequality, how much is attributable to each component of income? The methodology for disaggregation of inequality by factor components was first developed by Rao (1969) and subsequently refined by Kakwani (1977b, 1980a); Fields and Fei (1974); Fei, Ranis, and Kao (1978); Fields (1979); and Pyatt, Chen, and Fei (1980).[2] In this section, we use this methodology to analyze the contribution of each of these factor components to the inequality of total household income.

The income concept used is the gross household income (income received from all sources including government cash transfers by all members of the household). Suppose that there are n households who are arranged in ascending order of their incomes: $x_1 \leq x_2 \leq \cdots \leq x_n$. Supposing there are m factor incomes, then the Gini index of total household income may be decomposed as (Kakwani 1980a):

$$G = \frac{1}{\mu} \sum_{j=1}^{m} \mu_j C_j \qquad (6.1)$$

where $\mu = \sum_{j=1}^{m} \mu_j$ is the mean household income, μ_j the mean income of the jth factor income of all households, and C_j the concentration index of the jth factor income.[3]

Equation (6.1) expresses the Gini index of total household income as the weighted average of the concentration index of each factor income component, the weights being proportional to the mean of each factor income. This equation provides the quantitative framework to analyze the contribution of each of these components to the inequality of total household income.

The numerical results giving the contribution of each factor income to total inequality are presented in Table 6.3. The first row gives the mean income of each factor income. The second row gives the percentage share of each factor. The quintile shares of each factor income, when the households are arranged according to the total household income, are presented in the next five rows. The eighth row gives the concentration indices of each factor income, and the ninth row presents the contribution of each factor income to total income inequality. Finally, the last row expresses these contributions in percentages.

The concentration index of a factor income measures how evenly or unevenly that factor income is distributed over the total household income. It can be seen that the concentration index of employment income is 40.79, which is considerably higher than the Gini index of total income, 34.51. This implies that income from wages and salaries is unevenly distributed over the total income in favor of richer households. From quintile shares, it can be seen that wages and salaries are heavily concentrated in the third and fourth quintiles. This confirms our earlier findings that the commonly held belief that the larger the family's average income, the smaller the proportion derived from employment is not universally true.

Table 6.3. *Income inequality by factor components: Australia 1975-6*

	Wages and salaries	Business income	Individual government cash benefits					Total gov't cash benefits	Other income	Total household gross income
			Pensions	Unem-ployment benefits	Sickness & special benefits	Family allowance	Other gov't benefits			
Mean household income	170.63	24.03	12.52	1.47	.27	1.05	.89	16.20	15.34	226.20
% share of each factor	75.43	10.62	5.53	.65	.12	.47	.39	7.16	6.78	100.00
Quintile shares										
1	.62	1.82	56.01	24.54	37.45	5.49	21.57	47.65	15.75	5.14
2	11.00	11.28	18.66	31.91	41.20	23.38	25.08	20.90	18.43	12.24
3	19.18	14.88	11.38	17.41	13.65	25.53	20.30	13.38	16.73	18.12
4	27.72	18.23	6.76	11.08	2.01	20.61	16.09	8.49	18.06	24.68
5	41.47	53.79	7.14	15.04	5.68	24.99	16.96	9.58	31.40	39.81
Concentration index	40.79	49.88	-43.64	-13.07	-37.87	15.57	-7.08	-34.90	13.97	34.51
Contribution of each factor income to total income inequality	30.77	5.30	-2.41	-.08	-.04	.07	-.03	-2.50	.95	34.51
% contribution of each factor income to total inequality	89.16	15.35	-6.99	-.25	-.13	.21	-.08	-7.24	2.74	100.00

The concentration index of business income is 49.88, being considerably higher than that for income from wages and salaries, showing that the business income is even more unevenly distributed over the household income in the favor of richer households than the income from wages and salaries. This can also be seen from quintile shares which show that the top 20 percent households have 53.79 percent share of total business income, as against 1.82 percent for the bottom 20 percent households. This indicates that the business income contributes substantially to the inequality of total household income.

The concentration index of income from government transfers is −34.90, which implies that this income component is heavily concentrated at low income levels. The share of the first quintile is 47.65 of the total transfer income and it reduces to 9.58 percent for the fifth quintile. Among the five components of government transfers, the pensions have the lowest value of the concentration index, −43.64, and the family allowance the highest value, of 15.57. Households in the first quintile receive 56.01 percent of total pensions, whereas those in the fifth quintile receive only 7.19 percent. So, pensions have the maximum equalizing effects on income inequality; sickness and special benefits come next with a concentration index of −37.87. It is interesting to note that it is the second quintile that gets the highest share of sickness and special benefits.

The concentration index of unemployment benefits is −13.07, showing that it is more evenly distributed over the total income than pensions and sickness and special benefits. The second quintile gets the highest share of unemployment benefits whereas the fourth quintile has the lowest share. It is interesting to note that the top quintile receives as much as 15.04 percent share of total unemployment benefits, which suggests that a significant number of unemployed persons belong to households with high incomes. The reason may be that the rich households have a greater concentration of teenage children who receive unemployment benefits but still live with their parents.

The family allowance is given to all families with children irrespective of their incomes. We would expect it to be distributed evenly over the total income. This seems to be the case with an exception of the first quintile, which receives a share of only 5.49 percent of total family allowance. This may be due to the heavy concentration of elderly people in the first quintile, who generally have no dependent children. The concentration index of family allowance is 15.57, showing that it has the effect of making household income distribution more unequal.

The figures in the last row indicate that income from wages and salaries contributes as much as 89.16 percent to total income inequality. It would seem, then, that any policy that increases the labor share of the functional distribution may increase rather than decrease the inequality of the size distribution of total income. The share of business income is 10.62 percent but it contributes as much as 15.35 percent to total income inequality. This is what one would expect because business income is believed to have an adverse effect on income inequality.

The share of the other income is 6.78 percent but it contributes only 2.74 percent to total inequality. This result seems surprising because the major component of the other income is investment income, which is believed to be concentrated heavily at the higher income ranges. One reason for this phenomenon may be that a large number of retired persons, who receive a sizable proportion of their income from investment, belong to the lower income ranges.

6.4   Inequality of household income and expenditure

In this section we compare the inequality measures of various income concepts and total household expenditure. Three income concepts used are

1. *Original income,* which is defined as income received from all sources by all members of the households.[4]
2. *Gross income* is defined as the sum of original income and government cash benefits received by all members of the households.
3. *Disposable income* is equal to gross household income minus income tax paid.

In Chapter 3, "Income Concept in the Analysis of Income Distribution," it was mentioned that current income, measured over a short period, is subject to transitory fluctuations, and therefore shows greater inequality than permanent income. In a typical cross section of households, a number of these transitory components in measured income may not be relevant for the typical set of household spending decisions. It may be argued, therefore, that the observed current income may not adequately reflect the true economic position of a household. The total expenditure, on the other hand, is subject to less transitory fluctuations and may be considered a better indicator of the actual economic welfare of a household than its current income. Hence, in this chapter we also present the numerical estimates of various inequality measures for the household expenditure distribution.

The numerical estimates of various inequality measures are presented in Table 6.4. It should be mentioned that the generalized entropy measures I_0 and I_1 and Atkinson's measures $A(1.0)$ and $A(1.5)$ cannot be computed for negative values of income. Some households that had negative incomes were deleted when computations were performed for these in-

Table 6.4. *Inequality measures of various income concepts: Australia 1975-6*

Inequality measures	Original income	Gross income	Disposable income	Total expenditure
Quintile shares				
1	1.71	5.14	5.56	8.05
2	11.61	12.24	12.70	15.00
3	18.49	18.12	13.34	19.41
4	26.02	24.68	24.70	23.47
5	42.17	39.81	38.70	34.06
Generalized Gini index				
$G(1.0)$	40.11	34.51	33.05	25.55
$G(1.5)$	50.23	42.89	41.20	32.11
$G(2.0)$	57.67	48.94	47.15	37.03
Generalized entropy measures				
I_0	20.00	9.50	8.60	5.20
I_1	11.80	8.10	7.30	4.60
I_2	25.82	19.59	17.77	10.64
Kakwani's Lorenz measure	15.30	11.00	10.10	6.20
Atkinson's measures				
$A(1.0)$	36.90	19.70	18.00	11.30
$A(1.5)$	63.50	30.10	27.80	17.40
$A(2.0)$	89.20	38.50	36.10	23.70
Average household income or expenditure	210.00	226.20	196.55	172.39

equality measures. As a consequence, values of these measures are under-estimated but we expect the bias to be negligible because the proportion of such households was very small, with small negative values. Several conclusions can be drawn from this table.

First, Atkinson's measure $A(\epsilon)$ increases monotonically with ϵ for all income definitions. It may be recalled that the parameter ϵ measures the degree of inequality-aversion – or the relative sensitivity to income transfers at different income levels; the larger the value of ϵ, the more weight is attached to the lower end of the distribution than at the middle and at the top. The numerical values indicate that Atkinson's measures are highly sensitive to the degree of inequality aversion.

It was pointed out in Chapter 4 that the interpretation of parameter c in the generalized-entropy measures is similar to Atkinson's ϵ parameter – as c decreases, the index becomes more sensitive to transfers lower down the distribution. It is interesting to note that a monotonic relationship between the magnitude of inequality and the degree of inequality-aversion is not observed in the case of the generalized entropy family. As the degree of inequality-aversion decreases, the generalized-entropy measure decreases first and then increases. Thus, the two families of measures differ with respect to their sensitivity to the degree of inequality-aversion.

The generalized Gini index was computed for three values of k, viz., 1.0, 1.5, and 2.0, $G(1.0)$ being the well-known Gini index. The numerical results indicate that the higher the value of k, the greater is the value of the generalized Gini index, suggesting a monotonic relationship between the magnitude of inequality and the degree of inequality aversion. Thus, the sensitivity of these measures varies with k in much the same way as Atkinson's ϵ parameter alters his inequality measure.

Second, the inequality of original income is substantially higher than that of the gross income, showing that government benefits have a major impact on the distribution of income towards greater equality. This can also be seen from quintile shares; shares of the first two quintiles are increased and those of the remaining three decreased as a result of government cash transfers. Income tax also reduces income inequality, as shown by the inequality of disposable income; but its impact is significantly lower than that of the government benefits.

Third, the inequality of total household expenditure is considerably lower than that of disposable income; the Gini index of total expenditures is only 25.55, compared to 33.05 for disposable income. This can be explained in terms of inequality of savings. Since income is the sum of expenditures and savings, and since households with higher incomes tend to save a greater proportion of their income, inequality of saving will be high. This is an important reason why inequality of income is higher than that of expenditure.

Podder and Kakwani's (1975a) study based on the Australian Survey of Consumer Finances and Expenditures 1967–8 estimated inequality measures for the income concept used in the present study. Table 6.5 sets out these results.

It can be seen that the income shares of the first two quintiles are higher in 1967–8 than 1975–6 and the shares of the remaining three quintiles are lower. As a consequence, the inequality of income as measured by the Gini index has increased during the period from 1967–8 to 1975–6. This conclusion is supported by all the three income definitions; inequality of original income has increased by about 9 percent, that of gross income by 7.2 percent, and that of disposable income by 8.36 percent.

These increases in income inequality during the period from 1967–8 to 1975–6 are most striking. We would not expect inequality of income to be increasing at such a high rate. In fact, Richardson (1979) expected in-

Table 6.5. *Inequality measures of various income concepts: Australia 1967–8*

Inequality measures	Original income	Gross income	Disposable income
Quintile shares			
1	2.92	6.31	6.77
2	13.74	13.59	14.07
3	18.34	17.87	18.18
4	24.01	23.27	23.29
5	40.98	32.20	30.50
Gini index expressed in percentages	36.8	32.20	30.50

equality to decline rather than increase during this period. The available information is insufficient to provide a definitive explanation for our results, which may be due to the unreliability of the 1967–8 data. The inequality calculations given in the table are based on the second stage of the survey, which has a response rate of only 50 percent. The high nonresponse rate has the effect of making the sample nonrandom, which may have significantly affected the estimates of inequality measures.

6.5   An international comparison of household income distribution

A brief international comparison of household income distributions is attempted in this section. Before such a comparison is made it is necessary to point out that there are several difficulties associated with the use of income distribution data from different countries. These data are generally subject to large errors, and the magnitude of errors is not likely to be the same for all countries. There are problems associated with definitions of income and income units. These have been widely discussed elsewhere (see, for instance, Kuznets 1955; Titmus 1962; Adelman and Morris 1971; and Kravis 1960). Unavoidably, then, conclusions from international comparisons of inequality have severe limitations.

In spite of these limitations, the comparisons have some value. As noted by Roberti (1978), "the observation and comparisons of income distributions can help us to understand, though approximately and tentatively, where different nations stand with respect to each other and to some chosen objective of fair distribution of income."

This comparison is restricted to a few developed countries, the choice of which was based on three considerations: (a) the countries are similar

Table 6.6. *Distribution of pre- and post-tax personal income by households*

Country	Year	Quintile shares					Gini coefficient
		1	2	3	4	5	
Pre-tax household income							
Australia	1975–6	5.14	12.24	18.12	24.68	39.81	34.51
Japan	1971	3.80	10.90	16.30	22.80	46.20	40.70
France	1972	5.20	11.20	16.70	23.10	43.80	38.40
Republic of Ireland	1973	4.10	11.10	16.60	23.80	44.50	39.50
United Kingdom	1974	5.50	11.90	18.10	24.40	40.10	34.80
United States	1974	3.80	10.00	16.10	23.70	46.40	41.20
Post-tax household income							
Australia	1975–6	5.56	12.70	18.34	24.70	38.70	33.05
Sweden	1972	6.60	13.10	18.50	24.80	37.00	30.20
Germany	1975	6.20	10.50	15.60	22.50	45.30	38.80
United Kingdom	1973	6.30	12.40	18.00	24.10	39.30	33.30

Sources: Australia: Household Expenditure Survey, 1975–6. France: M. Sawyer, Income Distribution in OECD Countries, OECD Economic Outlook, Occasional Studies, July 1973. Japan: R. O. Wada, "Changes in the Size Distribution of Income in Post-War Japan," World Employment Program Research, ILO, October 1974. Republic of Ireland: Central Statistical Office: Household Budget Survey, Vol. 1 Summary Results, Dublin 1976. United States: Bureau of the Census, Dept. of Commerce, Current Population Reports, Consumer Income, Household Money Income and Selected Social and Economic Characteristics of Households. United Kingdom: Royal Commission on the Distribution of Income and Wealth, Reports Nos. 1 and 4. Sweden: National Central Bureau of Statistics, Swedish Survey on Relative Income Differences 1972, Stockholm 1974. Germany: DIW "Das Einkommen sozialer Gruppen in der Bundesrepublik Deutschland Jahre" Wochenbericht, 1976.

in political and socioeconomic structure, (b) estimates of the inequality indices are readily available for a period around 1975–6, and (c) the definitions of income and income-recipient unit are closest to the Australian definitions. The developing countries have been excluded from the list mainly because of the lower reliability of income-distribution data available in these countries. Moreover, these countries have a greater degree of heterogeneity with respect to political and socioeconomic structures, and as such the comparison of their income inequality with that of Australia may not be very meaningful.

Table 6.6 provides the basis for comparison of pre- and post-tax income distributions in the selected countries. The level of inequality in Australia, on the basis of the Gini index of the pre-tax household income, is less than elsewhere. The difference in the level of inequality between Australia and the United Kingdom is almost insignificant. The shares of total income accruing to various quintiles are of approximately similar magnitude in the two countries. The United States of America has the highest level of inequality, with Gini index 41.20, and Japan the second highest, with slightly lower Gini index. The quintile shares are also of similar magnitude in these two countries.

Roberti (1978), using 1968–9 Australian Bureau of Statistics data on family income distribution, concluded that the degree of inequality in Australia is "exceptionally low" whereas Canada, Germany, Italy, Norway, New Zealand, Spain, Sweden, and the United Kingdom have comparatively low inequality. However, this conclusion is not supported by the evidence presented in Table 6.6. The fact that the inequality of income in the United Kingdom is very similar to that in Australia immediately casts doubt on the validity of this conclusion. Further, comparing the post-tax income distribution, it is evident that Australia has considerably greater inequality than Sweden.

An important reason for the "exceptionally low" inequality observed in Australia compared to other countries, as noted by Ingles (1981), could have been due to the fact that Roberti based his study on family income distribution for 1968–9, which does not include single-member families; evidence based on the 1973–4 income distribution showed that the inclusion of these "nonfamily individuals" leads to significantly greater inequality.

To sum up, the conclusion that Australia has exceptionally low inequality in comparison with other developed countries may not be valid. But on the whole it may be concluded that there is some empirical ground to believe that Australia is one of the most egalitarian countries in the world as far as distribution of income is concerned. This conclusion should be regarded as tentative, because these comparisons did not take into account household size and composition, which is an essential consideration in any accurate measurement of income inequality.

6.6   Children and adults in the income distribution

In Chapter 2, "Income-recipient units and their differing needs," it was pointed out that the level of economic welfare enjoyed by a household cannot be adequately measured without taking into account household size and composition. The reason is that households of different size and composition require a different amount of income in order to enjoy the same level of economic welfare. The need for adjusting the household by its size and composition has been emphasized strongly by Kuznets (1976):

It makes little sense to talk about inequality in the distribution of income among families or households by income per family or household when the underlying units differ so much in size... before any analysis can be undertaken, size distribu-

Table 6.7. *Children and adults in the household income distribution in Australia 1975-6*

Range of weekly household income	Percentage of households	Average income per household	Persons per household	Children per household	Adults per household	Income per person
under $40	4.24	17.25	1.62	.35	1.27	10.65
$40-$80	11.41	60.10	1.82	.32	1.50	33.02
$80-$110	6.68	95.59	2.55	.82	1.73	37.49
$110-$140	7.74	127.15	2.73	1.00	1.73	46.57
$140-$170	9.97	156.32	3.11	1.20	1.91	50.26
$170-$200	9.51	186.18	3.36	1.37	1.99	55.41
$200-$230	8.26	216.66	3.41	1.35	2.06	63.54
$230-$260	7.94	245.61	3.37	1.34	2.03	72.88
$260-$300	9.92	281.23	3.41	1.25	2.16	82.47
$300-$340	6.58	319.18	3.57	1.24	2.33	89.41
$340-$400	7.12	370.34	3.69	1.27	2.42	100.36
$400 and over	10.63	530.89	3.90	1.19	2.72	136.12
All households	100.00	226.20	3.09	1.07	2.02	73.25

tions of families or households by income per family or household must be converted to distribution of persons (or consumer equivalents) by size of family or household income per person (or consumer).

Interestingly enough, most of the income-distribution studies carried out in Australia are based on household income. The conclusions emerging from these studies will be meaningful only if it can be assumed that households are more or less of the same size and composition. This is clearly not evident from the numerical results given in Table 6.7.

This table indicates that households in different income ranges vary substantially with respect to the number of persons per household. The average number of persons per household rises as we move from the low to the higher brackets of income per household. For instance the average household size in the lowest income bracket is 1.62 as against 3.90 in the highest income bracket. If we disaggregate the total number of persons per household by the number of adults and children per household, we find that the variation in the number of children per household is considerably greater than that in number of adults per household. The average number of adults per household appears to be increasing monotonically with the household income, but such a relationship does not exist with respect to the average number of children per household.

On the basis of the U.S. data, Kuznets (1981) observed that larger house-

Table 6.8. *Children and adults in the per capita gross household income distribution in Australia: 1975-6*

Range of per capita weekly household income	Percentage of persons	Income per person	Income per household	Persons per household	Children per household	Adults per household
under $30	12.68	20.05	91.04	4.54	2.64	1.90
$30-$50	26.07	40.60	127.00	3.13	1.28	1.85
$50-$70	22.03	60.22	212.57	3.53	1.42	2.11
$70-$100	18.18	83.40	262.83	3.15	.92	2.23
$100-$130	9.86	113.89	305.84	2.68	.49	2.19
$130-$160	5.51	142.96	310.31	2.17	.18	1.99
$160-$190	2.39	173.14	337.30	1.95	.12	1.83
$190-$220	1.40	204.39	406.05	1.99	.12	1.87
$220-$250	.80	235.03	423.16	1.80	.20	1.60
$250-$280	.47	268.68	459.64	1.71	.10	1.61
$280-$310	.14	292.84	541.13	1.85	.19	1.66
$310 and over	.47	428.38	447.09	1.54	.06	1.48
All households	100.00	73.25	226.20	3.09	1.07	2.02

holds usually have a higher proportion of children. If this observation is valid generally, then the positive association between the household size and income should at least imply an increasing monotonic relationship between the average number of children per household and the household income. This is clearly not supported by the evidence given in the table.

Despite the fact that there is a positive association between the average size of household and total income per household, income per person rises as we move from the lower to the higher income per household (as can be seen from the last column of the table). This might suggest a positive correlation between average size of household and income per person. But this correlation is clearly spurious, as can be seen from Table 6.8, where households are classified by the per capita household income. This table clearly shows that the average number of persons per household decreases more or less monotonically with rising per capita household income. The negative association between the size of household and household income per person was also observed by Kuznets (1981) in all five countries (United States, Germany, Israel, Taiwan, and the Philippines) covered by him. On the basis of this observation, he arrived at an important conclusion, that "the very identity of the lower and upper groups on the income scale shifts as we convert from a size distribution of households by income per household to a size distribution of persons (or consumers) by income per person (or consumer)."

The monotonic relationship between the income per person and the income per household (as observed in the last column of Table 6.7) may suggest that the ranking of households by household income will be identical to that by income per person. This conclusion may be misleading, as can be seen by the size distribution of persons by income per person in Table 6.8. This table indicates that the monotonic relationship between the two income concepts breaks down as the income per person exceeds $280. Thus, ranking of households according to these two criteria (one by total household income and other by per capita household income) will be different.

In order to compute the various inequality measures, an important first step is to establish appropriate ranking criterion for ranking the households. If the household income is adjusted for household size and composition, the appropriate ranking criterion is the adjusted household income. But, in most cases, the published data on income distribution rank the households by total household income and, therefore, are unsuitable for analyzing the effect of household size and composition on income distribution. This deficiency is corrected in the remaining parts of this study.

6.7 Inequality of household income distribution, adjusted for size and composition

To take account of the fact that the number of children and adults varies among households, we adjust the household income by an equivalent-income scale. This adjustment is done by dividing the income of each household by a certain number of equivalent-adults, obtained by the use of a certain equivalent-income scale. In Chapter 2, it was concluded that the estimation of equivalent-income scales in Australia raises several difficulties and the only solution to this seems to be to estimate the distribution of income using several alternative equivalent-income scales. This section attempts to investigate the sensitivity of income inequality with respect to alternative equivalent-income scales.

Let $v_i(\lambda_1, \lambda_2)$ be the number of equivalent adults in the ith household consisting of a_i adults and c_i children, given by

$$v_i(\lambda_1, \lambda_2) = 1 + \lambda_1(a_i - 1) + \lambda_2 c_i \tag{6.2}$$

where λ_1 is the weight given to the second and subsequent adult and λ_2 the weight given to each child in the household. The head of the household is assigned the weight equal to unity. Obviously, then, both λ_1 and λ_2 must be less than unity. A further restriction that $\lambda_2 < \lambda_1$ seems reasonable on the assumption that children need less than adults in order to have the same level of welfare.

The adjusted household income that is used as a proxy for the economic

Table 6.9. *Quintile shares and generalized Gini index of the distribution of households according to adjusted income or expenditure with differing weights: Australia 1975-6*

Weights									
λ_1	0.0	1.0	.9	.8	.8	.8	.7	.7	.7
λ_2	0.0	1.0	.5	.5	.4	.3	.5	.4	.3
Original income									
Quintile shares									
1	1.7	2.5	2.4	2.4	2.4	2.4	2.4	2.4	2.3
2	11.6	9.9	11.2	11.2	11.5	11.8	11.1	11.5	11.8
3	18.5	16.3	17.8	17.8	18.1	18.5	17.8	18.2	18.5
4	26.0	25.0	25.3	25.4	25.8	25.8	25.5	25.6	25.8
5	42.2	46.2	43.1	43.1	42.4	41.6	43.1	42.4	41.6
Generalized Gini index									
$G(1.0)$	40.1	43.5	40.4	40.5	39.8	39.1	40.5	39.8	39.1
$G(1.5)$	50.2	53.2	50.1	50.1	49.4	48.8	50.3	49.5	48.8
$G(2.0)$	57.7	60.0	57.1	57.2	56.5	55.9	57.3	46.6	56.0
Gross income									
Quintile shares									
1	5.1	6.8	7.3	7.2	7.3	7.2	7.1	7.1	7.1
2	12.2	11.4	12.0	11.9	12.1	12.4	11.9	12.1	12.5
3	18.1	15.9	17.4	17.4	17.7	17.9	17.3	17.7	17.9
4	24.7	23.7	23.7	23.8	23.9	24.1	24.0	24.0	24.2
5	39.8	42.2	39.6	39.7	39.0	38.3	39.7	39.0	38.4
Generalized Gini index									
$G(1.0)$	34.5	35.4	32.5	32.6	32.0	31.4	32.8	32.2	31.5
$G(1.5)$	42.9	42.9	39.7	39.9	39.3	38.7	40.2	39.5	38.9
$G(2.0)$	48.9	47.9	44.8	45.1	44.4	43.9	45.4	44.7	44.1
Disposable income									
Quintile shares									
1	5.6	7.4	7.9	7.9	7.9	7.9	7.8	7.8	7.8
2	12.7	12.0	12.6	12.5	12.7	13.0	12.4	12.7	13.0
3	18.3	16.2	17.7	17.7	18.0	18.2	17.7	18.0	18.2
4	24.7	23.8	23.8	23.9	23.9	24.1	24.0	24.0	24.2
5	38.7	40.6	38.0	38.1	37.4	36.8	38.1	37.5	36.8
Generalized Gini index									
$G(1.0)$	33.1	33.3	30.3	30.4	29.8	29.2	30.6	30.0	29.4
$G(1.5)$	41.2	40.5	37.2	37.4	36.8	36.2	37.7	37.0	36.4
$G(2.0)$	47.2	45.4	42.1	42.4	41.8	41.2	42.8	42.1	41.5
Total expenditure									
Quintile shares									
1	8.1	10.4	11.4	11.4	11.5	11.5	11.3	11.4	11.3
2	15.0	13.8	15.0	14.8	15.1	15.3	14.7	15.0	15.4
3	19.4	17.5	18.0	18.2	18.3	18.5	18.3	18.4	18.6
4	23.5	22.6	22.8	22.9	22.9	23.0	22.9	23.0	23.1
5	34.1	35.7	32.8	32.8	32.2	31.7	32.9	32.2	31.6

Table 6.9 (cont.)

Weights									
λ_1	0.0	1.0	.9	.8	.8	.8	.7	.7	.7
λ_2	0.0	1.0	.5	.5	.4	.3	.5	.4	.3
Generalized Gini index									
$G(1.0)$	25.6	25.4	21.7	21.7	21.0	20.5	21.9	21.1	20.5
$G(1.5)$	32.1	30.8	26.4	26.6	25.8	25.2	26.9	26.0	25.4
$G(2.0)$	37.0	34.6	29.8	30.1	29.3	28.7	30.4	29.6	28.9

welfare of a household is defined as

$$y_i(\lambda_1, \lambda_2) = \frac{x_i}{\nu_i(\lambda_1, \lambda_2)}$$

where x_i is the total income of the ith household. Note that when $\lambda_i = 0$, $\lambda_2 = 0$, the adjusted income is identical to the total household income. The per capita household income is obtained when both λ_1 and λ_2 are equal to unity, implying that each member of the household gets equal weight.

The inequality measures were computed by ranking the households according to the size of the adjusted income. Note that the ranking of households will be different for different values of λ_1 and λ_2. The numerical values of various inequality measures are reported in Tables 6.9 and 6.10 for three income definitions (original, gross, and disposable) and total expenditure. Several interesting points emerge from the results given in these tables.

First, the inequality indices based on per capita household income differ significantly from those based on household income. It is not possible to say which of the two distributions is more equal. For instance, on the basis of generalized Gini index and Kakwani's Lorenz measure, the distribution of households by original per capita income is more unequal than the distribution of households by original household income. This ranking is reversed, however, if we compare the two distributions on the basis of Atkinson's measure. If we use the total expenditure as a measure of household welfare, the distribution of the per capita household expenditure appears to be more equal than the total household expenditure distribution, as can be seen from the numerical values of all inequality measures except one, viz., I_2. The distribution of per capita household income is believed to be more equal than the total household income distribution[5] but this clearly is not evident from the results given here. The ranking of the two distributions in terms of inequality is sensitive to both the choice of income concepts and the choice of inequality measure used.

Table 6.10. *Inequality in the distribution of households according to adjusted income or expenditure with differing weights: Australia 1975–6*

Weights									
λ_1	0.0	1.0	.9	.8	.8	.8	.7	.7	.7
λ_2	0.0	1.0	.5	.5	.4	.3	.5	.4	.3
Original income									
Kakwani's Lorenz measure	15.3	16.8	15.0	15.1	14.7	14.4	15.1	14.8	14.4
Atkinson's measures									
$A(1.0)$	36.9	34.2	32.5	32.6	32.3	32.1	32.9	32.5	32.3
$A(1.5)$	63.5	54.2	53.7	54.1	54.1	54.3	54.5	54.7	54.7
$A(2.0)$	89.2	78.3	79.7	80.2	80.6	81.0	80.8	81.1	81.5
Generalized entropy measures									
I_0	20.0	18.2	17.0	17.2	17.0	16.8	17.3	17.1	16.9
I_1	11.8	13.5	11.8	11.8	11.4	11.1	11.8	11.5	11.1
I_2	25.8	34.5	28.3	28.1	26.9	25.8	27.9	26.7	25.6
Gross income									
Kakwani's Lorenz measure	11.0	11.1	9.5	9.6	9.3	9.0	9.7	9.4	9.1
Atkinson's measures									
$A(1.0)$	19.7	18.4	15.7	15.9	15.4	15.0	16.1	15.6	15.1
$A(1.5)$	30.1	26.5	23.1	23.3	22.8	22.3	23.7	23.0	22.5
$A(2.0)$	38.5	31.3	27.6	27.9	27.3	27.0	28.3	27.7	27.3
Generalized entropy									
I_0	9.5	8.8	7.4	7.5	7.3	7.0	7.6	7.3	7.1
I_1	8.1	8.7	7.2	7.2	6.9	6.7	7.3	7.0	6.7
I_2	19.6	24.4	19.5	19.4	18.4	17.6	19.3	18.4	17.5
Disposable income									
Kakwani's Lorenz measure	10.1	9.9	8.4	8.4	8.2	7.9	8.5	8.2	8.0
Atkinson's measures									
$A(1.0)$	18.0	16.3	13.7	13.8	13.4	13.0	14.0	13.5	13.1
$A(1.5)$	27.8	23.9	20.5	20.7	20.1	19.7	21.0	20.4	19.9
$A(2.0)$	36.1	28.8	25.1	25.4	24.9	24.5	25.8	25.2	24.8
Generalized entropy									
I_0	8.6	7.7	6.4	6.5	6.2	6.0	6.6	6.3	6.1
I_1	7.3	7.5	6.1	6.1	5.9	5.6	6.2	5.9	5.7
I_2	17.8	20.3	16.1	16.1	15.3	14.5	16.1	15.3	14.5
Total expenditure									
Kakwani's Lorenz measure	6.2	6.0	4.4	4.4	4.1	3.9	4.4	4.2	4.0
Atkinson's measures									
$A(1.0)$	11.3	10.0	7.3	7.4	6.9	6.6	7.4	7.0	6.7
$A(1.5)$	17.4	14.2	10.5	10.6	10.0	9.6	10.7	10.1	9.7
$A(2.0)$	23.7	18.1	13.4	13.6	12.9	12.4	13.8	13.1	12.6
Generalized entropy									
I_0	5.2	4.6	3.3	3.3	3.1	3.0	3.4	3.1	3.0
I_1	4.6	5.0	3.4	3.6	3.4	3.2	3.6	3.3	3.1
I_2	10.5	15.3	10.8	10.4	9.7	9.0	10.1	9.4	8.7

It can be seen that shares of the first and the fifth quintiles are consistently higher for the per capita household distribution than those for the household income distribution for all four concepts. It means that the households in the middle three quintiles suffer a relative income loss as a result of the change in the ranking criteria from total household income to per capita household income.

The ranking of households on the basis of per capita household income assumes that all persons within the household have exactly the same needs, irrespective of their age. As has been already pointed out, this assumption is difficult to justify, as adults do need more than children. Also, due to the economies of scale of family living, the expenditure or income required by the second and subsequent adult will be less than the first adult or head of the household in order to maintain the same living standard. It is, therefore, necessary to make a distinction between the first and the second adult and the children belonging to the household. So, the remaining columns in the table present the values of inequality measures for different weights given to the second and subsequent adult and the children in the household.

It should be noted that the inequality measures are more or less of the same magnitude despite wide variations in the weights given to the second and subsequent adults and children. This is an important finding. It implies that if our objective is to measure income inequality, inaccuracies occurring in the estimation of equivalent-income scales are of little consequence.

The inequality of adjusted household income distribution is generally lower than that of per capita and total household income distributions for each of the three income definitions (original income, gross income, and disposable income) and for total household expenditure. This means that if we make adjustment for household size and composition, the inequality of income or total expenditure is reduced. This is an important result because all the earlier income distributions studies carried out in Australia are based on household income and they could have overestimated the levels of inequality.

6.8 Individual income distribution

In the previous section we presented the values of inequality measures based on the distribution of households according to the household income adjusted for size and composition. In the construction of the size distribution, each household was given an equal weight irrespective of its size. This means that the welfare of a single-person household is given equal weight to that of a household consisting of, say, eight persons. This approach is unsatisfactory because there exists no welfare justification for giving larger weights to individuals belonging to smaller households and smaller weights to those belonging to larger households. In fact Danziger and Taussig (1979) point out that "conventional size" distributions, which weigh each family or household equally, violate the requirements for individualistic social welfare functions because they implicitly weight the welfare of an individual inversely to the size of the unit to which that individual belongs.

The second approach we might consider is to weight each household by the number of equivalent-adults in it. This approach appears attractive because it puts a weight on each household proportional to its consumption needs measured by the number of equivalent-adults in it. Unfortunately, the approach runs into a serious conceptual difficulty which Sen (1979) has highlighted: " I he scale of equivalent-adults indicates conversion factors to be used to find out how well off members of that family are, but ultimately we are concerned with the sufferings of everyone in the family and not of a hypothetical equivalent number. If two can live as cheaply as one and a half and three as cheaply as two, these facts must be taken into account in comparing the relative well-beings of two-member and three-member families, but there is no reason why the suffering of two three-member families should receive any less weight than that of three two-member families at the same level of illfare."

Since our objective is to measure the distribution of the economic welfare of individuals, the best approach seems to be to weigh each individual equally, irrespective of the size and composition of the household to which he or she belongs. This approach can be justified from the welfare point of view if one opts for an individualistic social welfare function (Danziger and Taussig 1979).

Under this approach the size distribution of individual welfare is constructed by assigning each individual in a household a welfare value equal to the income per equivalent-adults for that household. This approach will be appropriate if we assume that every member in the household enjoys exactly the same level of welfare. The validity of this assumption is difficult to assess because of the limited knowledge available on the internal structure of the household. It was pointed out in Chapter 2 that if we assume that the family members care about each other, then it may be reasonable to say that the family will allocate its resources so that each family member enjoys the same level of economic welfare. If this assumption is not satisfied, however, the inequality measures presented in this section will underestimate the true inequality in individual income distribution.

The numerical values of inequality in individual income distribution are presented in Tables 6.11 and 6.12 for different adjustment criteria for

Table 6.11. *Quintile shares and generalized Gini index of the distribution of individuals with differing weights: Australia 1975-6*

Weights								
λ_1	1.0	.9	.8	.8	.8	.7	.7	.7
λ_2	1.0	.5	.5	.4	.3	.5	.4	.3
Original income								
Quintile shares								
1	4.0	4.2	4.2	4.3	4.4	4.1	4.2	4.3
2	11.4	12.8	12.7	13.0	13.3	12.5	12.9	13.2
3	16.9	18.1	18.0	18.4	18.7	17.9	18.3	18.6
4	23.9	24.6	24.7	24.8	24.9	24.8	24.9	25.0
5	43.8	40.3	40.4	39.6	38.8	40.6	39.7	38.9
Generalized Gini index								
$G(1.0)$	39.3	35.7	35.9	35.1	34.2	36.2	35.3	34.4
$G(1.5)$	48.1	44.3	44.6	43.7	43.8	44.9	43.9	43.0
$G(2.0)$	54.4	50.8	51.0	50.1	49.3	51.3	50.4	49.5
Gross income								
Quintile shares								
1	6.9	7.6	7.5	7.7	7.7	7.4	7.6	7.7
2	12.1	12.9	12.9	13.1	13.5	12.8	13.0	13.4
3	16.6	17.8	17.8	18.0	18.3	17.7	18.0	18.2
4	23.2	23.6	23.7	23.8	23.8	23.8	23.9	23.9
5	41.2	38.0	38.1	37.4	36.7	38.3	37.5	36.8
Generalized Gini index								
$G(1.0)$	34.1	30.4	30.7	29.8	29.0	31.0	30.1	29.2
$G(1.5)$	41.4	37.4	37.7	36.8	35.9	38.1	37.1	36.2
$G(2.0)$	46.5	42.4	42.8	41.8	40.9	43.2	42.2	41.2
Disposable income								
Quintile shares								
1	7.5	8.2	8.1	8.3	8.3	8.0	8.2	8.2
2	12.5	13.4	13.4	13.6	14.0	13.3	13.5	14.0
3	16.8	18.1	18.0	18.3	18.5	17.9	18.3	18.5
4	23.3	23.6	23.8	23.8	23.9	23.8	23.9	24.0
5	40.0	36.6	36.8	36.0	35.3	37.0	36.2	35.4
Generalized Gini index								
$G(1.0)$	32.3	28.5	28.8	28.0	27.2	29.1	28.2	27.4
$G(1.5)$	39.4	35.2	35.6	34.6	33.8	36.0	35.0	34.0
$G(2.0)$	44.3	40.1	40.5	39.5	38.6	40.9	40.0	38.9
Total expenditure								
Quintile shares								
1	10.6	12.0	11.9	12.2	12.4	11.8	12.0	12.3
2	14.1	15.5	15.3	15.6	15.9	15.1	15.6	15.9
3	18.0	18.4	18.5	18.6	18.8	18.6	18.6	18.8
4	22.7	22.6	22.7	22.7	22.7	22.8	22.8	22.8
5	34.6	31.5	31.6	30.9	30.3	31.8	31.0	30.3

Table 6.11 *(cont.)*

Weights								
λ_1	1.0	.9	.8	.8	.8	.7	.7	.7
λ_2	1.0	.5	.5	.4	.3	.5	.4	.3
Generalized Gini index								
$G(1.0)$	24.9	19.6	19.9	18.9	18.1	20.2	19.2	18.3
$G(1.5)$	29.44	24.1	24.5	23.9	22.5	24.9	23.7	22.7
$G(2.0)$	33.1	27.4	27.8	26.6	25.63	28.3	27.0	25.9

household size and composition. The distribution of individuals by per capita income is more equal than that of households by household income. This observation is supported by all income concepts and inequality measures used in the analysis (with the exception of the generalized entropy measure I_2).[6]

Adjustment for household size and composition makes a great deal of difference to the inequality in individual income distribution. The inequality of adjusted household income is considerably lower than that of per capita income. The inequality decreases as the weight given to children decreases, indicating a positive association between the inequality and the weight given to each child in the household. But the variation in inequality with respect to the weight given to the second and subsequent adults in the household shows the negative association (i.e., the inequality increases as the weight to the second and subsequent adult decreases). Despite these patterns, the variation in inequality with respect to the variation in weights given to various household members is not wide enough to be concerned about the accurate estimation of equivalent-income scales.

A comparison of the distributions of individuals with those of households shows that the individual distributions are always more equal than the corresponding distributions of households for all income concepts and weighting criteria used. The magnitudes of differences in the values of inequality measures are significant and vary with respect to both the income concept and the weighting criterion. The variation is greater with respect to the income concept than with respect to the weighting.

6.9   Summary of conclusions

Several aspects of the distribution of income in Australia have been discussed in this chapter, from which a number of broad conclusions may be derived. Among them are

1. The commonly held belief – that the larger the family's average income, the smaller the proportion derived from employment –

Table 6.12. *Inequality in the distribution of individuals according to adjusted income or expenditure with differing weights: Australia 1975-6*

Weights								
λ_1	1.0	.9	.8	.8	.8	.7	.7	.7
λ_2	1.0	.5	.5	.4	.3	.5	.4	.3
Original income								
Kakwani's Lorenz measure	13.9	12.0	12.1	11.6	11.3	12.2	11.7	11.3
Atkinson's measures								
$A(1.0)$	26.7	24.2	24.4	23.9	23.4	24.7	24.1	23.6
$A(1.5)$	42.8	41.0	41.3	41.0	40.8	41.8	41.4	41.2
$A(2.0)$	63.5	64.5	65.1	65.5	66.0	65.8	66.1	66.7
Generalized entropy								
I_0	13.5	12.0	12.2	11.9	11.6	12.3	12.0	11.7
I_1	10.8	9.0	9.0	8.7	8.3	9.1	8.7	8.3
I_2	28.5	22.2	22.2	21.0	19.9	22.4	21.1	19.9
Gross income								
Kakwani's Lorenz measure	10.4	8.5	8.6	8.2	7.9	8.8	8.4	8.0
Atkinson's measures								
$A(1.0)$	16.9	13.7	13.9	13.3	12.7	14.2	13.5	12.8
$A(1.5)$	24.6	20.3	20.7	19.8	19.0	21.1	20.1	19.3
$A(2.0)$	28.0	23.1	23.5	22.5	21.7	24.0	23.0	22.1
Generalized entropy								
I_0	8.1	6.4	6.5	6.2	5.9	6.7	6.3	6.0
I_1	7.9	6.2	6.3	5.9	5.6	6.4	6.0	5.6
I_2	22.3	16.8	16.9	15.8	14.8	17.1	16.0	14.9
Disposable income								
Kakwani's Lorenz measure	9.5	7.6	7.8	7.4	7.0	7.9	7.5	7.1
Atkinson's measures								
$A(1.0)$	15.2	12.0	12.3	11.6	11.1	12.5	11.8	11.2
$A(1.5)$	22.3	18.1	18.4	17.6	16.9	18.8	17.9	17.1
$A(2.0)$	25.5	20.8	21.2	20.3	19.6	21.7	20.7	19.9
Generalized entropy								
I_0	7.2	5.6	5.7	5.4	5.1	5.8	5.5	5.2
I_1	7.0	5.3	5.4	5.1	4.8	5.5	5.5	5.2
I_2	19.2	14.3	14.4	13.5	12.6	14.7	13.6	12.7
Total expenditure								
Kakwani's Lorenz measure	5.3	3.6	3.7	3.3	3.1	3.8	3.4	3.1
Atkinson's measures								
$A(1.0)$	9.0	6.0	6.2	5.6	5.2	6.4	5.8	5.3
$A(1.5)$	13.0	8.8	9.0	8.3	7.7	9.3	8.5	7.8
$A(2.0)$	16.8	11.5	11.8	10.8	10.1	12.2	11.1	10.3
Generalized entropy								
I_0	4.1	2.7	2.8	2.5	2.3	2.9	2.6	2.4
I_1	4.3	2.8	2.9	2.6	2.4	2.9	2.6	2.4
I_2	12.1	7.6	7.6	6.9	6.2	7.7	6.9	6.2

is not supported by the empirical evidence presented here. In fact the relationship appears to be the reverse; income from wages and salaries is unevenly distributed over the total income in favor of richer households. It would seem, then, that any policy that increases the labor share of the functional distribution may increase rather than decrease the inequality of the size distribution of total income.

2. The income from investment has an equalizing effect on income distribution. This is a surprising conclusion because it is believed that this kind of income is heavily concentrated at the higher-income ranges. A possible explanation of this phenomenon is that a large number of retired persons who receive a sizable proportion of their income from investment belong to the lower-income ranges.

3. Australian National Accounts estimates of household income by factor components show that the wage share declined and the income share of government cash benefits increased during the period 1969–70 to 1979–80. Since both these factors have an equalizing effect on income distribution, we expect that the inequality of household income in Australia might have fallen during the 1970s.

4. A comparison of Podder and Kakwani's (1975) results based on the Australian Survey of Consumer Finances and Expenditure 1967–8 with those of this study show a considerable increase in income inequality during the period 1967–8 to 1975–6. This is an unexpected result in view of the observation made in the third conclusion. The available information is insufficient to provide a definitive explanation of this deviation but it may be partly due to the unreliability of the 1967–8 data.

5. The conclusion from earlier studies that Australia has an exceptionally low inequality in comparison with other developed countries of similar political and socioeconomic structure is not supported by empirical evidence from 1975–6 data. But, on the whole, it may be concluded that Australia is one of the most egalitarian countries in the world as far as the distribution of income is concerned.

6. The general belief that the distribution of per capita household income is more equal than the total household income distribution is not evident here. The ranking of the two distributions in terms of inequality is sensitive to both the choice of income concept and the choice of inequality measure used.

7. It is found that if our objective is to measure income inequality, inaccuracies in the estimation of equivalent-income scales are of

little consequence. This is an important finding because the accurate estimation of equivalent scales is not feasible.

8. The inequality of adjusted household income was found to be lower than that of per capita and total household income distributions for each of the three income definitions – original income, gross income, and disposable income – and for total household expenditure. This is an important result because all the earlier income distributions studies carried out in Australia, based on household income with no adjustment made for household size and composition, could have overestimated the levels of inequality.

9. A comparison of the distributions of individuals with those of households shows that individual distributions are always more equal than the corresponding distributions of households for all income concepts and alternative weighting criteria used. Since we are more concerned with the economic welfare of individuals, it is the inequality in the distribution of individual welfare that is most relevant, although much of the empirical literature is focused on the distribution of households' welfare.

CHAPTER 7

Tax rates and government benefit rates by income ranges

In this chapter we examine how the incidence of taxes and government benefits are distributed across income ranges. The two income concepts used for this purpose are total and per capita household income. In order to gain further insight into the issue of progressivity of taxes and government benefits, the indices of relative tax burdens and relative benefits received are computed for various income quintiles, and several policy implications indicated.

7.1   Tax incidence assumptions

Who actually pays the taxes is the key issue in the analysis of income redistribution. There is now a considerable literature on the incidence of taxation which attempts to answer this question, but with limited success. [1]

It is widely recognized that taxes may be shifted either forward or backward and that accurate quantitative measurement of these shifts is almost impossible. Generally speaking, the more direct the tax, the more difficult it is to shift to someone else; the more indirect the tax, the easier it is to shift it elsewhere (Schnitzer 1974: 9).

Indirect taxes, such as sales and excise taxes, are imposed on suppliers of goods and services, but their ultimate burden must be traced to individual households who pay these taxes in terms of increased prices. The process of shifting these taxes may be analyzed through the supply and demand mechanism of the taxed commodities. According to Dalton's (1936) law, the proportional shifting of tax on a commodity depends on the price elasticities of demand and supply of the commodity. It can be demonstrated that the more elastic the supply, the more the market price will rise and the greater will be the extent of shifting the tax to the buyers. Similarly, if demand of the taxed commodity is elastic, either because the good is not important to buyers or there are ready substitutes for it, the supplier will find it difficult to shift taxes to the buyer.

It should be emphasized that Dalton's law is based on partial equilibrium analysis, which makes no allowance for cross-price effects on the overall level of demand. It has, therefore, been suggested to analyze tax incidence within a general equilibrium framework. Piggott (1983) attempted to estimate the economic effects of tax changes under a general equilibrium model of the Australian economy. This model is of the algorithmic type and was first applied to the United Kingdom economy by Piggott and Whalley (1981). The policy changes considered were the abolition of the tax on corporate profits and the elimination of tax-favored treatment of owner-occupied housing. Although this study highlights the dangers of relying on partial equilibrium formulations in analyzing tax incidence, there still remains doubt among economists whether the empirical estimates of redistributive effects generated by general equilibrium tax models of the Piggott–Whalley type are necessarily more reliable than those based on the traditional approach employed in the present study.[2] The proper estimation of redistributive effects of taxes and government transfers, based on a general equilibrium approach, is a gigantic task which cannot as yet be attempted.

This chapter is concerned with the redistributive effects of direct taxes which are less likely to be shifted to someone else. This is explained by the fact that a direct tax is generally applied to a tax base closer to the individual, such as his or her income. Moreover, direct taxes do not directly interfere with market operations, although their indirect effects cannot be avoided. Indirect taxes, on the other hand, can be shifted more readily because of their closer association with market transactions.

In studying the redistributive effects of taxes and government cash benefits we will assume that the existing distribution of income before taxes and benefits would have been the same even in the absence of taxes and benefits. This assumption implies that the indirect effects of taxes and government benefits on market operations generating factor incomes are either negligible or neutral, in the sense of opposing effects canceling one another out. This assumption may sound unrealistic, particularly when it is alleged that progressive income taxation has a negative influence on work incentives.

In principle, an increase in tax rates can lead to either more or less work; more work if income effect dominates (i.e., people work harder in order to make up for the loss of disposable income) but less work if the substitution effect dominates (i.e., at the margin it becomes more attractive to substitute leisure for income). Existing empirical studies do not seem to provide conclusive evidence as to which of these two effects dominates. It appears that the net effect of taxation on work incentive is slight. (See, for example, Break 1957; Barlow, Brazer, and Morgan 1966.) This is probably due to the fact that workers have limited control over their work hours.

Table 7.1. *Effective rates of personal income tax by total household income ranges 1975–6*

Range of income	Percentage of households	Average income ($)	Average tax paid ($)	Effective tax rate ($)
Under $40	4.24	17.26	1.85	10.72
$40–$80	11.41	60.10	2.62	4.36
$80–$110	6.68	95.59	6.87	7.19
$110–$140	7.74	127.15	11.37	8.94
$140–$170	9.97	156.32	16.87	10.79
$170–$200	9.51	186.18	20.95	11.25
$220–$230	8.26	216.66	26.39	12.18
$230–$260	7.94	245.61	30.27	12.32
$260–$300	9.92	281.23	37.38	13.29
$300–$340	6.58	319.18	40.95	12.84
$340–$400	7.12	370.34	50.72	13.69
$400 and over	10.63	530.89	90.82	17.11
All households	100.00	226.20	29.64	13.10

7.2   Effective personal income-tax rates by income ranges

Table 7.1 presents the average tax rates and shows how the burden of the personal income tax varies with the level of total household income. As has already been pointed out, the incidence of the tax was assumed to be entirely on the taxpayer with no shift occurring. The overall tax rate of all households is just over 13 percent and the rate varies with the income ranges with the minimum of 4.36 percent to the maximum of 17.11 percent. The tax burden in the lowest income range is 10.72 percent, which is extremely high given the fact that the tax burden of the highest income group is only 17.11 percent. Clearly, the sharp progressiveness of income tax shown in the individual income-tax schedules is not reflected in the actual income taxes paid by the household. This situation may, however, be explained if we take into account the size and composition of households. We will investigate this issue at a later stage.

It can be seen that the income-tax rate is not progressive over the entire income range. Indeed, it turns out to be regressive at the bottom end of the income scale, the tax as a percentage of income being higher for the lowest income range than for the next income range. At the top end of the income scale the tax appears to be highly progressive, as shown by a sharp increase in the rate from 13.69 percent for the income range $340–400 to 17.11 percent for the top income range. This result casts doubt on

Table 7.2. *Effective rates of personal income tax by per capita household income ranges: Australia 1975-6*

Per capita income range	Percentage of persons	Average income per person ($)	Average tax paid per person ($)	Effective tax rate (%)
Under $30	12.68	20.05	1.47	7.3
$30–$50	26.07	40.60	3.54	8.7
$50–$70	22.03	60.23	6.81	11.3
$70–$100	18.18	83.45	10.83	13.0
$100–$130	9.86	113.96	15.53	13.6
$130–$160	5.51	142.96	19.58	13.7
$160–$190	2.39	173.11	23.94	13.8
$190–$220	1.40	204.39	33.88	16.6
$220–$250	.80	235.03	42.53	18.1
$250–$280	.47	268.59	70.87	26.4
$280–$310	.14	292.84	63.22	21.6
$310 and over	.47	428.38	126.76	29.6
All households	100.00	73.25	9.60	13.1

the commonly held belief that taxes are regressive at the top end of the income scale due to exploitation of tax loopholes by the very rich. The regressiveness at the bottom end is hardly mentioned in any debate on taxation. One reason for this phenomenon may be that the one-person households, who cannot claim any tax deductions or benefits for dependents, are concentrated in the lowest income range.

Next, we examine the progressiveness of taxes with respect to the per capita household income ranges. The effective tax rates are presented in Table 7.2, which has been constructed by arranging households according to their per capita income.

It can be seen that the tax rate in the lowest income range is now 7.3 percent, which increases with the income ranges to the maximum value of 29.6 percent. The rates appear to be more or less constant at the middle-income ranges, from $70–100 to $160–190, and then increase steadily to the value of 18.1 percent, followed by a sharp increase, decrease, and an increase again. Thus the tax is proportional in the middle-income ranges, then becomes progressive, regressive, and finally progressive again. However, the most striking thing to note is that the regressiveness at the bottom end of the income scale has now disappeared. From these observations we may conclude that the overall progressiveness of taxes increases somewhat when the size of the households is taken into account.

Table 7.3. *Relative burden index of personal income tax: Australia 1975–6*

Income quintiles	Total household income			Per capita household income		
	Income share	Tax share	Relative tax burden	Income share	Tax share	Relative tax burden
1	5.14	2.36	45.91	6.91	3.13	45.30
2	12.24	9.10	74.35	12.07	8.83	73.16
3	18.12	16.43	90.67	16.55	15.04	90.88
4	24.68	24.15	97.85	23.23	22.84	98.32
5	39.82	47.96	120.47	41.24	50.16	121.63
All households or persons	100	100	100	100	100	100

7.3   Relative tax burden of personal income tax for various quintiles

In order to gain further insight into issues of the progressiveness of taxation we computed the index of relative tax burden for various quintiles. The relative tax burden of each quintile is defined as the ratio (expressed in percentage terms) of its share of total taxes to its share of total income.[3] For instance, a quintile paying 10 percent of aggregate tax and receiving 15 percent of total income would have a relative tax burden of 66.6 percent. If the value of this index increases as we move up the income scale, the tax becomes progressive and will have equalizing effects on the income distribution.

Table 7.3 presents the numerical results giving the income share, the tax share, and the relative burden index of personal income tax for each quintile. It can be seen that the relative tax burden for each of the first two quintiles is decreased and that of the last three quintiles increased as income is adjusted in terms of per capita income. This result confirms our earlier observation that per capita income may indicate higher progressivity of personal income tax than household income.

7.4   Property taxes by income ranges

Australia is one of the few countries in the world where wealth attracts hardly any tax. As a result of the recent abolition of death and gift taxes at the federal level and in most states, the only form of wealth taxation that still remains is property tax.

Table 7.4. *Property tax rates by total household income: Australia 1975-6*

Range of household income	Water and sewerage	General council rates	Council rates, other dwellings	Land tax	Total property tax
Under $40	4.95	7.77	.56	.16	13.44
$40-$80	1.42	1.88	.06	.04	3.40
$80-$110	1.06	1.34	.07	.03	2.50
$110-$140	.69	.97	.04	.01	1.71
$140-$170	.63	.89	.06	.02	1.60
$170-$200	.59	.86	.05	.01	1.51
$200-$230	.60	.81	.06	.02	1.49
$230-$260	.45	.65	.05	.01	1.16
$260-$300	.39	.55	.07	.01	1.02
$300-$340	.39	.55	.06	.02	1.01
$340-$400	.42	.57	.06	.02	1.07
$400 and over	.31	.41	.08	.03	.83
All households	.50	.70	.07	.02	1.29

There are three types of property taxes – namely, land tax, water and sewerage rates, and general council rates – all of which are levied on the basis of unimproved capital value of the land. This tax base is subject to tremendous valuation problems, which have been highlighted by Neutze (1977) and Groenwegen (1976). The land tax, which is levied at the state level, has a further problem of having a limited tax base because of exemptions allowed for owner-occupied properties, which account for about 70 percent of all properties.

In this section, we examine how the various property taxes are distributed across the income ranges. Table 7.4 presents the average tax rates by household income. The water and sewerage rates account for 0.50 percent of total household income. This percentage is 4.95 for the lowest income group and decreases to only 0.31 for the highest income group. Clearly, the water and sewerage rates are highly regressive and have adverse effects on the distribution of income.

The general council rates are even more regressive than the water and sewerage rates. The tax burden of the lowest income range is 7.77 percent and decreases more or less monotonically to 0.41 percent for the highest income range.

The council rates for other dwellings appear to be less regressive than the other two rates. This is an expected result because other dwellings are

Table 7.5. *Property tax rates by per capita household income:*
Australia 1975–6

Ranges of per capita household income	Water and sewerage rates	General council rates	Council rates, other dwellings	Land tax	Total property tax
Under $30	.99	1.48	.11	.03	2.61
$30–$50	.77	1.02	.06	.02	1.87
$50–$70	.56	.81	.05	.01	1.43
$70–$100	.48	.73	.07	.03	1.31
$100–$130	.44	.57	.05	.02	1.08
$130–$160	.32	.41	.06	.02	.81
$160–$190	.33	.41	.05	.01	.80
$190–$220	.37	.51	.08	.01	.97
$220–$250	.28	.36	.09	.01	.74
$250–$280	.35	.36	.16	.09	.96
$280–$310	.27	.31	.02	.01	.61
$310 and over	.25	.34	.18	.02	.79
All households	.50	.70	.07	.02	1.29

owned generally by the households belonging to the higher income ranges. What is not expected is the highest tax rate of 0.56 percent in the lowest income range. It appears that there is a heavy concentration of households in the lowest income range who depend on rental income. These results should be qualified, however, because the taxes paid for other dwellings can be easily shifted to the renters. As a result, the true incidence cannot be determined.

The land tax accounts for only 0.02 percent of total household income. It appears to be regressive at the lower income ranges and then it becomes more or less proportional. The overall effect of this tax is probably regressive, but the degree of regressivity is lower than those for other property taxes.

The last column in the table gives the rates for the total property tax, which accounts for 1.29 percent of the total household income. These rates indicate that the total property tax is highly regressive when measured with respect to total household income. It will be interesting to see how this conclusion changes if we take into account the size of households. So, we examine the progressiveness (or regressiveness) of property taxes with respect to the per capita household income ranges. The effective tax rates are presented in Table 7.5, which has been constructed by arranging households according to their per capita income.

Table 7.6. *Relative burden index of property taxes: Australia 1975-6*

Quintiles	Water and sewerage rates	General council rates	Council rates, other dwellings	Land tax	Total property tax
Total household income					
1	309.34	305.45	132.68	NA	297.86
2	132.84	133.17	86.27	NA	130.55
3	113.52	115.78	74.89	NA	112.75
4	80.51	81.89	92.02	NA	81.89
5	68.85	67.34	116.40	NA	70.48
Per capita household income					
1	210.71	210.27	124.17	90.59	204.20
2	138.03	137.45	77.05	86.41	133.80
3	104.53	110.09	73.53	77.46	105.56
4	95.91	99.74	98.84	142.23	98.84
5	70.80	66.66	113.94	90.81	71.10

It can be seen that both the water and council rates decrease more or less monotonically, indicating their regressive nature. The tax rates in the lowest income bracket are considerably less than those observed in the case where households were arranged according to the total household income. From these observations we may conclude that the overall regressiveness of these local taxes decreases somewhat when the size of the households is taken into account. The council rates for other dwellings appear to be regressive at the bottom end of the income distribution and progressive at the top end. From this observation we cannot arrive at a definite conclusion as to whether the overall effect is progressive or regressive unless we compute a single measure of progressivity.

The degree of regressivity of the land tax is also reduced when the total household income is converted to the per capita household income. This tax may have become even progressive as a result of this adjustment, but in order to arrive at a more definitive conclusion this issue requires further investigation, which will be done in the next chapter.

Table 7.6 presents the relative index of property taxes. The values of this index for both the water and council rates decrease monotonically, confirming that these taxes are regressive. The council rates for other dwellings appear to be regressive up to the third quintile and then they become progressive. The land tax is regressive up to the third quintile and then it becomes progressive and regressive again. The total property tax

Table 7.7. *Effective government benefit rates by total household income: Australia 1975-6*

Income ranges	Pensions	Unem- ployment benefits	Sickness & special benefits	Family allowance	Other govt. benefits	Total govt. benefits
Under $40	128.99	4.12	0.00	2.11	.78	136.00
$40–$80	64.62	2.54	.76	.47	2.31	70.73
$80–$110	32.93	5.95	.80	.96	1.09	41.73
$110–$140	9.01	1.08	.49	.82	1.19	12.61
$140–$170	6.37	.95	.38	.76	.36	8.83
$170–$200	4.12	.55	14	73	.61	6.15
$200–$230	3.41	.37	.04	.60	.38	5.00
$230–$260	1.40	.43	.04	.51	.20	2.58
$260–$300	1.58	.20	0.00	.43	.28	2.49
$300–$340	1.27	.41	.02	.38	.18	2.26
$340–$400	1.16	.21	.03	.36	.26	2.03
$400 and over	.94	.27	.01	.20	.13	1.56
All households	5.53	.65	.12	.46	.39	7.16

is regressive, but the degree of regressivity measured with respect to per capita household income is lower than when it is measured with respect to total household income.

7.5   Effective government benefits by income ranges

Table 7.7 presents the government benefit rates (i.e., benefits expressed as a percentage of gross income by households arranged into 12 groups according to the total gross household income). In the first group the average benefits received by households exceed the average household income. This is due to the fact that several households who made business losses belong to the lowest income group.

Government cash transfers account for 7.16 percent of total household income. This percentage is 136 for the lowest income group and decreases monotonically to only 1.56 for the highest income group. Government cash transfers are highly progressive and have a significant effect on income distribution.

The most important point to be noted is that a significant amount of government cash benefits, particularly pension, accrue to households in all income ranges. This suggests that a significant component of these benefits is not means-tested. One reason for this phenomenon may be that age

Table 7.8. *Effective government benefit rates by per capita household income: Australia 1975-6*

Per capita income ranges	Pensions	Unemployment benefits	Sickness & special benefits	Family allowance	Other govt. benefits	Total govt. benefits
Under $30	10.47	8.38	1.15	3.69	2.29	25.98
$30-$50	19.78	1.01	.22	1.01	1.01	23.05
$50-$70	5.18	.53	.17	.58	.31	6.79
$70-$100	3.87	.31	.06	.27	.36	4.96
$100-$130	2.26	.19	0.00	.11	.10	2.68
$130-$160	.95	.16	0.00	.05	.05	1.22
$160-$190	.52	.10	0.00	.02	.19	.84
$190-$220	.87	0.00	0.00	.01	.04	.93
$220-$250	.26	0.00	0.00	.05	.02	.33
$250-$280	1.12	0.00	0.00	.02	0.00	1.15
$280-$310	.68	0.00	0.00	.02	.01	.71
$310 and over	.44	0.00	0.00	.01	0.00	.45
All households	5.53	.65	.12	.46	.39	7.16

pensions payable to people at the age of 70 or more ceased to be means-tested during 1974-5.

The important aspect of our investigation, however, is whether various government benefits are directed to those whose needs are the greatest. It is important, therefore, to examine the distribution of these benefits according to an income concept that takes into account the household size and composition. Table 7.8, which shows how various government benefits are distributed according to the income ranges of per capita household income, indicates that the pattern of distribution of benefits has changed substantially. For the lowest income range, the benefit-income ratio is only 25.98 percent. This ratio does not seem to fall as sharply with income ranges as was observed in the case of total household income. It can, therefore, be said that the progressivity of government benefits measured with respect to per capita household income is lower than when it is measured with respect to total household income.

Looking at various categories of benefits we observe that sickness and special benefits are the most progressive. It accrues only to the lowest four income ranges. Pensions appear to be the least progressive of all benefits, with a significant amount going to the higher income ranges. These results seem to suggest that the government needs to give more careful consideration to the eligibility requirements of pensions, and possibly make all pensions means-tested.

Table 7.9. *Relative benefit index of various government cash benefits*

Quintiles	Pension	Unem- ployment benefits	Sickness & special benefits	Family allowance	Other govt. benefits	Total govt. benefits
Total household income						
1	1090	477	729	107	411	927
2	152	261	337	191	205	171
3	63	96	75	141	113	74
4	27	45	8	83	65	34
5	18	38	14	63	43	24
Per capita household income						
1	496	735	569	487	530	520
2	256	125	175	214	174	235
3	59	81	154	130	89	69
4	69	53	51	62	72	67
5	22	20	6	11	26	21

7.6   Relative benefit index for various government benefits

Table 7.9 presents the relative benefit indexes of various categories of government benefits. Analogous to the relative burden index of taxes, we define the relative benefit index of a quintile as its share of total government benefits to its share of total income. This index, expressed in percentage terms, was computed for the total government benefits and for each of the five types of benefits considered in the present study. If the value of this index decreases as we move up the income scale, benefits tend to be progressive and will have equalizing effects on the income distribution.

For total household income, the relative benefit index for total government benefits is as high as 927 for the first quintile and it decreases monotonically to a value of only 24 for the fifth quintile, showing government benefits to be highly progressive. Looking at the individual benefits, pensions and sickness and special benefits appear to be highly progressive; unemployment and the other benefits are progressive but have a considerably lower degree of progressivity compared to pensions and sickness and special benefits, and the family allowance appears to be regressive first and then it becomes progressive.

Turning to the per capita household income, we note that in the first quintile, the relative benefit index of the total benefits has decreased quite

Table 7.10. *Relative benefit index of various types of government pensions*

Quintiles	Age pension	Invalid pension	Widow's pension	War pension	Service pension	War widow's pension	Total pension
Total household income							
1	1236	885	866	576	1129	877	1090
2	120	183	194	295	189	147	152
3	52	86	88	96	53	37	63
4	21	37	39	37	16	76	27
5	18	18	15	19	13	28	18
Per capita household income							
1	514	631	633	151	393	26	496
2	256	233	235	234	369	279	256
3	49	54	60	127	83	92	59
4	66	58	55	105	44	183	69
5	24	14	12	38	10	16	22

drastically from 927 to 520. Although the benefit index has increased in the second quintile from 171 to 235, it may still be concluded that the progressivity of total government benefits becomes less progressive when the income is adjusted in terms of per capita household income. Thus, total household income unadjusted for the household size tends to exaggerate the extent of progressivity of government cash benefits.

It is the pensions component which appears to cause this decline in the progressivity of total government benefits. The regressiveness of the family allowance at the lower income ranges has now disappeared, making the overall effect of this benefit progressive. Unemployment and sickness and special benefits show even greater progressivity when income is adjusted for household size.

Table 7.10 presents the relative benefit index for various types of pensions. With the exception of war widow's pension, all types of pensions are progressive as indicated by the monotonically decreasing value of the index as we move from the lower to the higher quintile. The war widow's pension appears to be progressive up to 60th percentiles and then it becomes regressive and finally progressive again. Although the age and service pensions appear to be highly progressive, the complete ranking of various types of pensions is not possible without computing a single index of progressivity.

When we change the base for measuring progressivity from total household income to per capita income, we note that the relative benefit index has fallen dramatically for the first quintile and increased for the second quintile for all types of pensions. For the war and war widow's pensions, the relative benefit index for the second quintile even exceeds that for the first quintile, showing these pensions to be regressive in the lower ranges of per capita household income. The age, invalid, and widow's pensions continue to remain progressive although the degree of progressivity is considerably reduced.

7.7   Summary of findings

In the foregoing sections, attempts were made to examine the distribution of taxes and government benefits across the income ranges. It has been found that the sharp progressivity of income tax shown in the individual tax schedules is not reflected in the actual taxes paid by the households. In fact, the income tax rates are not uniformly progressive over the entire income range – they turn out to be regressive at the bottom end of the income scale and highly progressive at the top end of the scale. When the progressiveness of taxes is measured with respect to per capita household income (instead of household income), the regressiveness at the bottom end of the income scale disappears and the overall degree of progressiveness is increased. These observations highlight the weakness of the existing Australian studies, which make no adjustment for the needs of the household.

Turning to property taxes, it is observed that they are highly regressive and have adverse effect on the distribution of income. The general council rates appear to be more regressive than the water and sewerage rates. As expected, the council rates for other dwellings are less regressive than the other two rates. What is not expected is the highest tax rate of .56 percent in the lowest income range. This result suggests a heavy concentration of households in the lowest income range who depend on rental income.

The overall regressiveness of the water and council rates decreases somewhat as income is adjusted in terms of per capita income. The land tax may have become even progressive as a result of this adjustment although a more definitive conclusion requires further investigation.

Government cash transfers appear to be considerably more progressive than the personal income tax. However, the progressivity of these transfers is reduced when household income is adjusted in terms of per capita income. Looking at various categories of benefits, it is observed that sickness and special benefits are the most progressive and pensions the least progressive. Since a significant amount of pensions accrue to the higher income ranges, the government should give more careful consideration to their eligibility requirements and possibly make all pensions means-tested.

CHAPTER 8

Effects of taxes and cash benefits on equity

The measures of horizontal and vertical equity developed in Chapter 5 are estimated in this chapter in order to analyze the distribution effects of taxes and government cash benefits. These effects have been measured with respect to three income concepts: (1) total household income, (2) per capita household income, and (3) adjusted household income. A comparison of these estimates with those based on the Australian Survey of Consumer Finances and Expenditures of 1967–8 is also provided in this chapter along with a discussion of several policy implications.

It is useful to recall that per capita household income and adjusted household income differ with respect to the weights given to various members of the household. Per capita household income gives equal weight to all persons in the household whereas the adjusted household income makes a distinction between the first and the second adult and the children belonging to the household. This adjustment was made by dividing the income of each household by a certain number of equivalent-adults obtained by the use of the following scale:

First adult in the household	1.0
Second and subsequent adults	0.7
Each child	0.4

This scale was chosen on the basis of subjective judgment of "reasonableness." The redistributive effects of taxes and government benefits were then measured with respect to the *adjusted household income*. The taxes paid and benefits received by a household were also adjusted for household size and composition by means of the above scale. Each individual in a household was assumed to be paying taxes equal to the *adjusted taxes* and receiving benefits equal to the *adjusted benefits*. Thus, the progressivity and redistributive effects of taxes and government benefits were measured against the frequency distribution of individuals by adjusted household income and not that of households. This approach gives equal weight to each individual's welfare, irrespective of the size and composition of the household to which he or she belongs, and is considered to be the most appropriate in view of our objective; that is, to measure the redistribution of the economic welfare of individuals.

Table 8.1. *Estimates of horizontal and vertical equity of personal income tax measured with respect to gross household income: Australia 1975-6*

Measures of equity	Total household income	Per capita household income	Adjusted household income
Tax progressivity	10.22	12.09	12.93
Inequality of pre-tax income	34.51	34.05	30.09
Inequality of post-tax income	33.05	32.28	28.22
Redistributive effect	4.23	5.20	6.21
Index of vertical equity	4.46	5.35	6.40
Index of horizontal equity	−.23	−.15	−.19

8.1 Estimates of horizontal and vertical equity for personal income tax

The estimates of horizontal and vertical equity developed in Section 5.5 for personal income tax are presented in Table 8.1. The first row in the table gives the overall measure of progressivity (the concentration measure discussed in Section 5.2); the second and third rows give the inequality of the pre- and post-income inequality measured in terms of the Gini index, respectively; and the redistributive effect of taxes – measured by the pre-tax income Gini index less the post-tax Gini index, divided by the pre-tax income Gini index and expressed in percentage terms – is presented in the fourth row. The fifth and sixth rows present the indices of vertical and horizontal equity, respectively.

For total household income, personal income tax is progressive, as shown by the positive value of the progressivity index, and reduces inequality of income by 4.23 percent. The vertical equity contributing to this reduction in inequality is 4.46 percent but the tax introduces horizontal inequality, which has the effect of increasing the inequality by 0.23 percent.

The redistributive effect of taxes as computed from Table 6.5 showed that in 1967-8 personal income tax reduced the inequality of income by 4.98 percent. Thus, the redistributive power of personal income tax has decreased from 4.98 to 4.23 during the period 1967-8 to 1975-6. This conclusion should be qualified, however, in view of the doubtful reliability of the 1967-8 survey data.

It can be seen that the overall effect of personal income tax based on adjusted household income is to decrease the income inequality by 6.21

Table 8.2. *Changes in quintile shares due to personal income tax in terms of horizontal and vertical equity: Australia 1975–6*

Quintiles	Quintile share of pre-tax income	Quintile share of post-tax income	Change in quintile shares due to taxes	Change in quintile shares due to horizontal equity	Change in quintile shares due to vertical equity
Adjusted household income					
1	7.58	8.18	.60	−.01	.61
2	13.04	13.52	.48	.01	.47
3	17.97	18.25	.28	−.04	.32
4	23.89	23.87	−.02	.00	−.02
5	37.52	36.18	−1.34	.04	−1.38

percent. As a result of the adjustment made for household size and composition, the progressivity of these taxes is increased from 10.22 to 12.93, which in turn increases the index of vertical equity from 4.46 percent to 6.40 percent. Interestingly enough, income taxes now have less effect in increasing horizontal inequity; the value of the horizontal equity index changes from −.23 to −.19.

Two conclusions may be drawn from these observations. First, the degree of horizontal inequity introduced due to taxes is very small compared to the extent of vertical equity. Second, the use of household income unadjusted for household size and composition tends to overestimate the extent of horizontal inequity and to underestimate the extent of vertical equity. As a result the net effect of the redistributive power of taxes is underestimated.

Table 8.2, based on the adjusted household income, presents the changes in the quintile shares introduced by personal income tax in terms of horizontal and vertical equity. The tax increases the income shares of each of the first three quintiles and decreases the shares of the remaining two quintiles.

It is interesting to note that the income share of the fourth quintile is completely unaffected by the introduction of horizontal inequity. The income shares of the second and the fifth quintiles are increased, however, whereas those of the first and the third quintiles are decreased. Vertical equity, on the other hand, increases the shares of the first three quintiles and decreases the shares of the remaining two quintiles. The magnitudes

Table 8.3. *Progressivity of various types of property taxes with respect to gross household income: Australia*

Type of tax	Total household income	Per capita household income	Adjusted household income
Water and sewerage rates	−23.28	−18.43	−21.13
General council rates	−23.78	−19.52	−21.91
Council rates for other dwellings	3.06	6.49	5.66
Land tax	−0.98	1.99	3.66
Total property tax	−21.84	−17.43	−19.82

of the changes in income shares brought about by horizontal inequity are much smaller than those by vertical equity.

8.2   Progressivity of property taxes

Table 8.3 presents the estimates of progressivity measure for various types of property taxes. Both water and sewerage and general council rates are fairly regressive, as shown by the negative values of the progressivity index. The general council rates are slightly more regressive than the water and sewerage rates. The degree of regressivity of both these taxes is reduced as the adjustment for the household size is made in terms of per capita income. This confirms our earlier observation (Section 7.4) made on the basis of distribution of tax rates across the ranges of total household and per capita household incomes. When the adjusted household income is used instead of per capita household income as a basis for measuring progressivity (or regressivity), the degree of regressivity of both these taxes is increased but still is lower than that with respect to total household income.

The council rates for other dwellings are mildly progressive but the degree of progressivity is increased as adjustment is made for household size and composition. Similarly, the land tax, which appears to be mildly regressive (or almost proportional) on the basis of total household income, becomes slightly progressive as a result of the adjustment for household size and composition.

When all types of property taxes are added, their overall effect is fairly regressive and should increase the inequality in post-tax income distribution. However, the use of household income unadjusted for household

Table 8.4. *Progressivity of government cash benefits measured with respect to gross household income: Australia 1975–6*

Types of benefits	Total household income	Per capita household income	Adjusted household income
Age pension	82.92	34.24	71.55
Invalid pension	70.44	65.42	74.91
Widow's pension	73.68	67.12	73.75
War pension	62.79	29.72	46.65
Service pension	81.17	60.09	74.20
War widow's pension	59.69	17.77	34.00
Total pensions	78.15	53.68	69.53
Unemployment benefits	47.58	73.49	75.52
Sickness and special benefits	72.38	72.55	82.88
Family allowance	18.94	64.38	51.17
Government home saving grant	6.40	−9.49	−5.07
Government maternity allowance	40.03	59.26	54.66
Other government benefits	43.23	60.33	55.56
Total government benefits	69.41	56.68	67.69

size and composition tends to overestimate the extent of regressivity of property taxes.

8.3   Progressivity of various government cash benefits

This section presents the estimates of the degree of progressivity (or regressivity) of various types of government cash benefits. These estimates have been obtained on the basis of gross household income, which includes all these benefits. The values of the progressivity index presented in Table 8.4 show that almost all types of cash benefits are progressive and lead to greater equality of income. However, the variation in the degree of progressivity of different types of benefits is considerable.

There are six types of pensions – all of which appear to be highly progressive. Age pension is the most progressive, with a progressivity index of 82.92. The least progressive pension is the war widow's pension, with a value of index equal to 59.69. After pensions, sickness and special benefits is the most progressive benefit. The least progressive benefit is the government home saving grant which is given to families to buy the first home.

Turning to the per capita household income, we note that the degree of progressivity of total government benefits has fallen dramatically from

69.41 to 56.68. Most of this reduction has been brought about by pensions, the progressivity index of which is reduced from 78.15 to 53.68. The progressivity index of all other benefits, with an exception of the government home saving grant, has increased. The government home saving grant, which was mildly progressive with respect to total household income, has now become regressive.

When adjusted income is used as a basis for measuring progressivity, we find that sickness and special benefits has the maximum progressivity index of 82.88. Unemployment benefits is the second most progressive benefit, with a value of index of 75.52. Among the six types of pensions, the invalid pension is the most progressive. Government home saving grant continues to be regressive, although the degree of regressivity is lower than that for per capita household income.

These observations clearly indicate that the adjustment for household size and composition can considerably change our conclusions regarding the relative degree of progressivity of various government cash benefits. This result is important, because most of the existing Australian incidence studies are based on household income with no adjustment made for the needs of the households and may have led to misleading conclusions.

8.4   Combined redistributive effect of taxes and benefits

Table 8.5 presents the numerical results on the measurements of redistributive effects of both taxes and government cash benefits. These effects have been measured with respect to original household income. It should be recalled that the numerical results presented in Table 8.1 measured the redistributive effects of taxes with respect to gross houshold income (i.e., original income plus government benefits).

It can be seen that the estimates of tax progressivity shown in the first row of Table 8.5 are considerably less than those in Table 8.1. That is, the progressivity of taxes measured with respect to original income is lower than that measured with respect to gross income. One reason for this result may be that the households who depend heavily on government transfers belong to the lower income ranges, and pay little or no tax.

The progressivity of personal income tax based on adjusted household income is higher than that based on total household income. It means that the total household income tends to underestimate the extent of tax progressivity. This conclusion conforms with the earlier one that emerged when the progressivity was measured with respect to the gross income.

The overall effect of personal income tax as measured by adjusted household income is to reduce the inequality of income by 3.22 percent, showing that the redistributive power of taxes is reduced considerably when the

Table 8.5. *Combined redistributive effect of personal income tax and cash benefits measured with respect to the original income of households: Australia 1975-6*

Measures of equity	Total household income	Per capita household income	Adjusted household income
Taxes only			
Progressivity	5.24	7.38	7.97
Vertical equity	2.15	3.09	3.64
Horizontal equity	−.26	−.14	−.42
Redistributive factor	1.89	2.95	3.22
Government cash benefits only			
Progressivity	80.92	81.46	81.93
Vertical equity	16.86	17.33	17.71
Horizontal equity	−2.90	−3.99	−3.07
Redistributive factor	13.96	13.34	14.64
Combined effect of taxes and government benefits			
Progressivity	109.09	114.15	101.58
Vertical equity	18.60	19.91	21.02
Horizontal equity	−1.00	−2.07	−1.08
Redistributive factor	17.60	17.84	19.94

basis of measurement is changed from gross income to original income. This raises the question as to which of the two bases should be used to measure the progressivity and redistributive effects of taxes. It is difficult to give a definitive answer, particularly when we know that some government benefits are subject to taxes and others are not. Podder and Kakwani (1975) base their entire analysis on original income, but – in view of the general belief that taxes should be levied on all incomes including government benefits – it seems that the gross income is the most appropriate concept to use for this purpose.

The redistributive effect of government cash benefits should, however, be measured with respect to the original income. It can be seen that the progressivity index of government benefits is almost 10 times the progressivity index of taxes. The overall effect of government benefits is to reduce the inequality of income by 14.64 percent, showing clearly that government cash benefits are far more redistributive than taxes.

The vertical equity introduced by government benefits has the effect of reducing the inequality of income by 17.71 percent, but this effect is offset with the introduction of horizontal inequity, which increases inequality by 3.07 percent. This result indicates that there can be a possible clash be-

Table 8.6. *Combined redistributive effect of personal income tax and government cash benefits measured with respect to original household income: Australia 1967–8*

Benefits/taxes	Average benefit or tax rate (%)	Progressivity index (%)	Horizontal equity (%)	Vertical equity (%)	Redistributive effect
Cash benefits	7.37	62.90	−.81	13.58	12.77
Tax	11.75	19.10	NA	6.93	NA
Combined effect of cash benefits and tax	4.39	156.8	−2.44	19.56	17.12

tween horizontal and vertical equity (i.e., the greater vertical equity may lead to greater horizontal inequity). However, the increase in vertical equity is far greater than the increase in horizontal inequity and as a result the net effect of government benefits is highly redistributive towards greater equality.

The combined effect of taxes and government benefits is observed to be highly progressive. The vertical equity introduced by the high degree of progressivity would have reduced the income inequality by 21.02 percent, but this effect was offset by accompanying horizontal inequity, which had the effect of increasing inequality by 1.08 percent. Thus, the resulting decrease in income inequality was 19.94 percent. The interesting observation to be made is that the degree of horizontal inequity introduced by the combined effect of taxes and government benefits is less than that calculated when the effects of taxes and government benefits are considered separately.

Table 8.6 presents the estimates of horizontal and vertical equity of government benefits and taxes based on the 1967–8 survey data. These estimates have been obtained on the basis of original income, with no adjustment made for household size and composition.

A significant finding that emerges from a comparison of the numerical values in Tables 8.5 and 8.6 is that the two instruments of redistributing income (namely, personal income tax and government cash benefits), together, are more egalitarian in 1975–6 than they had been in 1966–7. The shift toward greater equality has been brought about by government transfers, which increased the redistributive effect from 12.77 percent to 13.96 percent. Personal income tax, on the other hand, became less egalitarian but the net effect of the two instruments increased, increasing the redistributive effect from 17.12 percent to 17.60 percent.

Table 8.7. *Redistributive effects of various government cash benefits measured with respect to adjusted original household income: Australia 1975–6*

Type of benefit	Progres-sivity	Vertical equity	Horizontal equity	Redistributive effect
Age pension	88.06	7.71	−.85	6.86
Invalid pension	87.64	1.72	−.08	1.64
Widow's pension	94.63	1.83	−.13	1.70
War pension	60.85	.59	−.02	.57
Service pension	89.38	.66	−.01	.65
War widow's pension	60.93	.29	−.04	.25
Total pensions	86.22	13.21	−2.06	11.15
Unemployment benefits	82.35	1.81	−.11	1.70
Sickness and special benefits	94.39	.33	−.02	.31
Family allowance	52.30	.90	−.02	.88
Government home saving grant	−1.90	0.00	0.00	0.00
Government maternity allowance	54.67	0.00	0.00	0.00
Other government benefits	72.70	.86	.07	.79
Total government benefits	81.93	17.71	−3.07	14.64

8.5   Redistributive effects of various cash benefits

Table 8.7 presents estimates of progressivity and redistributive effects of various government cash benefits. These estimates have been obtained on the basis of adjusted original income of households and not the gross income as was the case earlier.

The estimates of progressivity index presented in the first column of Table 8.7 are considerably higher than those in Table 8.4. That is, progressivity of various government cash benefits measured with respect to adjusted original household income is considerably higher than that measured with respect to adjusted gross income. Of all benefits, widow's pension is the most progressive, with a progressivity index of 94.63, followed by sickness and special benefits, with a progressivity index of 94.39. In the earlier analysis, when the progressivity index was computed with respect to the adjusted gross household income, pensions were observed to be less progressive than unemployment benefits. This situation is reversed, however, as the basis of measurement is changed from the gross to the original income. Again, these results suggest the importance of selecting the appropriate basis before measuring the progressivity.

Pensions, which represent 77 percent of total benefits, have the maximum effect of income inequality. The vertical equity introduced by pensions reduces inequality by 13.21 percent, whereas the horizontal inequity increases the inequality by 2.06 percent. The net effect of pensions reduces income inequality by 11.15 percent.

Despite the fact that sickness and special benefits are the second most progressive component of all government transfers, the value of its redistributive factor is only .31 percent. This is because the redistributive factor of a transfer depends not only on progressivity but also on the average benefit rate; the higher the average benefit rate, the greater will be the effect on income redistribution. The average sickness and special benefit rate is only 0.12 percent and as a result this component has a very small effect on income inequality compared to other components such as pensions. It would seem that any policy that increases the share of sickness and special benefits will make the government transfers even more egalitarian.

Government home saving grant is mildly regressive and government maternity allowance highly progressive but both these benefits have negligible effects on income inequality. This is because they have very low average benefit rates, which have direct effects on income inequality. These observations suggest the importance of making a distinction between the concept of progressivity and the redistributive effect. Much of the empirical literature seems to have ignored such a distinction (see Chapter 5).

8.6   Summary of conclusions

This chapter demonstrates how the methodology developed in Chapter 5 relating to the measures of vertical and horizontal equity can be utilized to analyze the effects of taxes and government cash benefits on equity. It has been observed that both income tax and government cash benefits reduce inequality in income distribution in Australia, but cash benefits are far more important than income tax in this respect. In fact the progressivity index of government cash benefits is almost 10 times the progressivity index of personal income tax. The personal income tax reduces inequality of income by 3.22 percent, whereas the similar figure for cash benefits is 14.64 percent.

The degree of horizontal inequity introduced due to personal income taxation is very small compared to the extent of vertical equity. However, the use of household income unadjusted for size and composition tends to overestimate the extent of horizontal inequity and underestimate the extent of vertical equity. As a result the net effect of the redistributive power of the personal income tax is underestimated.

The available empirical analyses presented above show that there can be a possible clash between horizontal and vertical equity. However, the increase in vertical equity is far greater than the increase in horizontal inequity so that the net effect results in greater equality of income.

The total property tax is fairly regressive and should increase the inequality in post-tax income distribution. However, the adjustment for household size and composition tends to reduce the extent of regressivity of property taxes.

A comparison of Podder and Kakwani's (1975) results shows that personal income tax and government cash benefits together have a greater effect in redistributing income in 1975–6 than they had in 1966–7. This shift toward greater equality has been brought about by government transfers, which increased the redistributive effect from 12.77 percent to 13.96 percent. Personal income tax, on the other hand, became less egalitarian but the net effect of the two instruments became more egalitarian, increasing the redistributive effect from 17.1 percent to 17.60 percent.

Redistribution of income within and between socioeconomic and demographic groups

This chapter analyzes the differential impacts of government benefits and taxes on the distribution of income between and within groups classified according to certain socioeconomic and demographic characteristics of households. The household characteristics considered are household size and composition, sex and age of household head, predominant source of household income, marital and employment status of household head, geographical region, period of residence, country of birth, and occupation of the household head.[1]

9.1 Sex of household head

In 1976, 17.69 percent of Australian household units were headed by women. These households are likely to have relatively low incomes and high incidence of poverty. Several reasons may be given for this phenomenon, but the most important one is the fact that many such women did not expect to assume the responsibility of providing for a family and were not prepared for this task when faced with it. Since the range of choice for working women is significantly narrower than that available to males, it is always harder for women to get employment, particularly when they are unprepared for labor-market activities. Thus the families headed by women tend to depend much more on pensions, alimony, or other types of relatively fixed incomes than do other families. It is interesting, therefore, to look at Table 9.1, which gives major sources of household income classified by the sex of the household head.

It is evident that the two types of households differ significantly with respect to various sources of household income. Although the income from wages and salary remains the major component for both types of households, it contributes 77.39 percent of total income for the male-headed households as against 58.67 percent for the female-headed households. Income from business forms the second major component for households headed by men, and has a share of 11.49 percent. This component is least important for households headed by women, contributing only 3.21 percent of total income. Government and cash benefits, which form the second major component for these households, contribute as much as 24.08

Table 9.1. *Components of income, by sex of household head: Australia 1975–6*

Income components	Female head	Male head	Total population
Wages and salaries	58.67	77.39	75.44
Business income	3.21	11.49	10.62
Pensions	20.86	3.74	5.53
Unemployment benefits	1.02	.61	.65
Sickness and special benefits	.17	.11	.12
Other government benefits	1.74	.23	.39
Total government benefits	24.08	5.18	7.16
Other income	14.02	5.93	6.78
Total income	100.00	100.00	100.00
Average gross income per household	133.72	246.08	226.20

percent of total income, compared with 5.18 percent for the male-headed households. Among various government benefits, the pension remains the most dominant component, contributing 20.86 percent of total income. Other income – which among other things includes interest, dividends, royalties, rent, and alimony or maintenance allowances – is the third major component of income among female-headed households, with a share of about 14 percent. The percentage for male-headed households is only 5.93.

It may be concluded from the above observations that households headed by women are heavily dependent upon welfare payments and other unearned income, including alimony and maintenance allowances. As a result, we would expect their income to be lower than those of other households. This is clearly indicated by the last row in the table. The income per household with a female head is about .54 of the average with a male head.

Table 9.2 provides estimates of income redistribution by the sex of household head. It can be seen that the adjusted income per person in households with a female head is about .87 of the average with a male head. It means that the income differentials between the male-headed and the female-headed households are considerably narrowed when income is adjusted for household size and composition. This is due to the fact that households with a female head on average have to support only 1.46 equivalent-adults compared with the 2.28 equivalent-adults that are supported by the male-headed households.

Table 9.2. *Income redistribution by sex of household head: Australia 1975–6*

Variable	Female head	Male head	Total population
Percentage of persons	10.59	89.41	100.00
Adjusted original income per person	69.08	99.41	96.20
Adjusted gross income per person	90.58	104.49	103.01
Adjusted disposable income per person	82.77	90.48	89.66
Average tax rate	8.62	13.41	12.97
Average benefit rate	23.74	4.86	6.62
Inequality of			
original income	50.42	33.28	35.25
gross income	32.32	29.69	30.09
disposable income	29.62	27.96	28.22
Redistributive effect of			
government benefits	35.90	10.79	14.64
taxes	8.35	5.83	6.21
combined taxes and government benefits	41.25	15.99	19.94

The ratio of adjusted income before cash benefits of female-headed to male-headed households is only .69, which increases to .87 when income is adjusted for government transfers. The ratio is further increased to .91 when income tax is subtracted from the gross income. On average, female-headed households pay tax at the rate of 8.62 percent, but receive government benefits at the rate of 23.74 percent of gross income, whereas for the male-headed households these percentages are 13.41 and 4.86, respectively. These observations tend to support the conclusion that the Australian tax-transfer system plays a major role in reducing the income differentials between male- and female-headed households. This conclusion is also supported from the calculations of the between-group Gini index of various income concepts.[2] The values of this index for the adjusted original and gross income concepts are 2.99 and 1.28, respectively, showing a reduction of 57.19 percent in the between-group inequality caused by the government income-support programs. The adjustment of income for taxes further reduces the between-group inequality by about 37 percent, from the value of 1.28 to .81. As a result, the total reduction in the between-group inequality caused by the combined effect of taxes and government benefits is 72 percent.

The subtantial differences in the inequality of income within the groups are also quite evident. The Gini index of the original income within households with female head is 50.42, as against 33.28 for other households.

This demonstrates that the distribution of income among female-headed households is far more unequal than among those with a male head. Government transfers reduce income inequality among female-headed households by 35.90 percent, whereas they reduce inequality among the male-headed households by 10.79 percent.

Taxes also contribute to a reduction in income inequality within groups but their effect is considerably smaller than that of government transfers. The combined effect of taxes and government transfers amounts to a reduction of inequality of 41.25 percent among households with a female head and of 15.99 percent among those with a male head. Thus the Australian tax-transfer system brings about a large reduction in inequality between and within groups classified by sex of household head, the reduction being particularly marked among households headed by women.

9.2   Age of household head

The economic welfare of a household is closely associated with the age of its head. First of all, the age of the head has direct impact on the income per household. It has been observed in the United States and many other countries that income per household shows a marked rise, from the low for the under-25 age-of-head class, to a peak for the 45–54 age-class, and then a sharp decline to a trough in the 65-and-over class (Kuznets 1974). This phenomenon may be explained in terms of skills and experience acquired before a person finally settles down to a particular field of work. Up to the age of 25, a person goes through an apprenticeship or training phase, during which he or she is paid relatively little. From the age of 25 to 45 years, experience in the chosen career is gradually acquired, and income increases steadily until it reaches the peak when he or she is in the forties. This peak income is maintained until about the age of 55, and then income starts declining. At the age of 65, a sharp decline in income is faced, at retirement from the work force.

Secondly, the age of the head may have a close relationship with the household size and composition. Initially, the size of a household increases with the age of the head as children are born and added to the family. Then, as children mature and leave the family, the household size tends to shrink.

Thus, the redistributive effects of taxes and government benefits measured in terms of per equivalent-adult household income are closely associated with the age of the household head. Moreover, in Australia, the old age pension is the most dominant component among all types of government benefits. Table 9.3 gives the major sources of household income by age groups. It shows that the importance of income from wages and

Table 9.3. *Components of income by age of household head: Australia 1975-6*

Income components	Age groups			
	15–25	25–45	45–65	65 and over
Wages and salaries	90.52	80.21	77.89	24.58
Business income	4.16	12.34	9.75	11.14
Pensions	.37	1.02	4.78	38.27
Unemployment benefits	.70	.64	.77	.21
Sickness and special benefits	.12	.08	.16	.13
Family allowance	.12	.75	.27	.03
Other government benefits	.79	.41	.27	.40
Total government benefits	2.10	2.91	6.11	39.05
Other income	3.22	4.53	6.25	25.23
Total income	100.00	100.00	100.00	100.00
Average gross income per household $	230.00	252.00	247.00	116.00

salaries diminishes monotonically as the age of the head increases. Although the importance of business income seems to increase with the age, there is no monotonic relationship between the two. There is a steady increase with advancing age in the importance of government benefits and other income as a source of income. Government cash benefits form the major income component of households in the 65-and-over age group, contributing 39.05 percent of total income. Other income is the second major component for these households, with a share of 25.23 percent. From these observations, it may be concluded that households belonging to the 65-and-over age group depend heavily on unearned income, particularly government pensions.

Income per household increased from about $230 for the age group 15-to-25 years, to about $252 for the 25–45 age group, followed by a moderate decrease to about $247 for the 45–65 age group. Beyond age 65, income dropped sharply to about $116. The average equivalent number of adults in each household followed approximately the same pattern as income per household.

The relative economic position of various age groups must be assessed by computing the per equivalent-adults' income per person for each of these household groups. These calculations are presented in Table 9.4, along with estimates of income redistribution by age of the household head.

Table 9.4. *Income redistribution, by age of household head: Australia 1975–6*

Variable	15–25	25–45	45–65	65 and over	Total population
Percentage of persons	6.56	52.66	31.25	9.53	100.00
Adjusted original income per person	116.84	96.42	106.07	48.46	96.20
Adjusted gross income per person	119.74	99.56	112.92	78.16	103.01
Adjusted disposable income per person	106.57	86.28	97.74	78.25	89.66
Average tax rate	11.00	13.34	13.44	10.12	12.97
Average benefit rate	2.41	3.15	6.07	38.00	6.62
Inequality of					
original income	28.43	32.62	31.29	60.17	35.25
gross income	26.74	30.35	26.85	33.25	30.09
disposable income	25.74	28.73	24.87	29.91	28.22
Redistributive effect of					
benefits	5.94	6.96	14.19	44.74	14.64
taxes	3.74	5.34	7.37	10.04	6.21
combined taxes and government					
benefits	9.46	11.92	20.52	50.29	19.94

It is interesting to note that the 25–45 age group was the richest on the basis of total household income, but its ranking is only third from the top when the income is adjusted for household size and composition. The 65-and-over age group continued to remain the poorest group, despite the fact that it had on average the lowest number of equivalent-adults.

It is evident that the 65-and-over group pays income tax at the lowest rate, of 10.12 percent, and receives benefits at the highest rate, of 38.00 percent. This is what we would expect; but what is not expected is the magnitude of the tax rate, which appears to be quite high compared to the income level of this group. Among the remaining three groups, there appears to be no monotonic relationship between the tax rates and the level of income.

Government cash benefits increase substantially the income share of the 65-and-over age group. The tax payments also increase the share of this group in after-tax income, but the magnitude of the increase is considerably lower. As a result, we would expect the inequality between the age groups to fall. The values of the between-group Gini index for the original and gross income concepts were computed to be 7.36 and 5.23, respectively, showing a reduction of 28.94 percent in the between-group inequality as a consequence of government transfers. Taxes, on the other hand, reduced the between-group inequality from 5.23 to 5.16, a reduction of only 1.34 percent.

Turning to the within-group inequalities, we observe that the distribution of original income among households in the over-65 age group is far more unequal than among those in the other age groups. This reflects the fact that a large number of retired persons are not in the work force and, therefore, have little or no earned income. Government transfers reduce the inequality among these households by about 45 percent. Taxes further reduce this inequality by about 10 percent. Thus, the total reduction in inequality due to the combined effect of taxes and government benefits amounts to just over 50 percent.

9.3   Employment status of household head

During the 1970s, unemployment in Australia increased by almost three times. This is bound to have considerable impact on the distribution of income and poverty. It is, therefore, relevant to ask questions such as What is the income gap between the employed and unemployed? How effective are the government policies in providing relief to the unemployed? These and several other related issues are examined below.

To examine these issues, households were divided into four major categories:

1. *Employees and self-employed,* including (a) main job, self-employed, (b) main job, full-time employee (30 or more hours per week), and (c) main job, part-time employee (29 hours or less per week);
2. *Unemployed*;
3. *Retired,* persons who reported no earned income and who described themselves as being retired (e.g., having retired from work for reasons of age or sickness);
4. *Others,* including (a) full-time students; (b) on strike/laid off; (c) unpaid holiday, sickness/accident, leave without pay; (d) unpaid helper; (e) voluntarily idle; and (f) other.

Table 9.5 provides the major sources of income by the employment status of the household head. It shows that wages and salaries form a significant component of income for all types of households considered here. This unexpected result may be explained by the fact that households where the head has no earned income nevertheless have on average .25 persons other than the head who are working. Households with nonemployed heads depend heavily on government benefits and other income. Business income is of minor importance for these households. As a result, their

Table 9.5. *Income components, by employment status of household head: Australia 1975-6*

Income components	Employees and self-employed	Unemployed	Retired	Others	Total population
Wages and salaries	81.72	41.02	20.77	29.90	75.44
Business income	11.78	1.34	2.47	.74	10.62
Pensions	1.26	.74	44.78	38.40	5.54
Unemployment benefits	.02	.88	.50	1.34	.12
Family allowance	.48	1.83	.06	.51	.47
Other government benefits	.25	.17	.69	2.50	.39
Total government benefits	2.24	50.51	46.50	44.10	7.16
Other income	4.26	7.12	30.25	25.25	6.78
Total income	100.00	100.00	100.00	100.00	100.00
Average household income	265.11	116.17	111.56	98.25	226.20

income is considerably lower than those of other households, as is shown by the figures given in the last row. Income per household with a nonemployed head is about .39 of the average of other households.

Table 9.6 provides estimates of income redistribution by employment status. It can be seen that households with an unemployed head have the lowest per equivalent-adult or adjusted income. Their gross income per equivalent-adult is only .43 of the average of all households in the population. More than 46 percent of their income comes from unemployment benefits, which are much lower than the average earnings per worker. The most surprising finding, however, is the tax rate of 11.32 percent paid by these households, being only slightly less than that paid by all households. The available data are insufficient to provide explanation for this.

Government benefits appear to bring about a substantial reduction in income inequality within households headed by the unemployed and other nonemployed persons. The reduction, in the case of the unemployed category of households, is as much as 63.68 percent. Taxes further reduce this inequality by 5.66 percent. Thus, the combined effect of taxes and benefits leads to a reduction of inequality within this group by more than 65 percent.

9.4   The geographical location: urban and rural households

The geographical location of a household may have a sizable effect on the level and the source of its income. The residents of large metropolitan

Table 9.6. *Income redistribution, by employment status of household head: Australia 1975-6*

Variable	Employees and self-employed	Unem-ployed	Retired	Others
Percentage of persons	83.38	1.80	7.01	7.80
Adjusted original income per person	108.47	19.84	36.71	35.99
Adjusted gross income per person	111.01	44.25	67.63	62.84
Adjusted disposable income per person	95.97	39.24	61.49	59.03
Average tax rate	13.55	11.32	9.08	6.06
Average benefit rate	2.29	55.16	45.72	42.73
Inequality of				
original income	28.87	68.14	58.52	54.68
gross income	27.90	24.75	28.76	27.92
disposable income	26.26	23.35	26.79	26.50
Redistributive effect of				
government benefits	3.36	63.68	50.85	48.94
taxes	5.88	5.66	6.85	5.09
combined taxes and				
government benefits	9.04	65.73	54.22	51.54

areas generally have a wider choice of industries in which they may be employed. The choice is much more limited in the smaller towns and in the rural areas. In the rural areas, it may be restricted to the family farm. In order to examine these differences, we turn to Table 9.7, which provides the breakdown of major sources of household income by regions.

It can be seen that income from wages and salaries remains the major component for all types of households considered, even in rural areas. It may be that employment is available either in neighboring farms or in nearby country towns.

The regional differences in household income are not as great as one might have expected. The income per household in the rural areas is .80 of the average in the metropolitan areas. The ratio for urban to metropolitan households turned out to be .84.

Table 9.8, which presents estimates of income redistribution by regions, shows that the ratios of adjusted gross incomes per person of the rural to metropolitan and the urban to metropolitan households are .76 and .86, respectively. It means that income differences between the rural and metropolitan households decreased, and those between the urban and metropolitan households increased when the income was adjusted for household size and composition.

Table 9.7. *Components of income by regions: Australia 1975–6*

Income components	Metro-politan	Urban	Rural	Total population
Wages and salaries	79.12	73.71	46.66	75.44
Business income	7.98	10.30	36.25	10.62
Pensions	4.79	7.63	5.74	5.53
Unemployment benefits	.57	.66	1.31	.65
Sickness and special benefits	.11	.17	.07	.12
Family allowance	.42	.53	–	.47
Other government benefits	.37	.46	–	.39
Total government benefits	6.26	9.45	8.20	7.16
Other income	6.64	6.54	8.89	6.78
Total income	100.00	100.00	100.00	100.00
Average household income	240.38	202.81	192.12	226.20

Comparing the income shares of the three regions, it can be seen that both the government transfers and taxes tend to reduce the regional income differences. This conclusion is further supported by the calculations of the between-group Gini index of various income concepts. Government transfers reduced the between-inequality by about 11.5 percent from the value of 4.86 to 4.30, while income taxes contributed a further reduction of 4.88 percent in inequality; as a result the total reduction in the regional inequality was about 15.84 percent.

The distribution of original income among the rural households is far more equal than that of the other two groups. This may be explained in two ways. First, the rural households derive a sizable proportion of their income from farming and incomes of many farm operators are not as regular or predictable as those of city workers. Secondly, in rural areas the income from wages and salaries is generated in less unionized sectors of the economy, which is likely to produce wider income differences.

Government transfers and taxes reduce the inequality of income among the rural households by 16.54 percent, compared with similar reductions of 25.90 percent and 18.06 percent in the case of urban and metropolitan households, respectively. This shows that the government's redistributive policies are least effective among the rural households despite the fact that they have the lowest mean income.

9.5   Marital status of household head

Table 9.9 presents the breakdown of major sources of income by the marital status of the household head. The findings are summarized below.

Table 9.8. *Income redistribution, by regions: Australia 1975-6*

Variable	Metro-politan	Urban	Rural	Total
Percentage of persons	64.30	26.26	9.44	100.00
Adjusted original income per person	103.10	86.30	76.68	96.20
Adjusted gross income per person	109.46	94.43	82.97	103.02
Adjusted disposable income per person	95.04	82.16	73.87	89.66
Average tax rate	13.17	12.99	10.97	12.97
Benefit rate	5.81	8.61	7.58	6.62
Inequality				
original income	32.55	36.64	47.10	35.25
gross income	28.24	29.57	41.42	30.09
disposable income	26.67	27.15	39.31	28.22
Redistribution effect of				
government benefit	13.24	19.30	12.06	14.64
taxes	5.56	8.18	5.09	6.21
combined effect	18.06	25.90	16.54	19.94
Share of original income (%)	68.91	23.56	7.53	100.00
Share of gross income (%)	68.32	24.10	7.58	100.00
Share of disposable income (%)	68.16	24.06	7.78	100.00

Table 9.9. *Components of income, by marital status of household head: Australia 1975-6*

Income components	Never married	Married	Widowed, divorced, separated	Total population
Wages and salaries	81.72	77.25	56.01	75.44
Business income	4.48	11.97	5.13	10.62
Pensions	4.71	3.45	22.52	5.53
Unemployment benefits	.82	.60	.87	.65
Sickness and special benefits	.15	.11	.21	.12
Family allowance	.02	.54	.28	.47
Other government benefits	.71	.24	1.28	.39
Total government benefits	6.41	4.94	25.16	7.16
Other income	7.38	5.83	13.69	6.78
Total income	100.00	100.00	100.00	100.00
Average household income	205.78	250.68	134.29	226.20

Table 9.10. *Income redistribution, by marital status of household head: Australia 1975–6*

Variable	Never married	Married	Widowed, divorced, separated	Total population
% of persons	5.13	84.53	10.34	100.00
Adjusted original income per person	130.21	97.30	70.26	96.20
Adjusted gross income per person	139.48	102.06	92.70	103.02
Adjusted disposable income per person	121.42	88.47	83.58	89.66
Average tax rate	12.95	13.32	9.84	12.97
Average benefit rate	6.65	4.66	24.21	6.62
Inequality of				
original income	37.33	32.67	50.94	35.25
gross income	31.68	29.17	32.62	30.09
disposable income	29.11	27.43	29.88	28.22
Redistributive effect of				
benefits	15.13	10.71	35.96	14.64
taxes	8.11	5.96	8.40	6.21
combined effect	22.02	16.04	41.34	19.94

Although income from wages and salaries remains the major component for all the three types of households, its share is only 56.01 percent for the widowed–divorced–separated households. Income from government cash transfers is the second major component for these households, contributing just over 25 percent of total income. Other income is also a significant component for these households, with a share of 13.69 percent. Clearly, households whose head is widowed, divorced, or separated depend heavily on government benefits and other unearned income. Married households have the highest average income of about $250 a week. This may be due to a high concentration of multiple earners among these housholds.

Table 9.10 indicates that the income differences between the three groups are reduced considerably when the income is adjusted for differences in household size and composition. This is due to the fact that the married households have to support on average a considerably larger number of equivalent-adults, with a value of 2.52, as against 2.25 for households in the entire population. This resulted in higher per equivalent-adult income among households whose head never married than that of the other two groups.

The computed values of the between-group Gini index indicated a considerable redistribution of income between groups caused by the govern-

Table 9.11. *Income per household, average number of workers, and average number of equivalent-adults by states and territories: Australia 1975-6*

States or territories	Percentage of households	Average income per household	Average number of equivalent-adults	Average number of workers
New South Wales	35.37	220.78	2.15	1.33
Victoria	27.96	232.10	2.15	1.33
Queensland	14.60	220.39	2.13	1.32
South Australia	9.01	217.27	2.03	1.34
Western Australia	8.54	226.85	2.15	1.38
Tasmania	2.93	210.11	2.20	1.27
NT	.30	336.51	2.19	1.66
ACT	1.29	315.52	2.24	1.58
Australia	100.00	226.20	2.14	1.34

ment's redistributive policies. Government transfers alone reduced the between-group inequality by 38.73 percent from the value of 4.26 to 2.61. The personal income tax further reduced the between-group inequality by 11.88 percent so that the total reduction in between-group inequality was just over 46 percent.

9.6   Classification by states and territories

Table 9.11 provides the estimates of income per household along with the average number of equivalent-adults and the average number of workers in each of the six major states and the two territories. Average weekly household income shows a wide variation between states and territories, ranging from $210.11 in Tasmania to $336.51 in the Northern Territory (NT).

The highest average household income in the Northern Territory is rather surprising in view of the fact that this region is not as well developed as many other parts of the country. Two reasons may be given for this deviation. First, households in this territory have on average the highest number of working persons. Secondly, the sample covers Darwin and urban areas only, excluding the rural areas, which have markedly lower incomes.

Differences in income between states and territories may be explained in part by the differences in the average number of working persons. Although there is no strict monotonic relationship between the two vari-

Table 9.12. *Income distribution, by states and territories: Australia 1975-6*

	NSW	Vic.	Qld.	SA	WA	Tas.	NT	ACT
Percentage of persons	35.57	28.07	14.59	8.34	8.64	.07	.32	1.40
Adjusted original income per person	92.92	98.89	94.13	99.70	97.22	85.35	144.58	132.37
Adjusted gross income per person	100.40	105.44	101.02	105.89	103.05	93.25	146.08	135.63
Adjusted disposable income per person	87.89	91.32	87.54	92.38	90.20	81.69	127.83	112.43
Tax rate	12.46	13.39	13.34	12.76	12.47	12.40	12.49	17.10
Benefit rate	7.45	6.21	6.82	5.85	5.66	8.47	1.03	2.40
Inequality of								
original income	35.34	34.20	39.62	32.85	33.18	36.23	28.36	28.10
gross income	29.61	29.67	33.95	28.10	29.02	28.90	27.66	26.92
disposable income	28.09	27.67	31.01	26.53	28.16	26.86	27.12	25.16
Redistributive effect of								
benefits	16.21	13.25	14.31	14.46	12.54	20.23	2.47	4.20
taxes	5.13	6.74	8.66	5.59	2.96	7.06	1.95	6.54
combined effects	20.51	19.09	21.73	19.24	15.13	25.86	4.37	10.46
Share of original income (%)	34.36	28.85	14.28	8.64	8.73	2.72	.48	1.94
Share of gross income (%)	34.66	28.73	14.31	8.57	8.64	2.78	.45	1.86
Share of disposable income (%)	34.87	28.59	14.24	8.59	8.69	2.80	.46	1.76

ables, it seems that households with a larger number of working persons tend to have higher incomes.

The between-group Gini index for the gross income per household was 1.99. When the calculations were performed on the distribution of individuals according to the gross adjusted income, the value of this index became 2.03. This shows that the income differences between states and territories are widened as the income is adjusted for household size and composition. This is due to the fact that households in the poorer states have to support on average a larger number of equivalent-adults.

The results in Table 9.12 show that average benefits rates vary widely between states and territories, ranging from 1.03 percent in the Northern Territory to 8.47 percent in Tasmania. The variation in tax rates is relatively smaller, ranging from 12.40 percent in Tasmania to 17.10 percent in the Australian Capital Territory (ACT). Government benefits reduce the

Table 9.13. *Percentage of total household income from different income sources, by household income: Australia 1975–6*

| Weekly household income | Sources of income | | | | | |
	Wages and salary	Business income	Govt. benefits	Interest, rent, dividends	Other regular income	Total income
Under $80	4.4	6.8	72.8	8.0	8.1	100.00
$80–$140	48.8	11.9	23.4	6.9	9.0	100.00
$140–$200	77.5	8.6	6.7	3.1	4.2	100.00
$200–$260	82.5	8.4	3.1	2.9	3.0	100.00
$260–$340	84.9	8.4	2.0	2.5	2.2	100.00
$340 and over	78.4	14.7	1.4	3.3	2.2	100.00
All households	75.44	10.62	7,16	3.4	3.38	100.00

between-group inequality by 19.67 percent from the value of 2.44 to 1.96. Income taxes further reduce the inequality by 11.73 percent. Thus government redistributive policies bring about a sizable reduction in the income differences between states and territories.

The inequality of original income is considerably smaller in territories than that in states. One reason may be that the federal government is the main employer in the territories, employing people with similar abilities and other characteristics. The relatively greater homogeneity of the population contributes to the smaller inequality.

Among all states and territories, Queensland has the highest income inequality. Despite the fact that the government's redistributive policies reduce the inequality by 21.73 percent, it still remains the state with the highest inequality of disposable income.

9.7 Income inequality by predominant source of income

The size of a household's income is closely associated with its sources of income. This can be clearly seen from Table 9.13, which gives percentage of total household income from different income sources by household income. It is evident that low-income households are heavily dependent upon government transfers, although private means are of some significance. Households in the middle-income brackets receive most of their income from employment and households in the highest income brackets also depend mainly upon earned income, although business income is of greater importance.

Table 9.14. *Components of income, by predominant source of household income: Australia 1975–6*

Income components	Wages and salary	Business income	Interest, dividends, rent	Government benefits	Other income[a]
Wages and salaries	92.55	11.55	10.14	4.21	11.60
Business income	1.19	81.08	.83	.20	−8.22
Pensions	1.57	1.27	12.99	71.29	11.76
Unemployment benefits	.31	.13	.13	7.16	.96
Sickness and special benefits	.06	.00	.08	1.34	.00
Family allowance	.43	.60	.21	.56	1.10
Other government benefits	.24	.14	.01	2.95	1.77
Total government benefits	2.6	21.48	13.43	83.34	15.58
Other income	3.67	5.21	75.59	12.23	81.03
Total income	100.00	100.00	100.00	100.00	100.00
% of household	67.37	9.95	2.78	16.71	3.19
Average income per household	266.79	274.64	148.40	70.71	108.03

[a] This excludes interest, dividends, and rent.

Table 9.14 presents the income components of households classified by predominant source of income. The most striking finding emerging from this table is that as many as 16.71 percent of all households depend largely upon government benefits for their living. This group has the lowest average income of only $70.71 per week as compared with the highest income of $274.64 per week for the households dependent principally on business income. The between-group Gini index was computed to be 14.62, showing wide income differences between households differing with respect to their predominant source of income.

These income differences are narrowed considerably when the income is adjusted for household size and composition. The between-group Gini index reduced from the value of 14.62 to 8.24 as a result of this adjustment. This is explained by the fact that households dependent principally on earned income tend to have, on average, a larger number of equivalent-adults.

The results in Table 9.15 indicate that the variation in government benefit rates is considerably greater than in the income-tax rates. The benefit rates vary from the lowest of 2.13 percent to the highest of 82.97 percent. Although the strict monotonic relationship between the benefit rates and the adjusted original income is not evident, the poorer groups tend to

Table 9.15. *Income redistribution, by predominant source of household income: Australia 1975-6*

	Wages and salaries	Business income	Interests, dividends, rent	Government benefits	Other income[a]
Percentage of persons	73.02	12.04	1.81	10.36	2.77
Adjusted original income per person	109.59	106.45	78.12	7.77	43.25
Adjusted gross income per person	112.57	108.77	89.69	45.64	51.57
Adjusted disposable income per person	97.72	92.87	75.69	44.40	43.61
Average tax rate	13.19	14.62	15.61	2.72	15.43
Average benefit rate	2.65	2.13	12.90	82.97	16.13
Inequality of					
original income	24.99	40.64	45.42	52.36	67.90
gross income	24.11	39.71	43.16	15.01	62.01
disposable income	22.84	36.76	42.18	15.20	64.90
Redistributive effect of					
government benefits	3.52	2.29	4.98	71.33	8.67
taxes	5.27	7.43	2.27	−1.27	−4.66
combined taxes and benefits	8.60	9.55	7.13	70.97	4.42

[a] This excludes interest, dividends, and rent.

get greater benefits as a percentage of their original income. Government benefits reduced the between-group inequality by more than 35.6 percent, from the value of 11.98 for the original income to 8.52 for the gross income.

Although income taxes reduced the between-group inequality by 8.49 percent, from the value of 8.52 to 7.54, the tax rates paid by households principally dependent on interest, dividends, and rents and other income are higher than those dependent principally on wages and salaries and business income, despite their income being considerably lower. This is not what one would expect to happen with a progressive tax system. One reason may be that the Australian tax system is not insulated from the horizontal inequities introduced due to different income sources. A further investigation is necessary in order to arrive at a definite conclusion.

The distribution of income among households dependent mainly on wages and salaries is far more equal than those among the other groups. Households whose predominant source of income is government benefits

Table 9.16. *Income components, by period of residence of household head: Australia 1975-6*

Income components	Australian born	Less than 2 years	2-5 years	5-10 years	10 years or more	Total population
Wages and salaries	74.77	91.05	90.04	83.52	74.77	75.44
Business income	10.75	2.91	2.51	9.59	11.82	10.62
Pensions	6.13	1.16	.77	.88	5.28	5.53
Unemployment benefits	.51	.86	1.10	.97	1.04	.65
Sickness and special benefits	.13	.00	.00	.00	.14	.12
Family allowance	.46	.25	.44	.54	.49	.47
Other benefits	.46	.00	.32	.31	.17	.39
Total government benefits	7.70	2.27	2.64	2.70	7.12	7.16
Other income	7.11	3.77	4.81	4.19	6.62	6.78
Total income	100.00	100.00	100.00	100.00	100.00	100.00
Average household income	224.17	272.30	234.60	248.75	224.97	226.20

have the highest inequality of the original income, the Gini index being 52.36, but the inequality is reduced to only 15.01 as a result of government transfers. It is interesting to note that the taxes increase the income inequality by 1.27 percent, showing their effect to be regressive among these households. This regressive nature of taxes is also evident among households dependent principally on other income.

9.8   Period of residence of household head

Immigration has been of vital importance to Australia since World War II. Even now migrants are arriving here at the rate of more than 100,000 per year. It is important, therefore, to investigate the income differences between households classified according to the length of residence of household head. Length of residence may affect not only the level of income but the source of income as well. Table 9.16 gives the major sources of income by the length of residence of head.

The results indicate that the importance of income from wages and salaries diminishes monotonically as the length of residence increases. The importance of the remaining three income sources – namely, business income, government benefits, and other income – seems to increase steadily with increasing length of residence. These increases may be due to the age of household head, which increases steadily with the length of residence.

Table 9.17. *Income redistribution, by length of residence of household head: Australia 1975-6*

Variable	Australian born	Less than 2 years	2-5 years	5-10 years	10 years or more
Percentage of persons	72.20	1.21	1.95	5.20	19.44
Adjusted original income per person	96.52	112.85	100.50	100.85	92.35
Adjusted gross income per person	103.85	115.36	103.66	103.97	98.88
Adjusted disposable income per person	90.30	105.79	90.77	91.09	85.81
Average tax rate	13.05	8.30	12.43	12.39	13.22
Average benefit rate	7.06	2.18	3.05	3.01	6.60
Inequality of					
original income	35.94	19.45	33.20	33.80	33.65
gross income	30.45	18.07	30.75	31.13	28.93
disposable income	28.39	18.61	29.84	30.38	27.29
Redistributive effect of					
benefits	15.27	7.09	7.38	7.90	14.03
taxes	6.76	−2.99	2.96	2.41	5.67
combined benefits and taxes	21.01	4.32	10.12	10.12	18.90

It is interesting to note that households whose head has been here for less than two years have the highest average income of $272.30 per week. This is not what one would expect because new migrants have to go through the difficult process of adjusting to the new surroundings. There could be two possible explanations for this result. First, new migrants may be willing to work harder, doing greater amounts of overtime. Secondly, selection procedures may have changed recently, favoring highly skilled migrants, who earn higher incomes.

It is also interesting to note that income differences between the groups are very small, indicating that the period of residence of household head has an insignificant effect on the household income. However, these differences widened slightly as the income was adjusted for household size and composition. The between-group Gini index for income per household was computed to be .82, but it increased to .89 when the similar calculations were performed on the per equivalent-adult income.

The results given in Table 9.17 indicate that government benefit rates increase steadily with increasing length of residence. This is an expected result because migrants are not entitled to government pensions until they have completed the requirement of 10 years of residence. What is not expected is the lowest tax rate of 8.30 percent paid by households whose head has been here for less than two years, despite the fact that they have the highest average income. One reason for this may be that many of this group are not resident here during the entire financial year and, therefore, are subject to lower tax rates.

The values of the between-group Gini index for the original and gross income concepts were computed to be 1.18 and .89, respectively, showing a reduction of 24.58 percent in the between-group inequality from .89 to 1.03, an increase of 15.73 percent. So, the net effect of the taxes and government benefits was to reduce the between-group income differences by 12.71 percent.

Turning to the within-group inequalities, we observe that inequality computed on the basis of adjusted original income increases with the increasing length of residence. The highest inequality is found among households whose head was born in Australia. This is not what one would expect, since differences in characteristics may be assumed to be far wider among migrant households coming from a variety of countries. The available data are insufficient to provide a definitive explanation of this phenomenon. One reason may be that the migrant selection procedures ensure greater homogeneity of characteristics among migrant households.

It is evident that the government's redistributive policies bring out great equality of income among households whose head is either born in Australia or has been in Australia for more than 10 years than that in the other groups. The most striking thing to note is that the taxes are regressive among households who have been in Australia for less than two years. Again, this may be due to the fact that many recent arrivals are not residents of Australia for the entire financial year and, therefore, pay taxes at the lower rates.

9.9   Country of birth of household head

In 1976, just under 18 percent of the Australian population lived in households whose head was not born in Australia. These people are likely to have different ethnic backgrounds, which may have bearing on the levels of their income. In this section we investigate the income differences between households classified according to the country of birth of household head.

The results in Table 9.18 indicate that wages and salaries form a major component of income for all types of households considered. However, different types of households differ significantly with respect to various sources of household income. The share of wages and salaries varies from the lowest of 71.11 percent for households whose head was born in Italy, Greece, or Yugoslavia to the highest of 91.89 percent for those whose

Table 9.18. *Income components, by country of birth of household head: Australia 1975–6*

Income components	Australia	U.K. and Ireland	Italy, Greece, and Yugoslavia	Germany and Netherlands	Other Europe	Asia	Oceania, including New Zealand	America	Other
Wages and salaries	74.77	80.75	71.11	77.57	82.19	72.96	73.81	91.89	84.94
Business income	10.75	6.71	18.56	13.83	6.12	13.61	12.85	−.33	3.89
Pensions	6.13	5.57	1.98	1.56	3.63	3.30	4.31	3.63	3.61
Unemployment benefits	.51	.53	.57	2.06	1.23	3.47	1.47	.52	.93
Sickness and special benefits	.13	.02	.33	.20	0.00	0.00	0.00	0.00	0.00
Family allowance	.46	.35	.68	.58	.52	.62	.35	.33	.50
Other benefits	.46	.25	.23	.27	.09	.16	.09	.03	.02
Total government benefits	7.70	6.72	3.79	4.67	5.47	7.55	6.22	4.51	5.06
Other income	7.11	5.82	6.54	3.93	6.22	5.88	7.12	3.93	6.11
Total income	100.00	100.00	100.00	100.00	100.00	100.00	100.00	100.00	100.00
Average household income	224.17	233.42	230.76	227.08	228.25	234.81	235.47	228.42	239.55
Average household size	3.30	2.94	3.81	3.35	3.20	3.44	3.00	2.96	3.69

head was born in America. The variation in the share of business income is even greater; it varies from the lowest, −.33 percent, to the highest, 18.56 percent. Households whose head was born in America, on average, make business losses. Government cash benefits contribute a maximum of 7.70 percent to the total income of households whose head is born in Australia, as compared with a minimum of 3.79 percent to the income of those whose head was born in Italy, Greece, or Yugoslavia. This is an expected result because, as observed earlier, migrants are not entitled to government pensions during the first 10 years of their residence. What is not expected is the contribution of 7.55 percent by government cash benefits for households whose head was born in Asia. Of all government benefits, the unemployment benefit is the major component for these households, contributing 3.47 percent of total income. This may be attributed to high incidence of unemployment among the Asian population.

Despite wide variations in shares of various income components, the differences in household income between the different groups appear to be very small. This is reflected by the low value of the between-group Gini index which was computed to be .70 (expressed in percentage terms). These differences widened slightly as income was adjusted for household size and composition. The between-group Gini index increased from the value of .70 to 1.87 as a result of this adjustment.

Since there is no monotonic relationship between the tax rates or benefit rates and the adjusted household income, it is difficult to say whether taxes or benefits widened or narrowed the income differences between various groups classified according to country of birth of household head. Therefore, we computed the between-group Gini index of various income concepts. The values of this index for the adjusted original and gross income concepts were 1.70 and 1.87, respectively, showing an increase of about 10 percent in the between-group inequality caused by government cash benefits. The adjustment of income for taxes further increased the between-group inequality by about 3.7 percent from the value of 1.87 to 1.94.

Turning to the within-group inequalities, we observe from Table 9.19 that inequality computed on the basis of adjusted original income is highest among individuals in households whose head is born in Asia. Although the government's redistributive policies reduce the inequality by 20.11 percent, it still remains the group with highest inequality of adjusted disposable income.

9.10   Household size and composition

The economic welfare of households depends not only on income but on needs of households as well. The household size and composition is an

Table 9.19. *Income redistribution, by country of birth of household head: Australia 1975–6*

Variable	Australia	U.K. and Ireland	Italy, Greece, and Yugoslavia	Germany and Netherlands	Other Europe	Asia	Oceania, including New Zealand	America	Other
Percentage of persons	72.20	10.48	6.82	2.63	3.61	2.04	.99	.40	.82
Adjusted original income per person	96.52	103.13	87.54	91.88	93.49	87.61	103.03	100.97	88.52
Adjusted gross income per person	103.85	109.83	90.78	96.97	98.88	95.49	109.28	105.21	92.77
Adjusted disposable income per person	90.30	96.42	79.08	86.40	83.57	83.72	93.42	93.11	81.00
Average tax rate	13.05	12.21	12.89	10.90	15.48	12.33		14.51	12.69
Average benefit rate	7.06	6.10	3.57	5.25	5.45	8.25	5.72	4.03	4.58
Inequality of									
original income	35.94	32.87	29.62	37.24	32.76	40.23	35.81	33.16	25.55
gross income	30.45	28.50	27.20	32.37	28.35	32.98	30.45	29.36	23.90
disposable income	28.39	27.02	26.64	31.61	26.29	32.14	27.32	27.36	22.87
Redistributive effect of									
benefits	15.27	13.29	8.17	13.08	13.46	18.02	14.97	11.46	6.46
taxes	6.76	5.19	2.06	2.35	7.27	2.55	10.28	6.81	4.31
combined benefits and taxes	21.01	17.80	10.06	15.12	19.75	20.11	23.71	17.49	10.49
Original income (%)	72.44	11.23	6.21	2.51	3.51	1.86	1.06	.42	.76
Gross income (%)	72.78	11.17	6.01	2.48	3.46	1.89	1.05	.41	.75
Disposable income (%)	72.71	11.27	6.01	2.53	3.36	1.90	1.03	.41	.78

important demographic variable that has impact on both the needs of a household and its income. Clearly, a large household has greater needs than a smaller household. It has been observed in several studies that the larger households also tend to have higher incomes (Chapter 6). This may be explained in two ways. First, the larger households are likely to have on average a greater number of persons in the work force. Secondly, the greater needs of the larger households may induce their income earners to greater work effort.

The question whether the larger households are relatively better off or worse off has important policy implications because of the closer association between the government tax-transfer programs and the number of dependent persons in households Although government cash transfers are received by individuals, the size of these benefits depends on the number of dependents a person has to maintain. In the Australian tax system, an individual is allowed some concessional deductions, the amount of which depends crucially on the size and composition of his or her family.

The impact of the government's redistributive policies on households with differing size and composition is analyzed below. Households have been divided into 15 groups according to their size and composition. The numerical results are presented in Table 9.20.

Several interesting findings emerging from the numerical results can be briefly summarized. Adjusted income varies widely among the various households composition groups. The lowest adjusted original income is observed among households with one adult and three or more children. The mean adjusted original income among these households is only $42.57 a week compared with the highest mean income of $126.52 among households with three or more adults and one child. It seems that households with one adult and two or more children and with two adults and five or more children are characterized by low incomes. The high incomes are found among households with three or more adults. It is interesting to note that one-adult households, who are likely to have a high concentration of older people, are not as badly off as one might expect. Two-adult households are quite well off if they have few children but their economic situation worsens steadily as the number of children in the household increases. The hypothesis that the larger a household the higher its adjusted income does not seem to be supported by these observations.[3] A more conclusive finding is the positive correlation between the number of adults in a household and its adjusted income. Households with the larger number of adults tend to have the larger number of persons in the working category. There were on average 2.38 persons working in the three-or-more adults households as against the averages of 1.25 and 0.50 in the two-adult and one-adult households (with or without children), respectively.

Table 9.20. *Income redistribution, by household composition: Australia 1975–6*

Household composition	Percentage of persons	Adjusted income per person based on			Tax rate	Benefit rate	Inequality of			Redistributive effects		
		Original	Gross	Disposable			Original	Gross	Disposable	Benefits	Taxes	Combined
1 adult	5.06	83.65	105.25	90.32	14.18	20.52	58.79	40.21	36.46	31.60	9.32	37.98
2 adults	18.25	111.71	123.98	106.88	13.79	9.90	42.78	33.71	31.34	21.20	7.03	26.74
3 or more adults	8.22	118.22	127.01	110.60	12.92	6.92	23.83	19.64	18.84	17.58	4.07	20.94
1 adult, 1 child	1.18	82.05	97.56	88.31	9.48	15.90	48.05	32.26	29.22	32.86	9.42	39.19
1 adult, 2 children	.81	65.87	80.84	75.80	6.23	18.52	40.91	25.52	24.77	37.62	2.94	39.45
1 adult, 3 or more children	1.26	42.57	60.37	58.21	3.58	29.48	46.22	27.65	26.59	40.18	3.83	42.47
2 adults, 1 child	9.76	107.22	110.17	95.22	13.57	2.68	28.70	26.65	25.91	7.14	2.78	9.72
2 adults, 2 children	20.49	97.71	99.61	85.71	13.95	1.91	28.12	26.92	25.30	4.27	6.02	10.03
2 adults, 3 children	11.94	78.98	81.35	71.09	12.61	2.91	26.24	25.20	23.77	3.96	5.67	9.41
2 adults, 4 children	5.61	70.61	73.74	65.86	10.69	4.24	31.57	28.75	27.70	8.93	3.65	12.26
2 adults, 5 children	2.67	55.25	59.28	53.21	10.24	6.80	35.13	30.73	28.39	12.52	7.61	19.19
2 adults, 6 or more children	1.57	47.94	56.28	51.22	8.99	14.82	33.56	22.21	17.80	33.82	19.86	46.96
3 or more adults, 1 child	4.61	126.52	131.22	112.51	14.26	3.58	22.67	20.96	19.01	7.54	9.30	16.14
3 or more adults, 2 children	4.31	104.35	110.88	97.61	12.00	5.89	20.45	18.36	16.93	10.22	7.79	17.21
3 or more adults, 3 or more children	5.40	83.00	91.15	82.76	9.20	8.94	26.22	20.88	20.11	20.37	3.69	23.30

It can be seen that households with different composition pay different tax rates. The rates vary from the lowest of 3.58 percent to the highest of 14.26 percent with an average of 12.97 percent for all households. Since personal income tax is progressive, it is expected that the tax rates would increase monotonically with income. Although there is a general tendency for the rates to increase with adjusted household income, the monotonic relationship is not evident. This is supported by the fact that the ranking of household groups by the adjusted gross income is different from that by the average tax rate.

The variation in government benefits rates is considerably greater than that in tax rates. The rates vary from the low of 1.91 percent to the high of 29.30 percent, with an average 6.62 percent for all households. Again, the monotonic relationship between the benefits rates and the adjusted original income is not evident but the poorer groups tend to get the greater benefits. The one-adult households, with or without children, seem to receive greater benefits than other households, an exception being the two-adult households with six or more children. This may be explained in two ways. First, these households are largely concentrated in the lower ranges of original income, where the largest proportion of benefits usually goes. Secondly, the government income-support programs may be biased in favor of the one-adult households. It seems that both these factors are playing an important role in the income-support policies of the government.

The question whether government benefits and taxes narrowed or widened the income differences among the various household composition groups can be answered by examining the values of the between-group Gini index calculated for various income concepts. The values of this index for the adjusted original and gross income concepts were computed to be 13.14 and 10.64, respectively, showing a reduction of 19.03 percent in the between-group inequality caused by the government transfers. Income taxes, on the other hand, reduced the between-group inequality by only 4.23 percent from a value of 10.64 to 10.19. As a result, the taxes and government benefits together resulted in a 22.45 percent reduction in the between-group inequality.

The substantial differences in the inequality of income within various household composition groups are quite evident. It is readily seen that one-person households have the highest inequality of original income. The value of the Gini index for these households is 58.79 compared with the lowest value of only 20.45 for households with three or more adults and two children. This is an unexpected result, since differences in size of the household and in other characteristics may be assumed to be far wider among households of two and more persons. The available data are insufficient to provide a definitive explanation of this phenomenon, but the reason is probably that one-person households include a large number of pensioners and other supplementary-income recipients along with a substantial number of income earners of prime working age. About 17 percent of the one-person households had retired persons who reported no earned income and depended mainly on government benefits. There were about 43 percent of households that had persons working in a job or business receiving earned income. Thus the remaining 40 percent of these households had "other income" as the main source of income. They included persons living on alimony or maintenance allowances, workers' compensation, and other regular allowances. These observations suggest that one-person households do have a mixture of primary and supplementary income earners who probably contribute to the wide inequality among them.

The inequality of original income was also found to be very high among households with one adult and children. Interestingly enough, 82 percent of these households had a working head engaged in a job or business. The occurrence of high inequality of income among these households is rather surprising in view of their greater homogeneity with respect to the employment status of household head. A further investigation is necessary in order to provide a definitive explanation of this result.

It can be readily seen that government benefits bring about a substantial reduction in inequality among one-adult households (with or without children). The reduction in inequality varies from 31.60 percent for the one-adult households to 40.18 percent for the one-adult, three-or-more children households. The reduction in inequality due to government benefits is also very high among households with 2 adults and 6 or more children (33.56 percent). In the remaining groups the reduction is considerably lower, varying from the minimum value of 3.96 percent to the maximum value of 21.20 percent. It may be concluded that the government cash transfers play a more vital role in reducing income differentials among one-adult households than among those with two or more adults.

9.11 Summary of conclusions

This chapter has been concerned with the redistribution of income within and between several socioeconomic and demographic groups, providing considerable insight into issues concerning the impact of the government tax-transfer policies on particular groups in the community. Some of the major findings of the chapter are as follows:

1. Households headed by women have considerably lower incomes than those headed by men. These differences are considerably narrowed, however, when income is adjusted for household size

and composition. The Australian tax-transfer system also plays a major role in reducing the income differentials between the two types of households.

2. The importance of income from wages and salaries diminishes monotonically as the age of the household head increases. Although the importance of business income tends to increase with the age, there is no monotonic relationship between the two. The households belonging to the 65-and-over age group depend heavily on unearned income, particularly government pensions. Although the 25–45 age group was the richest on the basis of total household income its ranking is only third from the top when the income is adjusted for household size and composition. The 65-and-over age group continues to remain the poorest group despite the fact that government cash benefits substantially increase the income share of this group. The tax payments also increase the income share of this group, but the magnitude of the increase is considerably lower.

3. As expected, the households with an unemployed head have the lowest per equivalent-adult or adjusted income per person. Their gross income per equivalent-adult is only .43 of the average of all households in the population. The most surprising finding, however, is the tax rate of 11.32 percent paid by these households, being only slightly less than that paid by all households.

4. Both the government transfers and taxes tend to reduce the regional income differences. It is interesting that government's redistributive policies are least effective among the rural households despite the fact that they have the least mean income and the highest inequality of original income.

5. A wide variation in average household income was observed between states and territories. The highest average household income in the Northern Territory is rather surprising in view of the fact that this region is not as well developed as many other parts of the country. However, the government's redistributive policies bring about a sizable reduction in income differences between states and territories. Among all states and territories, Queensland has the highest income inequality. Despite the fact that the government's redistributive policies reduce the inequality by more than 21 percent, it still remains the state with the highest inequality of disposable income.

6. As many as 16.71 percent of all households depend largely upon government benefits for their living. This group has the lowest average income of only $70.61 per week as compared with the

highest income of $274.64 per week for the households depen-
dent principally on business income. The wide income differences
that exist between households differing with respect to their predominant source of income are narrowed considerably when income is adjusted for household size and composition. The tax
rates paid by households principally dependent on interest, dividends, and rents and other income are higher than those dependent principally on wages and salaries and business income,
despite their income being considerably lower. This result suggests the existence of horizontal inequities due to different income sources. Since the proportion of persons in these groups is
small, the effect of horizontal inequity so introduced on the income inequality of the total population is likely to be small (see
Chapter 8).

7. The period of residence of household head has an insignificant
    effect on the household income. However, these differences are
    widened slightly as the income is adjusted for household size and
    composition. The government cash benefits tended to reduce the
    between-group inequality while the personal income tax increased
    it, but the net effect of the two was to reduce the between-group
    income differences. The government redistributive policies bring
    about greater equality of income among households whose head
    is either born in Australia or has been in Australia for more than
    10 years than in the other groups. The most striking finding is
    that the personal income tax is regressive among households who
    have been in Australia for less than 2 years.

8. The income differences among households classified according to
    the country of birth of household head are not as large as one
    would have expected. Both government cash benefits and taxes
    tended to widen these income differences. The inequality com-
    puted on the basis of adjusted original income was highest among
    individuals in households whose head was born in Asia. Although
    government's redistributive policies reduced the inequality by
    more than 20 percent, it still remained the group with highest
    inequality of adjusted disposable income. Of all government
    benefits, the unemployment benefit was the major component of
    income for those households indicating a high incidence of un-
    employment among the Asian population.

9. Households with one adult and two or more children and with
    two adults and five or more children are characterized by low in-
    comes. The high incomes are found among households with three
    or more adults. The hypothesis that the larger a household, the

higher its adjusted income does not seem to be supported by the observations. However, there is an evidence of the positive correlation between the number of adults in a household and its adjusted income.

CHAPTER 10

Progressivity of sales tax on individual expenditure items

In reviewing the Australian tax system in Chapter 1, it was pointed out that Australia relies heavily on personal income tax as a major source of the government's revenue. However, in the past few years this pattern has been changing towards taxing consumer items. Still, the sales tax and excise duty play a relatively minor role in the overall Australian tax system.

In 1975, the Australian Taxation Review Committee, also known as the Asprey Committee, reached the general conclusion that the taxation system should place greater reliance on goods and services by the inclusion of a broad-based tax. The government did not implement these recommendations probably due to its concern about the immediate boost to inflation that would come from introduction of such a broad-based tax.[1] During the 1980–1 financial year the government did consider the introduction of a broad-based direct tax, such as a retail turnover tax, a wholesale tax, and a value added tax, but again abandoned such an idea because of its potential inflationary effect.

Instead, in the 1981–2 budget the government announced the introduction of a limited sales tax measure which amounted to the broadening of the sales tax base by including many consumption items previously exempt.[2] Although the rate on the new items is only 2.5 percent, the inclusion of these items in the sales tax base will have far-reaching effects on the future structure of the Australian tax system. The present base of the consumption tax system is rather narrow and is restricted to only a few goods and services. Therefore, a significant increase in revenue cannot be achieved even with a large increase in tax rates. The broadening in sales tax base will provide the government with an opportunity to achieve a significant increase in tax revenue with a moderate change in tax rates. It seems that in future the government will place greater reliance on indirect taxes and lesser reliance on direct taxes despite the fact that indirect taxes are regressive and will hit the poor harder than the rich.

If the government is to rely heavily on taxes on goods and services, an attempt must be made to reduce the degree of regressivity of such taxes by making a distinction between goods consumed mainly by the rich and the necessary goods consumed by most people. This raises the question

171

of finding the appropriate tax rates for different goods and services in order to avoid the adverse effect of these taxes on income distribution.

This chapter, based largely on an earlier paper by Kakwani (1983a), provides estimates of the degree of progressivity (or regressivity) of the sales tax or excise duty on more than 350 individual consumption items. This is the first tax-incidence study which considers such a fine classification of goods and services. These estimates based on the Australian Household Expenditure Survey of 1975–6 provide a guideline for determining the tax rates on individual consumption items. These results should be of interest because they provide some quantitative basis for formulating a structure of indirect taxes with least regressive impact.

10.1   The index of progressivity (or regressivity) used

It may be recalled that a tax is said to be progressive (regressive) if richer (poorer) individuals pay a higher proportion of their income in taxes. If the tax liability is distributed among individuals in proportion to their income, the tax is said to be proportional. Therefore, a measure of progressivity (regressivity) shows the extent to which a tax system deviates from proportionality in favor of poorer (richer) individuals.

The concentration measure of progressivity proposed by Kakwani (1977a) (discussed in Section 5.4) is used here to measure the progressivity (or regressivity) of sales tax on each expenditure item. The positive value of this index implies a progressive tax and the negative value implies a regressive tax.

In order to gain further insight into issues of the progressiveness of sales tax on individual expenditure items, we computed the relative tax-burden index for various quintiles. This index, as defined in Chapter 7, measures the relative tax burden of each quintile and is given by the ratio of its share of total taxes to its share of total income. If the value of this index for a quintile is greater (less) than 100, then that quintile is paying a greater (smaller) proportion of their income in tax. The tax tends to be progressive (regressive) if the value of this index increases (decreases) as we move up from the lower to higher quintiles.

10.2   The appropriate basis for measuring progressivity

The progressivity (or regressivity) of a tax is measured in order to estimate the effect of that tax on the distribution of economic welfare. If income is used as a measure of economic welfare, then the progressivity must be measured with respect to an income base. In that case, the definition of income should be as comprehensive as possible. It should include all its components that affect the economic well-being of individuals or households.

Alternatively, one may measure the degree of progressivity (or regressivity) with respect to an expenditure base. An argument in favor of the expenditure base is that the total expenditure may be considered a better indicator of the long-term economic position of a household than its current income. But the measurement of the long-term economic position of a household involves several conceptual problems, which have been highlighted in Chapter 3. The major difficulty with an expenditure base is that it includes outlays for current as well as for durable consumer goods. For the purpose of measuring the economic welfare of an individual, it is the consumption of durable goods, rather than expenditure on them, that is of interest (Kay and Keen 1980).

A recent OECD (1981) study has given arguments for and against each of these two bases. It concluded that "the choice between income or consumption as the basis for measuring progressivity is essentially one of methodology and the solution adopted is, wherever possible, to show the results on both bases." But we take the view that for policy purposes the choice must be made between the two alternatives. In view of all the arguments put forward in the literature it seems that the income base should be preferred provided the income definition is sufficiently comprehensive.

Almost all the incidence studies on indirect taxation of which we know invariably allocate the tax burden to the total household income and then draw conclusions about the redistributive effect of taxes. (See, for instance, Musgrave 1964; Gillespie 1965; Bentley, Collin, and Drane 1974; Nicholson 1974, 1977; Pechman and Okner 1974; Reynolds and Smolensky 1974; Dodge 1975; and OECD 1981.) There are two major weaknesses with these studies. First, they relate to the distribution of households and not that of individuals. Secondly, they completely neglect the needs of the household, which differ as a result of differences in household size and composition. In this chapter, the income as well as the tax burden was adjusted for the household size and composition by giving weights of unity to the first adult (head), 0.7 to the second and subsequent adults, and 0.4 to each child in the household. The progressivity (or regressivity) index is then computed from the resulting distribution of the tax paid by each individual.

10.3 The tax-incidence assumptions

Suppose there are n goods consumed by households, and $t_1, t_2, \ldots, t_n$ are the corresponding unit indirect-tax payments on them. Further assume that the indirect tax is partly paid by producers and partly by consumers.

If h_i denotes the proportion of the indirect tax on the ith commodity that is passed on to the consumers, the observed price of the ith commodity will be given by

$$p_i = \bar{p}_i + h_i t_i \tag{10.1}$$

where $\bar{p}_i$ is the price of the ith commodity in the absence of indirect taxes.

Let $q_i(x)$ be the quantity per equivalent adult of the ith commodity consumed by an individual in the household with per equivalent-adult income x, then

$$T_i(x) = \alpha_i v_i(x) \tag{10.2}$$

where $\alpha_i = h_i t_i / p_i$ and $v_i(x) - p_i q_i(x)$ is the indirect tax paid by that individual by consuming the ith commodity.

If the individuals are arranged according to the ascending order of their per equivalent-adult income x, then equation (10.2) gives the concentration curve of the indirect tax on the ith commodity to be equal to the concentration curve of the expenditure on the ith commodity.[3] The concentration curve of each expenditure item was estimated by the new equation for the Lorenz curve discussed in Chapter 4. The concentration curve of the indirect tax so derived enables us to compute the quintile shares of the tax paid on each commodity. These quintile shares when divided by the corresponding income shares provide the estimates of the relative tax-burden index. The estimates of this index are presented in the first five columns of Table 10.1.

Applying Theorem 8.5 of Kakwani (1980a) on (10.2) gives the progressivity (or regressivity) of the indirect tax paid on the ith commodity as

$$P_i = C_i - G \tag{10.3}$$

where C_i is the concentration index of the expenditure on the ith commodity and G is the Gini index of income x. The numerical values of the progressivity (or regressivity) index so obtained are presented in the last column of Table 10.1.

The progressivity (or regressivity) index of the overall indirect tax system will be

$$P = \left(\sum_{i=1}^{n} \mu_i \alpha_i P_i \right) \Big/ \left(\sum_{i=1}^{n} \mu_i \alpha_i \right) \tag{10.4}$$

where μ_i is the mean per equivalent-adult expenditure on the ith commodity.

Equation (10.4) shows that the progressivity of the overall indirect tax system is the weighted average of the progressivity indices of all expenditure items, the weights being proportional to the taxes paid by consumers on commodities. It can be seen that if the progressivity is measured with

Table 10.1. *Progressivity (regressivity) index of sales tax on individual expenditure items: Australia 1975-6*

Expenditure item	Relative tax burden index of sales tax on individual expenditure items					Progressivity (regressivity) index
	1	2	3	4	5	
Current housing cost						
Rent payments	207	133	105	75	81	−17.96
Mortgage payment on dwelling	134	125	116	93	81	−10.94
Mortgage payment on dwelling and land combined	137	105	113	93	89	−5.75
Water and sewerage rates	224	130	110	90	66	−21.13
General rates	222	131	112	92	63	−21.91
Housing insurance	238	132	102	86	68	−22.03
Payments to contractors	187	97	90	50	120	−3.90
Material for repairs and maintenance	164	185	77	83	79	−19.28
Council rates for other dwellings	106	87	75	93	120	5.66
Other housing payments for other dwellings	70	65	93	62	145	14.01
Fuel and power						
Electricity	243	144	110	83	62	−25.59
Mains gas	222	138	123	88	59	−24.03
B.P. gas	254	156	91	97	56	−26.63
Heating oil	218	163	114	95	51	−27.13
Kerosene and paraffin	339	141	107	97	36	−37.23
Other fuels	347	127	68	151	24	−39.34
Food						
Bread, cakes, and cereals						
Bread	280	163	113	83	46	−30.13
Flour	346	167	105	69	45	−40.81
Cakes, tarts, puddings, desserts (ready to eat), etc.	198	124	122	94	65	−19.10
Biscuits	260	150	120	86	50	−30.58
Prepared breakfast cereals	278	158	118	82	47	−33.53
Other cereals	270	165	138	74	41	−35.56
Meat and fish						
Fresh and frozen beef and veal	203	144	113	98	59	−22.49
Fresh and frozen mutton and lamb	282	138	106	86	56	−29.94
Fresh and frozen poultry and game	239	151	109	88	57	−26.46
Fresh and frozen pork	134	128	109	104	77	−12.62
Fresh and frozen offal	333	125	101	90	50	−33.22
Bacon	204	124	118	88	69	−19.65
Ham	195	136	112	90	69	−19.80
Sausages (not continental)	252	148	118	91	50	−29.36

Table 10.1 *(cont.)*

Expenditure item	Relative tax burden index of sales tax on individual expenditure items					Progressivity (regressivity) index
	1	2	3	4	5	
Canned meat (excluding bacon and ham)	163	158	109	109	57	−18.29
Other processed meat	236	147	108	99	54	−26.26
Meat unspecified	288	115	127	80	56	−27.41
Fresh fish and other seafoods	132	113	114	91	81	11.91
Frozen, canned, bottled, and processed seafoods	217	139	115	89	62	−23.31
Dairy products, oils, and fats						
Eggs	272	148	113	81	54	−30.51
Fresh milk and cream	259	161	119	82	50	−31.61
Cheese	220	135	112	97	60	−22.86
Butter	284	150	109	85	51	−31.87
Other dairy products	313	158	102	83	47	−34.97
Margarine	262	158	117	84	49	−31.63
Oils and fats	262	138	139	81	48	−31.49
Fruit and vegetables						
Fresh citrus fruit	262	139	117	86	54	−28.60
Fresh stone fruit	182	126	120	91	71	−18.00
Apples and pears	239	146	119	90	53	−27.40
Other fresh fruit	254	145	111	85	57	−27.25
Fresh fruit, unspecified	350	117	76	115	45	−30.68
Canned, frozen, and bottled fruit	231	142	119	87	58	−25.51
Dried fruit	243	134	112	87	62	−24.84
Nuts	186	130	118	105	60	−19.65
Fruit juice	141	117	107	99	83	−9.88
Potatoes	275	158	111	88	47	−32.74
Onions	279	139	109	86	55	−29.66
Tomatoes	244	140	112	85	61	−25.79
Fresh green vegetables	239	138	116	86	60	−25.68
Other fresh vegetables	245	138	111	85	62	−24.90
Fresh vegetables, unspecified	352	118	71	106	53	−29.80
Frozen vegetables	209	145	117	97	56	−24.13
Canned and bottled vegetables	197	150	112	87	65	−21.67
Other processed vegetables (including dried)	275	132	95	90	62	−25.65
Vegetable juice	154	60	51	120	114	4.45
Miscellaneous food						
Sugar	318	169	109	81	39	−39.34
Marmalades, jams, and conserves	328	150	109	76	47	−35.73
Honey	276	129	109	85	59	−28.09

Table 10.1 *(cont.)*

Expenditure item	Relative tax burden index of sales tax on individual expenditure items					Progressivity (regressivity) index
	1	2	3	4	5	
Syrups, spreads, etc.	299	172	79	82	36	−46.05
Cake mixes, jellies, desserts (mixes, powders, etc.)	237	167	118	84	50	−29.70
Savoury confectionery	193	157	128	91	54	−24.89
Other confectionery	192	144	121	90	62	−22.03
Ice confectionery	218	167	122	88	50	−28.54
Tea	297	148	109	84	49	−32.91
Coffee	244	145	111	85	60	−25.82
Other proprietary food/drinks (excl. soups)	278	182	105	86	42	−34.68
Food additives, spices	259	154	110	86	53	−29.69
Canned and packeted soup	235	142	106	92	60	−24.56
Baked beans and canned spaghetti	245	190	108	85	46	−33.28
Canned and bottled baby foods	402	193	135	46	24	−54.97
Prepared meals (canned, frozen, dried, etc.)	167	152	128	105	52	−23.10
Other foods necessary	229	86	127	90	72	−20.89
Food, undefined	334	97	102	90	59	−26.50
Soft drinks and aerated waters	181	150	113	91	65	−20.29
Meals out and take-away foods						
Meals in restaurants, hotels, clubs, etc.	85	71	74	94	130	11.11
Snacks, take-away foods (not frozen)	133	127	104	104	79	−10.27
Alcohol and tobacco						
Cider, stout, etc.	156	110	139	104	60	−13.29
Draught beer	129	124	104	96	86	−8.65
Packaged beer	153	131	91	95	86	−10.90
Wine	102	83	83	86	123	6.23
Spirits	127	84	102	95	103	−.73
Drinks undefined	67	60	55	117	132	15.51
Ice	130	180	81	57	102	−9.56
Cigarettes	192	132	113	90	70	−18.88
Other tobacco items	308	149	92	90	51	−32.60
Clothing and footwear						
Men's clothing						
Suits	30	119	70	110	115	12.07
Coats	256	27	106	51	122	−5.45
Trousers (excl. jeans)	139	96	96	119	83	−6.86
Cardigans, jumpers, etc.	166	101	93	94	94	−7.45

Table 10.1 *(cont.)*

Expenditure item	Relative tax burden index of sales tax on individual expenditure items					Progressivity (regressivity) index
	1	2	3	4	5	
Other outer clothing	162	147	81	85	90	−10.93
Shirts	121	141	88	89	94	−8.08
Underwear	181	105	99	133	62	−13.98
Nightwear	83	162	76	90	100	−5.51
Women's clothing						
Dresses, suits, shirts, trousers (excl. jeans)	134	87	128	86	93	−4.56
Coats	108	68	106	97	108	1.17
Cardigans, jumpers, etc.	174	88	103	80	100	−5.68
Other outer clothing	97	103	103	104	96	−1.50
Underwear	228	107	127	85	68	−20.37
Nightwear	122	112	120	118	70	−9.66
Stockings, pantyhose, etc.	163	108	115	115	68	−13.36
Children and infants' clothing						
Boys' suits	5	7	59	43	207	38.79
Boys' coats	354	89	180	95	17	−40.52
Boys' trousers (excl. jeans)	261	160	109	83	53	−27.86
Boys' cardigans, jumpers, etc.	317	99	163	54	55	−30.04
Other outer clothing (boys)	168	167	138	84	55	−22.80
Boys' shirts	177	163	122	84	62	−22.98
Boys' underwear	126	208	58	108	73	−14.38
Boys' nightwear	202	85	106	65	104	−7.03
Girls' dresses, suits, skirts, trousers (excl. jeans)	204	114	108	102	69	−20.33
Girls' coats	512	106	67	106	26	−45.00
Girls' cardigans, jumpers, etc.	217	200	82	97	52	−28.54
Other outer clothing (girls)	117	132	133	107	53	−24.17
Girls' underwear	338	135	115	68	53	−34.90
Girls' nightwear	190	132	94	135	51	−23.95
Infants' clothing	205	152	175	73	42	−30.28
Miscellaneous clothing materials						
Socks	192	138	108	101	64	−20.00
Jeans	164	146	100	94	75	−16.51
Other miscellaneous clothing	148	125	105	84	89	−9.40
Clothing, undefined	159	70	164	90	74	−10.79
Clothing materials	183	121	96	121	64	−16.28
Haberdashery	202	145	116	94	60	−21.55
Dry cleaning						
Dry cleaning	144	78	109	97	96	−2.92

Table 10.1 *(cont.)*

Expenditure item	Relative tax burden index of sales tax on individual expenditure items					Progressivity (regressivity) index
	1	2	3	4	5	
Footwear						
Men's footwear	181	120	106	86	83	−12.74
Women's footwear	158	85	111	119	76	−8.08
Children's footwear (including) infants)	239	137	159	77	45	−30.37
Footwear, undefined	39	85	211	50	96	1.07
Repairs to footwear	195	87	75	101	97	−5.67
Household equipment and operation						
Furniture and floor covering						
Kitchen furniture	594	54	99	10	74	−44.80
Bedroom furniture	115	43	112	85	121	3.32
Lounge/dining room furniture	145	66	81	128	94	1.59
Other furniture and furniture, undefined	44	96	148	81	102	1.87
Repair and maintenance of furniture	22	17	59	130	145	30.21
Carpets	296	140	116	74	56	−35.70
Linoleum, plastic floor coverings	444	130	80	25	78	−43.94
Other floor coverings	102	123	89	92	102	1.18
Repairs and maintenance of floor coverings	0	367	133	31	56	−25.33
Textiles, other household furnishings						
Bedding	236	81	110	88	82	−13.67
Toweling	237	115	82	70	95	−12.49
Table and kitchen linen	214	105	50	47	133	1.21
Curtains	61	64	74	50	165	17.76
Other household textiles	111	53	102	81	125	3.36
Awnings, blinds	128	53	355	23	38	−28.01
Other furnishings and ornaments	116	64	67	100	125	8.46
Repairs to houehold textiles and furnishings	2	40	362	47	49	−12.39
Household appliances						
Cooking stoves	33	30	114	15	185	32.44
Refrigerators	104	104	47	78	137	8.45
Washing machines	150	189	62	136	54	−19.47
Other household appliances, electrical	110	121	58	108	106	−4.23
Other household appliances, nonelectrical	108	148	114	116	65	−9.75
Repairs to household appliances	166	174	56	106	78	−13.02
Repair insurance for household appliances	148	136	61	168	53	−13.37

Table 10.1 *(cont.)*

Expenditure item	Relative tax burden index of sales tax on individual expenditure items					Progressivity (regressivity) index
	1	2	3	4	5	
Kitchen, tableware, and other utensils						
Tableware	124	75	76	102	114	6.17
Glassware	153	98	80	98	101	−3.04
Cutlery	230	52	112	118	73	−16.88
Other kitchenware and tableware	157	113	87	107	85	−7.55
Cleaning utensils	244	120	116	87	64	−22.13
Nails, screws, and other fasteners	142	139	80	61	112	−4.30
Other minor household durables	143	115	99	109	81	−8.69
Repairs to kitchenware, tableware, and utensils	0	0	34	30	231	49.06
Tools						
Gardening tools	139	272	94	47	69	−26.75
Other tools	256	78	136	100	59	−22.46
Repairs to tools	270	106	135	69	66	−22.96
Household nondurables						
Household soaps, detergents	247	149	115	86	55	−28.13
Laundry nondurables	191	139	146	81	58	−24.07
Polishes, oils	236	158	135	78	49	−30.27
Household paper products	215	152	114	92	60	−24.95
Gardening nondurables	134	120	82	72	113	.23
Other household nondurables	231	141	116	90	58	−25.44
Nonfood groceries, unspecified	340	100	106	88	56	−28.00
Household and domestic services						
Household services	90	58	114	165	68	−.79
Domestic services (excl. child minding)	127	17	59	70	162	22.24
Child-minding and other nursery fees	66	47	172	135	68	−5.71
Insurance contents of dwellings						
Insurance of contents of dwelling	156	119	116	85	84	−10.89
Medical care and health expenses						
Accident and health insurance						
Hospital, medical, dental insurance	165	132	116	99	69	−16.15
Ambulance fund	221	129	116	94	62	−22.61
Sickness and personal accident insurance	213	142	91	89	74	−19.43
Doctors' fees						
General practitioners' fees	202	171	127	79	55	−26.86
Specialists' fees	254	99	94	91	78	−17.06

Table 10.1 *(cont.)*

Expenditure item	Relative tax burden index of sales tax on individual expenditure items					Progressivity (regressivity) index
	1	2	3	4	5	
Medicines, pharmaceutical products						
Prescriptions	175	133	112	100	68	−17.45
Headache powders and tablets	238	158	106	89	56	−27.90
Other proprietary medicines	247	144	109	89	58	−26.10
Ointments, lotions	228	126	123	90	61	−23.04
Surgical dressings	234	145	158	66	51	−29.65
Other pharmaceutical goods	212	164	80	106	61	−22.35
Other therapeutic appliances	644	63	9	63	70	−45.50
Repairs to therapeutic appliances	0	0	0	419	0	12.33
Other health charges						
Hospital charges	161	110	68	185	45	−14.21
Ambulance charges	328	371	64	0	41	−60.42
Dental charges	114	147	116	89	80	−11.49
Opticians' fees (including spectacles)	152	161	130	88	61	−19.45
Home nursing	1182	0	58	0	0	−100.04
Other medical and health practitioners	329	149	96	72	57	−33.43
Transport and communication						
Purchase of car (net)						
Purchase of car	123	132	114	102	76	−10.64
Sale or insurance claim on car	75	109	157	78	89	−4.14
Petrol, oils, and lubricants						
Petrol and other motor vehicle fuels (excl. holiday)	155	136	104	97	77	−13.56
Oils and lubricants	147	166	88	110	66	−16.98
Vehicle registration and insurance						
Registration of motor car, utility, etc.	172	139	106	96	71	−16.88
Insurance of motor car, utility, etc.	148	124	105	100	79	−11.48
Registration of other vehicle (incl. motorcycle)	175	122	113	112	63	−17.65
Insurance of other vehicle (incl. motorcycle)	129	104	121	120	70	−10.92
Other running repairs of vehicles						
Driver's license	180	135	108	97	69	−17.87
Tires and tubes	42	102	135	102	93	.58
Other spare vehicle parts and accessories	178	121	81	93	91	−10.59
Crash repairs	12	237	32	116	93	−2.33
Other vehicle servicing	112	113	90	104	95	−4.28
Other vehicle charges (excl. holiday)	28	63	122	99	117	12.40

Table 10.1 *(cont.)*

Expenditure item	Relative tax burden index of sales tax on individual expenditure items					Progressivity (regressivity) index
	1	2	3	4	5	
Fares and freight charges						
Rail fares (excl. holiday fares)	166	95	105	106	82	−10.68
Bus, tram fares (excl. holiday fares)	202	123	124	91	66	−19.51
Taxi fares (excl. holiday fares)	171	108	100	103	81	−11.36
Water-transport fares (excl. holiday fares)	26	90	103	76	133	13.25
Air fares (excl. holiday fares)	13	16	115	6	200	31.62
Freight	133	32	39	185	92	1.85
Postal charges						
Postal charges	248	112	97	97	70	−20.63
Telephone and telegram charges						
Telephone and telegram charges	195	117	113	92	74	−16.58
Recreation and education						
Television and sound equipment						
Television	189	85	90	131	72	−13.18
Hire of television	81	121	120	89	94	−2.17
Radio	216	92	20	39	157	3.55
Record, tape, or cassette players	35	145	122	78	101	4.45
Combination units	122	50	31	60	171	16.75
Other electronic accessories	5	6	32	150	153	33.69
Repairs to TV, radio, record player, etc.	240	175	55	99	68	−23.01
Repair insurance for audiovisual appliances	289	181	86	86	50	−32.66
Other recreational equipment						
Photographic equipment	173	94	128	23	123	−8.06
Photographic film (incl. developing)	141	129	103	105	77	−10.34
Optical goods (excl. spectacles and optical sunglasses)	158	128	96	80	93	−7.96
Repairs (optical and photographic)	0	404	119	0	69	−26.28
Musical instruments	43	24	5	372	10	4.99
Records, cassettes	78	107	95	106	100	1.28
Hobbies	200	84	45	75	128	3.69
Purchase of boat	70	108	52	91	132	9.23
Sale or insurance claim on boat	0	79	87	72	152	23.14
Other sports and other recreational equipment	85	102	151	83	89	−6.57

Table 10.1 *(cont.)*

Expenditure item	Relative tax burden index of sales tax on individual expenditure items					Progressivity (regressivity) index
	1	2	3	4	5	
Toys and games	189	217	115	93	39	−31.63
Repairs (sports and recreational equipment)	32	28	39	170	123	25.00
Animals and animal products						
Animal purchases	110	72	64	64	148	14.82
Animal food	203	127	122	81	71	−19.81
Other animal expenses	151	62	104	75	117	3.28
Entertainment and recreational services						
Cinema admission charges	103	111	110	122	77	−5.38
Live-theatre admission charges	90	80	121	79	113	4.94
Day trips and excursions	228	139	111	108	50	−24.03
Cultural and other nonsporting lessons	149	124	76	134	72	−10.56
Other entertainment and recreation services (nonsport)	126	109	110	110	81	−8.59
Club and association subscriptions (excl. sports clubs)	74	86	211	76	73	−10.53
Sporting-club subscriptions	151	99	132	52	105	−9.11
Spectator admission fees to sports	88	124	94	101	96	−3.08
Other sports services	131	141	124	93	73	−14.24
Registration and insurance of boats	57	69	108	99	116	9.02
Books, newspapers, and magazines						
Books and other printed matter (excl. newspapers, magazines)	19	93	157	94	95	3.74
Newspapers	202	135	104	90	72	−18.91
Magazines and comics	154	126	106	94	81	−12.42
Educational fees						
Primary school, government	273	166	121	93	36	−35.58
Primary, independent	242	105	131	96	58	−27.47
Secondary school, government	211	134	126	116	43	−26.36
Secondary school, independent	112	73	71	86	129	8.71
Tertiary fees, university, training colleges, CAE	74	110	109	77	112	2.35
Fees paid to other educational institutions	86	125	152	59	95	−10.12
Miscellaneous goods and services						
Hairdressing and beauty services						
Hair services (men's and boys')	182	140	110	94	69	−18.23
Hair services (women's and girls')	159	96	118	109	75	−10.47
Other beauty and health services	160	145	55	94	98	−3.59

Table 10.1 *(cont.)*

Expenditure item	Relative tax burden index of sales tax on individual expenditure items					Progressivity (regressivity) index
	1	2	3	4	5	
Toiletries and cosmetics						
Toiletries and other personal products	173	134	115	90	73	−15.91
Cosmetics, skin care goods, beauty aids, etc.	121	107	134	104	74	−8.54
Other miscellaneous goods						
Jewelery, watches, clocks, etc.	90	125	106	117	79	−6.07
Travel goods, handbags, umbrellas, etc.	139	120	100	104	82	−9.44
Pens	185	145	86	108	69	−16.89
Paper stationery	182	157	103	103	60	−20.82
Other stationery, writing, etc. equipment	170	149	109	99	65	−18.88
Baby carriages, bassinets, etc.	94	131	71	62	131	3.62
Other miscellaneous goods	148	139	89	113	74	−11.51
Goods, undefined	189	104	171	106	42	−19.34
Repairs to miscellaneous goods	161	80	92	88	106	−3.13
Holidays						
Holiday fares, Australia	184	123	79	90	91	−9.52
Holiday petrol, Australia	111	164	108	96	75	−13.34
Holiday accommodation, Australia	114	112	96	98	96	−3.65
Holiday package tour, Australia	112	76		93	129	10.73
Holiday fares, overseas	98	85	25	151	109	6.27
Holiday accommodation, overseas	5	21	3	168	149	30.06
Holiday package tour, overseas	66	54	91	64	150	18.06
Miscellaneous services						
Stamp duty, shown separately	91	128	107	78	103	−2.28
Customs duty, paid direct	0	0	0	66	225	48.05
Other financial services	132	116	92	105	89	−6.57
Cash gift, money allowance, charity, pocket money	144	117	102	95	87	−9.03
Union dues, professional association subscription	39	73	79	119	120	12.52
Fines, legal fees, etc.	391	144	57	64	69	−39.52
Personal-belongings insurance	88	54	95	88	128	11.14
Short-term accommodation (less than 4 nights)	75	119	103	94	101	.45
Other misc. services	183	90	93	69	110	−5.65
Selected other payments						
Income tax	46	76	88	101	125	12.93
Gambling (net of winnings)	128	116	111	109	78	−10.28

Table 10.1 *(cont.)*

Expenditure item	Relative tax burden index of sales tax on individual expenditure items					Progressivity (regressivity) index
	1	2	3	4	5	
Superannuation and annuities	24	71	87	116	122	14.73
Life insurance	114	100	114	97	92	−3.94
Capital housing costs (net)	108	83	87	93	115	3.66

respect to the total expenditure base and if a uniform tax is paid on all commodities (i.e., $\alpha_1 = \alpha_2 = \cdots = \alpha_n$), the progressivity index P will be zero, that is, the overall indirect-tax system will be proportional.[4]

It is interesting to note that the estimation of the progressivity (or regressivity) index of the indirect tax on individual goods and services does not require the knowledge of α_i. In fact, the estimation of α_i is the most difficult problem encountered in the tax-incidence literature. α_i depends on two unknown quantities t_i and h_i, the estimation of both of which is quite troublesome. Consider, first, the tax rate, t_i, which consists of two components: (1) the tax imposed directly on the commodity and (2) the tax imposed on the commodities that are used as inputs in producing this commodity. In order to determine the second component, it is necessary to trace the indirect taxes on intermediate goods through the economy and to estimate the proportion of final goods prices due to indirect taxes paid on intermediate goods. Although Bentley et al. (1974) have attempted to trace the indirect tax through the economy using the Australian National Accounts Input–Output Tables 1962–3, their procedure is based on highly restrictive assumptions. For instance, one of the main limitations of their model is that it depends heavily upon the assumed shifting behavior embodied in the estimation technique (Bentley, Collin, and Rutledge 1977).

The estimation of the tax-shifting parameter h_i is even more complex. According to Dalton's (1955) law it depends on the price elasticities of demand and supply of the ith commodity. The estimation of these elasticities for a fine classification of goods such as is given in Table 10.1 is virtually an impossible task. Moreover, Dalton's law is based on partial equilibrium analysis which makes no allowance for cross-price effects or the effects of expenditure of the tax revenue. The proper estimation of shifting parameters is a gigantic task, which cannot as yet be attempted. In practice, the tax studies make arbitrary shifting assumptions, the most popular among them in this context being the 100-percent shifting of taxes on goods and services to the final consumers. The numerical results given in Table 10.1 do not require any of these arbitrary assumptions because they measure the progressivity (or regressivity) of the tax which is actually shifted to the final consumers. If the purpose is to measure the degree of progressivity (or regressivity) of the overall indirect-tax system, the knowledge of each α_i is essential as can be seen from equation (10.4). Such an attempt has not been made in this study for the reasons given above.

10.4   Interpretation of the results and policy implications

The last column in Table 10.1 presents the progressivity (or regressivity) index of indirect taxes on more than 350 consumption items. This is the first tax-incidence study that considers such a fine classification of goods and services. Most of the other studies have been restricted to allocating the total indirect tax to income classes and, therefore, are not very useful in formulating an appropriate indirect-tax scheme.[5]

The results show that indirect taxes on most goods and services are regressive. This observation casts doubt on the commonly held belief that indirect taxes can be made progressive by making a distinction between luxuries and necessities.[6] Since there is a considerable variation in the degree of regressivity for different commodities, the appropriate choice of the tax rates can reduce the degree of regressivity of the overall indirect-tax system.

The degree of progressivity (or regressivity) is measured by the magnitude of the index P_i given in the last column. It is convenient to discuss these magnitudes in terms of the following broad categories:

$P_i < -30$	Highly regressive
$-30 < P_i < -15$	Fairly regressive
$-15 < P_i < -5$	Moderately regressive
$-5 < P_i < +5$	Almost proportional
$+5 < P_i < +15$	Moderately progressive
$+15 < P_i < +30$	Fairly progressive
$+30 < P_i$	Highly progressive

Current housing cost

Under the item current housing cost, it can be seen that taxes on none of the items are highly regressive. The fairly regressive items are rent payments, water and general rate payments, insurance, and the material for repairs and maintenance. It is interesting to note that payments to contractors are almost proportional. This shows that the poorer households tend to do the repairs and maintenance themselves, whereas richer households get these tasks done by contractors. Rates and other payments for other dwellings are progressive because the other dwellings are owned by rich households. Water and general council rates are more regressive than rent payments which may be due to high concentration of homeowners in the low-income ranges. This is also confirmed by the relative tax burden of the first quintile, values of which for water and general rates are 224 and 222, respectively, as against 207 for the rent payment.

Fuel and power

The items under fuel and power are considerably more regressive than those under the current housing cost. The relative tax-burden index for the first quintile varies from the minimum of 222 to the maximum of 254, whereas that for the fifth quintile varies from 24 to 62, showing that the poorest 20 percent of the population has to bear considerably greater tax burden than the richest 20 percent of the population. Highly regressive items are kerosene and paraffin and other fuels, whereas the remaining items – including electricity, main gas, and heating oils – are fairly regressive. The contemplated increase in electricity prices in New South Wales will clearly affect poor households more than the rich ones.

Food items

Taxes on most of the food items are either highly regressive or fairly regressive. Taxes on items under the bread, cakes, and cereals category are highly regressive with the one exception of the item cakes, tarts, puddings, and dessert, which is fairly regressive. The most regressive item is flour; the relative tax burden for the poorest 20 percent of the population is 346, compared to 45 for the richest 20 percent of the population.

Taxes on most of the items under the meat and fish category are fairly regressive with the exception of three items, two of which are fresh and frozen pork and fresh fish and other seafoods, both being moderately regressive, and the third item, fresh and frozen offal, highly regressive. With the one exception of taxes on cheese, taxes on all other items under the category of dairy products, oils, and fats are highly regressive.

Expenditure on fruits and vegetables is generally fairly regressive. One item in this category, namely fruit juice, is moderately regressive. The vegetable juice item is slightly progressive or almost proportional. The highly regressive items under this category are fresh fruit, unspecified, potatoes, and onions.

Among the miscellaneous foods, marmalades, jams, syrups, tea, baked beans and canned spaghetti, and bottled baby food are highly regressive. It is interesting to note that tea is more regressive than coffee. Canned and bottled baby food is by far the most regressive item; the relative tax burden for the first quintile being 402 as against 24 for the top quintile.

Among all the food items, meals in restaurants, hotels, and clubs is the only progressive item, while the take-away food is moderately regressive. These results seem to suggest that the government should resist the temptation of broadening the sales tax base by including food items (though with the possible exception of meals in restaurants, hotels, and clubs). These observations also indicate the importance of taxing services in comprehensive sales taxation.

Alcohol and tobacco

For revenue purposes, expenditure items under the alcohol and tobacco category are always a major target of the government. Although it is believed that taxes on alcohol and tobacco are highly regressive, they still do not attract much public opposition mainly because of the effect of these consumption items on the health of the consumers. It is not known how much these taxes discourage the consumption of alcohol and tobacco but they certainly provide a significant amount of tax revenue to the government.

The numerical results in Table 10.1 indicate that the taxes on alcohol and tobacco are in fact mildly regressive. These results cast doubt on the commonly held belief that they are highly regressive. It is interesting that there is no excise duty on wine in Australia although the effect of such a tax is progressive. The effect of tax on undefined drinks is fairly progressive while on spirits it is almost proportional. These results seem to suggest that there still remains scope for further increasing the revenue from alcohol and tobacco without significantly increasing the regressivity of the tax system, by imposing a tax on wine and by taxing more heavily spirits and undefined drinks.[7]

Clothing and footwear

Expenditure on clothing and footwear is generally considered to be a necessity, with taxes on such things being highly regressive. But this belief does not seem to be supported by the numerical results. In fact, the effect of a tax on men's and women's clothing, as shown by the numerical values in Table 10.1, is only mildly regressive. Among all these expenditures, a tax on women's underwear is the only item which is fairly regressive.

Taxes on children's and infants' clothing are considerably more regressive than those on men's and women's clothing. Taxes on miscellaneous clothing, which includes items such as socks, jeans, and clothing material, are fairly regressive. Similarly, a tax on children's footwear is considerably more regressive than on men's and women's footwear. It can, therefore, be concluded that the children's and infants' clothing and footwear should be tax-exempt. The imposition of tax on men's and women's clothing and footwear, however, will not significantly affect the degree of tax regressivity.

Household equipment and operation

Among the furniture and floor covering items, a tax on kitchen furniture and linoleum plastic floor coverings is highly regressive. The effect of taxes on other furniture will be either proportional or progressive. A tax on curtains is progressive whereas on awnings and blinds it is highly regressive. Among all the items of expenditure under the category of household equipment and operation, taxing repairs to kitchenware and tableware utensils is most progressive; but the imposition of tax on this item will not significantly increase the tax revenue because of its very low mean expenditure. Taxing expenditures on tools and household nondurables is fairly regressive with the exception of one item, gardening nondurables, a tax on which is proportional.

Among the items in the household and domestic services category, a tax on domestic services excluding child-minding would be fairly progressive whereas one on child-minding would be moderately regressive. Note that the child-minding expenditure falls more heavily on the households in the third and fourth quintiles. This observation seems reasonable because the proportion of the two earner households is likely to be larger in these two quintiles.

Medical care and health expenses

Expenditure on accident and health insurance are fairly regressive. Doctors' fees, which are net of benefits received from medical funds, are more regressive than expenditures on accident and health insurance. Other medical care and health expenses are either fairly regressive or highly regressive with one exception of repairs to therapeutic appliances, which is progressive. Home-nursing expenditure is by far the most regressive; more than 90 percent of this expenditure is borne by the bottom 20 percent of the population, resulting in the relative tax burden of 1182 for the lowest quintile. The other two items with an extremely high degree of regressivity are ambulance charges and expenses on other therapeutic appliances.

Although the government greatly subsidizes medical and health care, poor households are still overburdened with these costs. These results seem to suggest that poor individuals have greater medical needs than rich individuals. Thus, there is a clear-cut need for a health scheme that is linked with needs in a more direct fashion.

Transport and communication

Expenditures on transport and communication are either moderately regressive or proportional. The petrol and other motor vehicle fuel excise duty, which contributes a sizeable amount of revenue, is only mildly regressive.[8] Bus and tram fares are fairly regressive whereas water transport and air fares are progressive. Postal and telephone and telegram charges are fairly regressive. These results are clearly useful in formulating appropriate price policies for these services, which are provided by the government.

Recreation and education

The variation in the degree of progressivity (or regressivity) is considerable among the recreation and education items. The expenditure on television is moderately regressive whereas that on radio is almost proportional. The expenditure on other electronic accessories is highly progressive but, interestingly enough, repair insurance expenditure for audiovisual appliances is highly regressive. The other highly regressive item is toys and games.

Recently, there has been a considerable debate on the possible introduction of a sales tax on books, newspapers, and magazines. It is only the tax on newspapers which is fairly regressive; the tax on books is almost proportional and on magazines it is moderately regressive.

The education fees on primary school, government, are highly regressive whereas those on primary school, independent, and secondary school, government, are fairly regressive. It is interesting that fees on secondary school, independent, are moderately progressive while the tertiary education fees, which include university, training college, and college of advanced education, are almost proportional.

It is surprising that fees paid to other educational institutions are regressive. The relative burden of these fees falls more heavily on persons in the second and third quintiles.

Miscellaneous goods and services

A wide variation in the degree of progressivity (or regressivity) is observed among miscellaneous goods and services. Hairdressing, beauty services, toiletries, and cosmetics are generally regressive; the most regressive item being hair services for men and boys. Other miscellaneous goods, which includes jewelery, watches, stationery, baby carriages, and travel goods, are either moderately regressive or fairly regressive, with the one exception of baby carriages (including bassinets), which is slightly progressive (or almost proportional).

It is interesting to note that expenses on holiday taken in Australia are moderately regressive, whereas those taken overseas are progressive. Holiday accommodation overseas is the most progressive item in this category. Holiday package tour taken overseas is fairly progressive while that taken in Australia is only moderately progressive. These observations support the view that rich people tend to take holidays overseas whereas the poor stay in the country.

Among miscellaneous services, custom duty paid directly is by far the most progressive item. The bottom 60 percent of the population do not pay any custom duty at all. This observation supports an earlier observation that the rich tend to travel overseas more than the poor. The most regressive item under this category is fines and legal fees; the relative tax burden of the first quintile being 391 as compared with 69 for the fifth quintile. This is an important result, suggesting that the government should resist the temptation to increase fines and legal fees, which for revenue purposes are always an easy target.

10.5   Some further comments on the results

It should be noted that Table 10.1 also provides the progressivity index of items such as electricity, postal, telephone, and public charges which are essentially the services provided by the government and, therefore, are not subject to any indirect taxes. The government sets the prices of these services, generally based on revenue considerations only. Numerical values of the progressivity indexes of these items can be of considerable value in arriving at the most equitable pricing policy.

It must be emphasized that most of the results presented are intuitively natural. There are, however, some exceptions that need to be mentioned. For example, cooking stoves receive a progressivity index of 32.44, the refrigerator index is 8.45, but the washing machine index is -19.47. The available data are insufficient to provide definitive explanation for these results. One reason may be that poorer households generally live in rented houses where cooking stoves and refrigerators are provided by landlords. Washing machines are generally not provided with rented homes. Another exception that needs mention is the expenditure on animal purchase, which receives a progressivity index of 14.83, but for animal food the index is

−19.81. One possible explanation for these results is that the poorest households do not spend money buying animals, which they may be getting free from their friends, whereas the rich households may indulge in buying fancy-looking but expensive animals. When it comes to feeding these animals, the expenditure should almost be the same for all households irrespective of their income. Clearly, then, the poorer households will be spending a higher proportion of their income on animal food than the richer households and, as a consequence, the progressivity index must be negative for this expenditure item.

The progressivity index for the purchase of a boat is observed to be 9.23 showing that this item is only moderately progressive. This is the most surprising result that emerges from the numerical results because only the rich people can afford to indulge in the purchase of a boat, and, therefore, this item should be highly progressive. No explanation can be given for this deviation in absence of any information on the wealth holdings of households. It must be pointed out, however, that expenditures on durables are seldom reliable and, therefore, the policy implications concerning items such as purchase of a boat must be drawn with caution.

We have commented on only a few results given in Table 10.1. It provides a wealth of information and one can draw many additional policy conclusions from it.

10.6   Concluding remarks

This chapter provides the estimates of the degree of progressivity (or regressivity) of the sales or excise tax on more than 350 individual consumption items. These estimates provide a quantitative basis for formulating a comprehensive indirect-tax scheme. Several interesting findings that emerge from the numerical results given in this chapter suggest the usefulness of considering such a fine classification of goods and services.

This study has several limitations which must be pointed out. First of all, it ignores efficiency considerations. It may be possible to overcome this by implementing a solution to the many-person Ramsey tax problem such as that found in Diamond (1975). Second, the chapter does not consider the issue of administration of different tax rates. Finally, the major limitation of the study is that it measures only the degree of progressivity of tax which is actually shifted to the final consumers. It does not, therefore, help us to measure the degree of progressivity (or regressivity) of the overall indirect-tax system. Despite these limitations, we believe that the contribution will be a useful addition to the tax-incidence literature.

PART IV

Welfare and poverty

CHAPTER 11

Distribution of welfare in Australia

The inequality measure, discussed in Chapter 4, focuses only on the distributional aspects of welfare ignoring completely the magnitude of mean income. In this chapter the measures of inequality are combined with the mean of the distribution of income in order to arrive at single measures of welfare that provide the welfare ranking of distribution with different means. These measures are then used to analyze the direct impact of Australian personal taxes and government cash transfers on the distribution of economic welfare across the income ranges and by other household characteristics.[1]

Van Praag and his group at the University of Leyden have generated considerable literature on estimating welfare functions using the survey data on individual perception of welfare in the income hierarchy (Van Praag 1968, 1971, 1978; Van Praag and Kapteyn 1973; Kapteyn 1977; Bryze 1982). In these studies it is assumed that individuals can evaluate their own welfare positions with respect to their income levels on a zero-one scale in a cardinal way. A description of this evaluation may be given by the individual welfare function of income which is approximated by a lognormal distribution function. This approach to measuring welfare will not be followed here because of the nonavailability of special surveys required for this purpose.[2]

The other works that have recently appeared on this subject are those of Sen (1973b, 1974) and Kakwani (1980a, 1981a), their welfare measures differing with respect to the assumptions made about the relative deprivation aspect of inequality. Sen's measure captures the sense of relative deprivation of a person by taking into account the number of persons who are richer. On the other hand, Kakwani's measure focuses only on the aggregate income of those who are richer. In a recent paper, Kakwani (1981a) has derived a class of welfare measures that capture the sense of deprivation by taking note of both these factors: the actual incomes enjoyed by those who are richer, and the number of such persons who enjoy these incomes.

This chapter discusses an alternative approach to measuring welfare, proposed by Kakwani (1985), which captures the sense of envy felt by individuals when they compare their incomes with each other. The approach adopted is similar to that of Sen (1973a) which is also closely related to Pyatt's (1976) interpretation of the Gini index in terms of the expected gain in a game in which each player compares his or her income with other individuals who are drawn from the population at random. The major contribution of this chapter is to provide several extensions of Pyatt's approach to the measurement of welfare with applications to Australia.

Total household income may be broken down according to income from various sources such as wages, capital income, and transfer income. Then the question is posed: Of total welfare enjoyed by the society, how much is attributed to income from wages, how much to income from capital, and how much to income from different types of government transfers? In order to answer this question we need to disaggregate total welfare by factor components. So, in this chapter, we develop this methodology to analyze the contribution of these factor components to total welfare in Australia.

If the population is divided into different groups according to certain socioeconomic characteristics of households, it is useful to know how the total welfare enjoyed by the society is distributed among these groups, and how the tax-transfer system affects such a distribution. It is proposed to develop the appropriate methodology to analyze the contribution of each of these socioeconomic groups to the total welfare of the society.

Finally, this chapter analyzes the welfare disparity between the sexes in Australia. The method developed in this chapter will be used to compare the welfare levels of female and male wage and salary earners over the period May 1974 to May 1979. This analysis throws some light on how the legislation introduced in 1975 for equal pay for women has affected the welfare disparity between the sexes in Australia.

11.1   Sen's axiomatic approach to measuring welfare

Suppose, in a society, there are n individuals who are arranged in ascending order of their incomes: $x_1 \leq x_2 \leq \cdots \leq x_n$, which we denote by vector $\mathbf{x} = (x_1, x_2, ..., x_n)$. Then the welfare measure $W(\mathbf{x})$ is defined to be a unique function of $x_1, x_2, ..., x_n$. Sen (1974) considered the following welfare function

$$W = \sum_{i=1}^{n} x_i v_i(\mathbf{x}) \tag{11.1}$$

where $v_i(\mathbf{x})$ is the weight given to a person i with income x_i. It should be emphasized that $v_i(\mathbf{x})$ has been defined as a function of the whole income distribution vector $\mathbf{x}$ and not of x_i alone; which implies a more general welfare function than the one that is additive-separable. A brief discussion of Sen's (1974) axioms will now be provided.

Axiom 11.1 (Relative equity): For any pair of individuals i and j, if $W_i(\mathbf{x}) < W_j(\mathbf{x})$, then $v_i(\mathbf{x}) > v_j(\mathbf{x})$, where $W_i(\mathbf{x})$ and $W_j(\mathbf{x})$ are the welfare levels of i and j under a given income configuration $\mathbf{x}$.

This axiom implies that if i is considered to be worse off than person j in a given income configuration $\mathbf{x}$, the income of the ith person should have higher weight than the income of the jth person. $W_i(\mathbf{x})$ is assumed to be ordinally measurable, which only indicates who is worse off than whom, but says nothing about the welfare differences.

Axiom 11.2 (Monotonic welfare): For any i and j, if $x_i < x_j$, then $W_i(\mathbf{x}) < W_j(\mathbf{x})$.

This axiom implies that a person i with lower income is always considered to be worse off than person j with higher income.

Axiom 11.3 (Rank order): The weight $v_i(\mathbf{x})$ on the income of the ith person equals the rank order of i in the interpersonal welfare ordering of all the individuals.

This axiom implies that weights $v_i(\mathbf{x})$ depend on the ranking of all individuals, which in some ways captures the relative deprivation aspect of inequality. The lower a person is on the welfare scale, the greater the sense of deprivation with respect to others in the society. Therefore, the poorest person in the society has the largest rank value of n, while the richest person has the rank value of 1. The axiom is equivalent to saying that the weight $v_i(\mathbf{x})$ on the income of the ith person is proportional to the number of persons with income as high as that of person i.

Axiom 11.4 (Normalization): If all the persons have the same income, then $W = \mu$, where μ is the mean income of the society.

The following theorem, which is due to Sen (1974), emerges from these axioms.

Theorem 11.1: For a large number of individuals, the only social welfare function satisfying Axioms 11.1, 11.2, 11.3, and 11.4 is given by

$$W = \mu(1 - G), \tag{11.2}$$

where G is the Gini index of the distribution $\mathbf{x}$.

11.2 An alternative approach to measuring welfare

Suppose the income x of an individual is a continuous random variable with mean income μ and probability density function $f(x)$. An individual with income x compares his or her income with all other individuals in the society. He (or she) selects other individuals one by one and makes all possible pairwise comparisons. Let $g(x, y)$ be the welfare of an individual with income x when the compared income is y, then in all pairwise comparisons, his (or her) expected welfare will be

$$E[\text{welfare} \mid x] = \int_0^\infty g(x, y) f(y) \, dy \tag{11.3}$$

considering that the probability of selecting an individual with income y from the population is $f(y) \, dy$.

In order to make this idea of welfare empirically operational, it is necessary to specify the function $g(x, y)$. This is an issue in which some value judgment is inevitable because there can be many defensible alternative functional forms. For instance, in the derivation of his inequality measure, Atkinson (1970) assumed that each individual has the same utility function, which depends only on his or her income. This implies that $g(x, y) = u(x)$ for all y, which means that the satisfaction that the individual derives is independent of the income of others. But this is a highly restricted assumption because people do compare themselves with others and feel envious of those with higher income. The following functional form captures the sense of envy in a simple way

$$g(x, y) = x \text{ if } x \geq y$$
$$= x - k(y - x) \text{ if } y > x \tag{11.4}$$

This formulation implies that if the individual finds that the compared incomes are lower than his, then his welfare is given by his own income x. If, on the other hand, the compared incomes selected are higher than his, then the individual feels envious and loses welfare. This loss in welfare is proportional to the differences in incomes. The parameter k measures the degree of envy; if $k = 0$, individuals do not feel envious and, therefore, suffer no welfare loss. On the other hand, if $k = 1$, the measure of welfare loss suffered by an individual is exactly equal to the difference between his income and the income of the richer individual selected by him for comparison. The value chosen for k should depend on one's judgment about the degree of envy felt by individuals.

In connection with measuring poverty, Pyatt (1980) proposed an alternative formulation of $g(x, y)$ as

$$g(x, y) = \min(x, y) \tag{11.5}$$

which implies the welfare of an individual to be equal to minimum of his income and the income of some other individual drawn at random from the population. According to this formulation, each individual is completely indifferent to the incomes (or living standards) of those who are better off, implying no sense of envy whatsoever when the compared incomes selected are higher than his. But the loss of welfare occurs when the compared incomes selected are lower than his. This may be explained in terms of the guilt feelings an individual may have when he finds that the person selected for comparison has income lower than his.

These two formulations give quite different results with respect to the levels of individual welfare. Which one should be used for measuring individual welfare is a matter of value judgment. However, we would be confined to the sense of envy which we consider to be most widely prevalent.

If individuals are arranged in ascending order of their income, then $F_1(x)$ defined as

$$F_1(x) = \frac{1}{\mu} \int_0^x Xf(X)\, dX \tag{11.6}$$

is interpreted as the proportion of income enjoyed by individuals with income less than or equal to x. Substituting (11.4) into (11.3) and using (11.6) gives the welfare curve:

$$W(x) = x - k\mu[1 - F_1(x)] + kx[1 - F(x)] \tag{11.7}$$

where $W(x)$ is the expected welfare enjoyed by an individual with income x, and

$$F(x) = \int_0^x f(y)\, dy$$

is the probability distribution function. Differentiating (11.7) twice yields

$$W'(x) = 1 + k[1 - F(x)] > 0$$
$$W''(x) = -kf(x) < 0$$

which imply that the individual (expected) welfare is an increasing function of income and is concave.

Suppose that income x corresponds to the 100th percentile, then the Lorenz curve is represented by a function $L(p)$ given by $L(p) = F_1(x)$ where $p = F(x)$ and $0 \leq p \leq 1$. Then using (4.1) in (11.7) yields the expected welfare enjoyed by an individual at the $100p$th percentile:

$$\phi(p) = \mu[L'(p)(1 + k - kp) - k + kL(p)] \tag{11.8}$$

where $L'(p)$ is the first derivative of $L(p)$.

For a finite collection of n individuals or income units who are arranged in ascending order of their incomes: $x_1 \leq x_2 \leq \cdots \leq x_n$, equation (11.8) yields the welfare of the ith individual as

$$w_i = w_i - k[\mu - x_i + (x_i - \bar{x}_i)p_i]$$

where $p_i = i/n$ and $\bar{x}_i$ is the mean income of the first i individuals. The welfare of the poorest and the richest individuals in the society will be $x_1 - k(\mu - x_1)$ and x_n, respectively. If every individual in the society gets exactly the same income, $w_i = \mu$ for all i.

Let p_μ be the population of individuals who have income less than or equal to the mean income μ of the population, then the relation $x = \mu L'(p)$ gives $L'(p_\mu) = 1$. Substituting $p = p_\mu$ and $L'(p_\mu) = 1$ in (11.7) will then yield the welfare enjoyed by an individual with income level μ:

$$\phi(p_\mu) = \mu\{1 - k[p_\mu - L(p_\mu)]\},$$

where $[p - L(p)]$ is the distance between the egalitarian line $L(p) = p$ (when each individual receives exactly the same income) and the Lorenz curve. It can be proved that this distance at $p = p_\mu$ is equal to the relative mean deviation which is a well-known measure of income inequality.[3] Thus, the following theorem is proved.

Theorem 11.2: *The welfare enjoyed by an individual with average income is equal to* $\mu(1 - k\delta)$, *where* δ *is the relative mean deviation.*

$\mu(1 - k\delta)$ may be used as a measure of social welfare as it takes into account both the size and distribution of income. However, it has one important drawback: It is completely insensitive to transfers of income among individuals on one side of the mean income. A utilitarian welfare measure in which individual utilities are interdependent follows from the following theorem.

Theorem 11.3: *The average welfare enjoyed by the society is given by*

$$W_k = \mu(1 - kG) \qquad (11.9)$$

where G is the Gini index of the entire population.

Proof: The area under the welfare curve (11.8) gives the average welfare enjoyed by the society as

$$\int_0^1 \phi(p)\,dp = \mu \int_0^1 [L'(p(1 + k - kp) - k + kL(p)]\,dp$$

which on evaluating the integrals leads to

$$W_k = \mu\left[1 - k + 2k \int_0^1 L(p)\,dp\right].$$

Since the Gini index is defined as one minus twice the area under the Lorenz curve, this equation immediately leads to (11.9). This completes the proof of Theorem 11.4.

When $k = 0$, $W_k = \mu$, a welfare measure that is completely insensitive to changes in the distribution of income. It assumes that individuals feel no envy whatsoever when they compare their incomes with other richer persons in the society. If $k = 1$, W_k leads to Sen's welfare measure, given in 11.2.[4]

It can be demonstrated that a pure transfer of income from an individual to anyone richer (poorer) will decrease (increase) the value of W_k for all $k > 0$. This property corresponds to the principle of transfer of income proposed by Dalton (1920) in connection with the measurement of income inequality. Thus, in order to make the welfare measure sensitive to an income transfer at all income levels, it is essential to choose k strictly greater than zero.

Suppose that on the basis of some accepted poverty line, a society is most concerned about the poorest $100h$th percent of its population. The average welfare of these persons will be

$$W_k(h) = \frac{1}{h} \int_0^h \phi(p)\, dp$$

which on using (11.8) leads to

Theorem 11.4: *The average welfare enjoyed by the poorest 100th percent of the population is given by*

$$W_k(h) = \mu_h - k[(\mu - \mu_h) + h\mu_h G_h], \qquad (11.10)$$

where μ_h and G_h are the mean income and the Gini index of the bottom 100h percent of the population, respectively.

It can be seen that, as h approaches unity, $W_k(h)$ approaches the utilitarian welfare function as given in (11.9).

It is interesting to note that the average welfare of the poor is independent of the distribution of income among the nonpoor. Thus the average welfare enjoyed by the bottom $100h$th percent of the population is not sensitive at all to income transfers among individuals belonging to the top $100(1-h)$th percent of the population.

Note that $pW_k(p)$ is the area under the welfare curve up to the $100p$th percentile. Therefore, the area under this curve between $100p_1$ to $100p_2$ percentiles will be

$$p_2 W(p_2) - p_1 W_k(p_1) \qquad (11.11)$$

which gives the average welfare enjoyed by individuals between $100p_1$ to $100p_2$ percentiles as

$$W_k(p_1, p_2) = \frac{1}{p_2 - p_1} [p_2 W_k(p_2) - p_1 W_k(p_1)]$$

This equation can now be used to compute the average welfare enjoyed by any decile, quintile, or quarter. For instance, the average welfare for the third quintile will be obtained when $p_1 = .4$ and $p_2 = .6$.

Income shares of deciles or quintiles are often used to describe income inequality and can be readily obtained from the Lorenz curve. These measures, although they provide a useful description of distributions, ignore the inequality of income within a decile or a quintile, which means that the measures are completely insensitive to income transfers within these deciles or quintiles. On the other hand, shares of welfare enjoyed by different deciles or quintiles, which are computed from equation (11.11), do take into account the inequality of income within deciles and quintiles when $k > 0$ and, therefore, will be more useful in analyzing the size distribution of income and wealth.

11.3   Numerical estimates of social welfare

This section presents numerical estimates of social welfare measures as developed in the previous section. The three income definitions used are original, gross, and disposable income adjusted for household size and composition. Again, this adjustment is done by giving weights of unity to the first adult, .7 to the second and subsequent adults, and .4 to each child. The level and distribution of social welfare were estimated by assuming that each individual within a household enjoys the same level of welfare, which means that each individual was weighted equally irrespective of the size and composition of the household to which they belong.

The numerical estimates of social welfare measures based on the three income definitions are presented in Table 11.1. The last three rows in the table measure the effect of personal income tax and government cash benefits on social welfare.

The loss of welfare due to income inequality increases directly with k. When $k = 0$, the measure becomes independent of income inequality and the social welfare is given by the mean income of the society. The numerical results show large reductions in welfare values when k exceeds zero.

The overall tax rates of all households are just under 13 percent whereas the overall benefit rate (i.e., government cash benefits as a percentage of income) is only 7.08 percent. It is therefore expected that the welfare loss due to taxes will be greater than the welfare gain from government cash benefits. As a result, the combined effect of taxes and government benefits should reduce the overall welfare. This is of course true when k takes values 0.0 and 0.5. But if $k = 1.0$, taxes and government benefits together increase the social welfare by 3.32 percent. The main reason for this result is that the sensitivity of the welfare measure to income inequality increases with k and the loss of welfare due to higher taxes is offset by the improve-

Table 11.1. *Effect of taxes and government benefits on social welfare: Australia 1975-6*

	Values of k		
Variable	0.0	0.5	1.0
Social welfare based on			
original income	96.20	79.24	62.29
gross income	103.01	87.51	72.01
disposable income	89.66	77.01	64.36
% change in social welfare due to			
taxes	−12.96	−12.00	−10.62
government benefits	7.08	10.44	15.60
combined taxes and government benefits	−6.80	−2.81	3.32

ment in the resulting income distribution brought about by the progressiveness of both taxes and government benefits.

It is evident from the results that the percentage loss of welfare due to taxes decreases from 12.96 percent to 10.62 percent as k increases from 0.0 to 1.0 indicating that taxes are progressive and lead to more equal distribution of income. Government cash benefits, on the other hand, bring about considerably greater improvement in welfare, increasing it from 7.08 percent to 15.60. From these results, it may be concluded that government cash benefits are far more redistributive than taxes and have considerably greater impact on social welfare.

In order to know how the welfare is distributed among households, we computed the quintile shares of welfare for all three definitions of income. The results are presented in Table 11.2.

It can be seen that the welfare share for each of the first two quintiles is decreased and that of the last three quintiles increased as k varies from zero to unity. These results, in fact, indicate that the higher the value of k, the more unequal is the distribution of economic welfare. Thus, the distribution of welfare measured by average income alone (for which $k = 0$) tends to underestimate the true inequality of economic welfare (for which k is greater than zero).

It is further evident that government cash benefits when added to the original income increase the welfare share for each of the first two quintiles and decrease that for the last three quintiles. Similarly, the income tax when subtracted from the gross income, increases the welfare share for each of the first two quintiles and decreases that for the last three quintiles. From these observations, it can be concluded that both government cash benefits and taxes tend to improve the distribution of economic welfare for all values of k.

The welfare curve based on three income definitions, namely, original income, gross income, and disposable income is given in Figures 11.1, 11.2, and 11.3 for three values of k. Table 11.3 presents the numerical values of the welfare levels at various percentiles. It can be seen that all three curves increase with income and are more or less concave in the entire income range. When $k = 0$, the welfare curves based on gross income are higher than those based on original and disposable incomes. This situation changes, however, as k exceeds zero. When $k = 1.0$, the welfare curve based on disposable income becomes higher than that based on gross income up to about 30th percentile, where the two curves intersect. The welfare curve based on the original income is lower than that based on gross and disposable incomes up to about 50th percentile. From these observations, it may be concluded that the welfare of all persons up to the bottom 50 percent of population is increased as a result of government cash benefits. When the income tax is subtracted from the gross income, the welfare of all persons up to the bottom 30 percent of the population is increased and that of the remaining 70 percent decreased.

11.4   Welfare by factor components

The disaggregation of the Gini index by factor components was discussed in Section III of Chapter 6. In this section, we extend this methodology to analyze the contribution of each of these factor components to the total welfare enjoyed by the society.

Suppose there are m factor components, then substituting (6.4) into (11.9) and using the fact that $\mu = \sum_{j=1}^{m} \mu_j$, μ_j being the mean of the jth factor income of all individuals, yields

$$W = \sum_{j=1}^{m} \mu_j (1 - kC_j)$$

C_j being the concentration index of the jth factor. This equation provides the framework to analyze the contribution of each factor income to the total welfare.

The numerical results giving the contribution of each factor income to total welfare are presented in Table 11.4. It is noted from the first column that income from wages and salaries is the major functional component, contributing 75.72 percent of total adjusted income. The welfare contribution of this component is decreased substantially to 69.31 percent as k is increased from zero to unity. This decrease in welfare share is attributed to the fact that income from wages and salaries is unevenly distributed over the total income in favor of richer households. It would seem, then, that any policy that increases the labor share of the functional distribution

Table 11.2. *Quintile shares of welfare in Australia: 1975–6*

Quintiles	Original income values of k			Gross income values of k			Disposable income values of k		
	0.0	0.5	1.0	0.0	0.5	1.0	0.0	0.5	1.0
1	3.71	−5.62	−20.44	7.36	1.12	−7.98	7.96	2.36	−5.57
2	12.32	9.32	4.57	12.62	9.95	6.07	13.10	10.50	6.81
3	17.95	18.32	18.91	17.60	17.66	17.75	17.91	18.07	18.29
4	24.97	28.68	34.57	23.88	26.58	30.50	23.83	26.37	29.96
5	41.05	49.30	62.39	38.54	44.69	53.65	37.21	42.71	50.51
All households	100	100	100	100	100	100	100	100	100

Table 11.3. *Welfare levels at various percentiles in Australia: 1975–6*

Percentiles	Original income values of k			Gross income values of k			Disposable income values of k		
	0.0	0.5	1.0	0.0	0.5	1.0	0.0	0.5	1.0
10th	14.62	−25.24	−65.11	38.99	7.59	−23.81	38.18	12.94	−12.31
20th	40.95	12.33	−16.29	51.22	25.08	−1.06	47.89	26.78	5.68
30th	57.90	35.77	13.65	62.00	39.92	17.83	57.08	39.39	21.70
40th	68.27	49.51	30.76	76.47	59.13	41.79	66.88	52.41	37.95
50th	83.26	68.69	54.12	88.81	74.86	60.90	79.32	68.29	57.26
60th	98.83	87.75	76.66	102.19	91.21	80.23	89.78	81.04	72.30
70th	116.26	108.21	100.16	121.92	114.31	106.70	106.74	100.56	94.97
80th	134.63	128.91	123.19	136.29	130.52	124.75	117.55	113.03	108.51
90th	172.68	170.02	167.37	175.43	172.81	170.19	148.11	146.12	144.12
100th	477.18	477.18	477.18	477.19	477.19	477.19	373.35	373.35	373.35

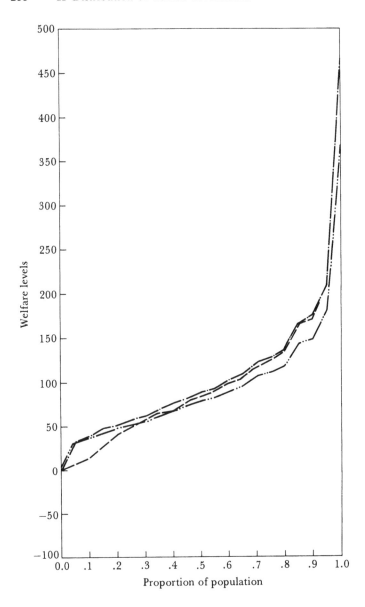

Figure 11.1   Welfare curve based on original, gross, and disposable in-comes when $k = 0.0$: Australia 1975-6. Key: – – – original income, – · – · – gross income, – ·· – ·· – disposable income.

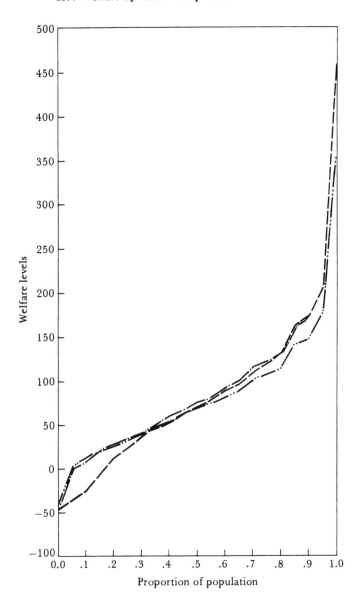

Figure 11.2 Welfare curve based on original, gross, and disposable incomes when $k = 0.5$: Australia 1975-6. Key: – – – original income,
– · – · – gross income, – · · – · · – disposable income.

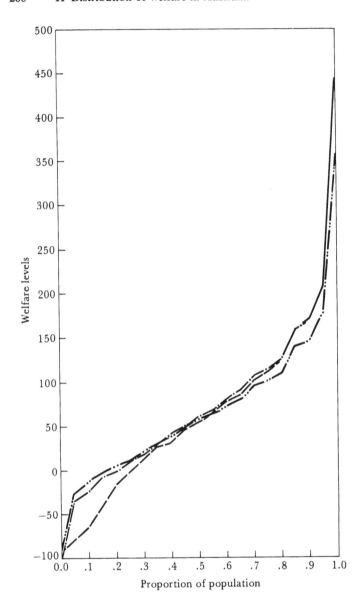

Figure 11.3   Welfare curve based on original, gross, and disposable incomes when $k = 1.0$: Australia 1975-6. Key: − − − original income,
− · − · − gross income, − · · − · · − disposable income.

Table 11.4. *Percentage contribution of each factor income to total social welfare: Australia 1975-6*

Sources of income	Values of k		
	0.0	0.5	1.0
Wages and salaries	75.72	73.08	69.31
Business income	11.18	10.67	9.94
Pensions	4.79	6.74	9.54
Unemployment benefits	.72	1.03	1.49
Sickness and special benefits	.12	.17	.25
Family allowance	.56	.73	.97
Other government benefits	.43	.59	.78
Total government cash benefits	6.62	9.26	13.03
Other income	6.48	6.99	7.72
Social welfare	100.00	100.00	100.00

may decrease rather than increase the total welfare unless, of course, the distribution of wage income is changed in the favor of poorer households. This constitutes an important finding because it casts doubt on the commonly held belief that any increase in wage share is good for society from the welfare point of view.

Income from business forms the second major functional component and has a share of 11.18 percent. The welfare contribution of this component is reduced to 9.94 when k is increased from zero to unity. It shows that the adverse effect of business income on welfare is not as high as it is believed to be, compared to the employment income.

The third major component is the income received from the government in the form of cash benefits and has a share of 6.62 percent in total income. The welfare contribution of this component is almost doubled when k is increased from zero to unity; the main reason being that it is heavily concentrated at low income levels. Among the five components of government transfers, sickness and special benefits have the greatest effect on total welfare compared to the magnitude of this transfer. Other income, which includes investment income such as interest, dividends, and rents, has a share of 6.48 percent in total income but this share is increased to 7.72 percent when k is increased to unity. Thus, this income component also has a favorable effect on welfare although the magnitude of increase in welfare due to an increase in its share of total income is considerably smaller than that of government cash benefits.

11.5   Analysis of welfare disparity between the sexes in Australia

The existence of earning differences between men and women is widely prevalent in almost all the countries of the world and Australia is no exception. Prior to 1970, the wage structure in Australia discriminated against women by giving them only a proportion of the male marginal rate prescribed for a skill. But this situation changed drastically between the period 1969 and 1974, when the Conciliation and Arbitration Commission handed down a series of judgments that narrowed the wage differences between men and women. Under the Labour Government in 1975 equal pay for women became universal in Australia.

Despite the introduction of equal-pay legislation, women are likely to have lower earnings than men. Several reasons may be given for this phenomenon, but the most important one is the fact that the range of choice for working women is significantly narrower than that available to males. Although it will be interesting to isolate various factors that explain the income differences between men and women, this aspect will not be pursued here due to lack of data on different factors. Instead, the purpose of this section will be to compare the affluence of women relative to that of men over the period May 1974 to May 1979. This analysis should throw some light on how the legislation for equal pay for women introduced in 1975 has affected the income disparity between the two sexes in Australia.

In a recent paper, Dagum (1980) has proposed a measure of *economic distance* between two income distributions that reflect the disparity of incomes of one population relative to another. This measure has been criticized by Shorrocks (1982b) on the grounds that it does not reflect the relative affluence of one population compared to another as intended. This section attempts to tackle this problem by comparing the average welfare levels of female and male wage and salary earners using the social welfare function developed in previous chapters. The methodology to measure the welfare disparity between the two sexes as given below rests heavily on the earlier work of Pyatt (1976) in connection with the disaggregation of the Gini index.

Assume that the probability density functions of the two groups (women and men) are $f(x)$ and $g(x)$, respectively. Then a person with income x in the first group selects a person in the second group at random. Her expected welfare in all possible pairwise comparisons will be

$$E_{12}(x) = \int_0^x xg(y)\,dy + \int_x^\infty [x - k(y-x)]g(y)\,dy \qquad (11.12)$$

where $g(y)\,dy$ is the probability of selecting a person with income y in the second group.

If the means of the first and second groups exist and are given by μ_1 and μ_2, respectively, then the first moment distribution functions are defined as

$$F_1(x) = \frac{1}{\mu_1} \int_0^x X f(X) \, dX$$

and

$$G_1(x) = \frac{1}{\mu_2} \int_0^x X g(X) \, dX$$

are interpreted as the proportion of income received by individuals belonging to groups I and II with income less than or equal to x, respectively. Equation (11.12) can then be simplified as

$$E_{12}(x) = x + kx[1 - G(x)] - k\mu_2[1 - G_1(x)]$$

where $G(x)$ is the probability distribution function of the second group. Averaging these expected welfares over all individuals in group I yields the expected welfare of all individuals in group I when they compare their incomes in group II as

$$E_{12} = \mu_1 - k(\mu_2 - \mu_1) - k \int_0^\infty x G(x) f(x) \, dx + k\mu_2 \int_0^\infty G_1(x) f(x) \, dx \quad (11.13)$$

Integrating the third term in this equation by parts gives

$$\frac{1}{\mu_1} \int_0^\infty x G(x) f(x) \, dx = 1 - \int_0^\infty F_1(x) g(x) \, dx$$

which on substituting in (11.13) gives

$$E_{12} = \mu_1 - k\mu_2 + k\left[\mu_2 \int_0^\infty G_1(x) f(x) \, dx + \mu_1 \int^\infty F_1(x) g(x) \, dx\right] \quad (11.14)$$

Similarly, the expected welfare of the individuals in the second group when they compare their incomes with the first group is obtained from (11.13) as

$$E_{21} = \mu_2 - k\mu_1 + k\left[\mu_2 \int_0^\infty G_1(x) f(x) \, dx + \mu_1 \int_0^\infty F_1(x) g(x) \, dx\right] \quad (11.15)$$

Subtracting (11.15) from (11.14) gives

$$E_{12} - E_{21} = -(1 + k)(\mu_2 - \mu_1), \quad (11.16)$$

which implies that if the mean income of the second group is higher than the mean income of the first group, the expected welfare enjoyed by the individuals in the first group (when they compare their incomes with the individuals in the second group) will always be lower than the expected welfare enjoyed by the second group individuals who are comparing their incomes with the first group individuals.

Substituting $\mu_1 = \mu_2$, $G_1(x) = F_1(x)$ and $f(x) = g(x)$, equation (11.14) yields the expected welfare enjoyed by individuals in the first group when they compare their incomes within their own group as

$$E_{11} = \mu_1 \left[1 - k \left\{ 1 - 2 \int_0^\infty F_1(x) f(x) \, dx \right\} \right]$$

where the second term in the bracket is equal to one minus twice the area under the Lorenz curve of the income distribution in the first group. This equation gives, therefore,

$$E_{11} = \mu_1 [1 - kG_1] \tag{11.17}$$

where G_1 is the Gini index of the income distribution in the first group. Similarly for the second group $E_{22} = \mu_2[1 - kG_2]$ must hold.

Let W be the expected welfare enjoyed by individuals in the two groups when they are combined, then

$$W = \sum_{i=1}^{2} \sum_{j=1}^{2} E_{ij} a_{ij} \tag{11.18}$$

where a_{ij} is the probability of an individual being in group i and comparing his income with individuals in group j. Since individuals are selected at random

$$a_{ij} = a_i a_j \tag{11.19}$$

where a_i is the proportion of individuals in group i, must hold.

Using (11.9) along with (11.19) into (11.18) gives

$$\mu(1 - kG) = a_1^2 \mu(1 - kG_1) + a_2^2 \mu_2(1 - kG_2) + a_1 a_2 (E_{12} + E_{21})$$

which in conjunction with (11.16) yields [5]

$$E_{12} = \mu_1 - \frac{k}{2a_1 a_2} [A + a_1 a_2 (\mu_2 - \mu_1)] \tag{11.20}$$

and

$$E_{21} = \mu_2 - \frac{k}{2a_1 a_2} [A + a_1 a_2 (\mu_1 - \mu_2)] \tag{11.21}$$

where $A = \mu G - a_1^2 \mu_1 G_1 - a_2^2 \mu_2 G_2$.

The expected welfare of the first group is given by

$$W_1 = a_1 E_{11} + a_2 E_{12}$$

which consists of two components; the first component relates to the expected welfare when the individuals in the first group compare their incomes within their own group and the second component relates to the expected welfare when individuals in the first group compare their incomes with the individuals in the second group. This equation on using (11.17) and (11.20) becomes

$$W_1 = \mu_1 - k\left[a_1\mu_1 G_1 + \frac{A}{2a_1} + \frac{1}{2}a_2(\mu_2 - \mu_1)\right]$$

Similarly, the expected welfare enjoyed by the second group will be

$$W_2 = \mu_2 - k\left[a_2\mu_2 G_2 + \frac{A}{2a_2} + \frac{1}{2}a_1(\mu_1 - \mu_2)\right]$$

It can be easily demonstrated from (11.18) that

$$W = a_1 W_1 + a_2 W_2 \tag{11.22}$$

which expresses total welfare in the two groups as the weighted average of the welfare enjoyed by each group, the weights being proportional to the number of individuals in each group. This equation provides the quantitative framework to analyze the contribution of each group to the total welfare of society. The ratio of the welfare levels of the two groups, viz., W_1/W_2 will be used below to measure the welfare disparity between the two sexes in Australia.[6]

The data used for the analysis in this section were obtained from the Australian Bureau of Statistics sample household surveys conducted throughout Australia in order to obtain information about the weekly earnings of wage and salary earners. The first survey of this kind was conducted in May 1974 and was subsequently extended for other periods.

The income in the survey refers to the weekly earning, which is the gross earning before taxation and other deductions have been made. It comprises overtime and ordinary-time earnings including week's proportion of payments made other than on a weekly basis (e.g., salary paid fortnightly or monthly and paid annual or other leave taken during the specified pay period).

The income-distribution data were available in grouped form giving relative frequency in each income class and the mean income of the entire population. It was assumed that observations were spaced evenly across class intervals, so that the midpoint of each income class could be used as an approximation to the class mean. The mean for the last open-ended income class was obtained as a residual given the mean income of the entire income distribution. Since the number of income classes was more than 25 for each income distribution, this approximation of using midpoint for the mean income in each income class will not affect the accuracy of the results.

The numerical results on average welfare levels of female and male earners are presented in Table 11.5 for three values of k, viz., 0.0, 0.5, and 1.0. The adjustment for the price increases was made using the con-

Table 11.5. *Welfare of wage and salary earners, by sex, in Australia*

Variable	May 1974	May 1975	May 1976	May 1977	May 1978	May 1979
$k = 0.0$						
E_{11}	81.90	89.23	91.93	91.53	92.10	90.61
E_{12}	81.90	89.23	91.93	91.53	92.10	90.61
E_{22}	133.20	132.95	136.22	133.70	134.07	133.86
E_{21}	133.20	132.95	136.22	133.70	134.07	133.86
Average welfare of female earners	81.90	89.23	91.93	91.53	92.10	90.61
Average welfare of male earners	133.20	132.95	136.22	133.70	134.07	133.86
Average welfare of all earners	155.70	118.52	121.16	119.29	119.55	118.61
Ratio of welfare of female earners to welfare of male earners (%)	61.49	67.12	67.48	68.46	68.69	67.69
$k = 0.5$						
E_{11}	72.03	79.12	81.29	81.25	81.43	79.70
E_{12}	52.25	63.33	65.15	65.91	67.62	64.83
E_{22}	118.19	118.55	121.24	118.95	119.42	119.16
E_{21}	129.20	128.91	131.60	129.16	130.58	130.58
Average welfare of female earners	58.97	68.54	70.63	71.15	72.40	70.07
Average welfare of male earners	121.93	121.96	124.76	122.43	123.28	122.88
Average welfare of all earners	100.47	104.25	106.20	104.91	105.68	104.26
Ratio of welfare of female earners to welfare of male earners (%)	48.36	56.19	56.62	58.11	58.73	57.03
$k = 1.0$						
E_{11}	62.15	69.02	70.65	70.96	70.76	68.80
E_{12}	22.60	37.42	38.38	40.29	43.15	39.06
E_{22}	103.18	104.14	106.25	104.20	104.76	104.45
E_{21}	125.20	124.86	126.96	124.62	127.09	125.57
Average welfare of female earners	36.05	47.84	49.35	50.78	52.70	49.54
Average welfare of male earners	110.67	110.98	113.29	111.18	112.49	111.90
Average welfare of all earners	85.24	90.06	91.40	90.54	91.80	89.91
Ratio of welfare of male earners to welfare of male earners (%)	32.57	43.11	43.56	45.67	46.85	44.27

sumer price index. So the figures in the table represent the real levels of welfare.

The numerical results show that male wage and salary earners enjoy considerably higher welfare than female wage and salary earners. Recall that when $k = 0$, the disparity of welfare between female and male wage earners is measured by the ratio of their mean incomes. This ratio in May

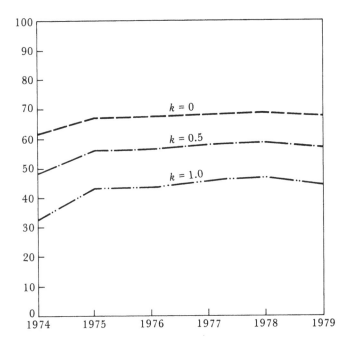

Figure 11.4   Welfare disparity between female and male wage and salary earners in Australia from 1974 to 1979.

1974 was 61.49, but it increased monotonically to 68.69 in May 1978, and then decreased to 67.69 in May, 1979. During the period May 1974 to May 1975, the real mean income of the male wage and salary earners decreased slightly and that of female earners increased substantially, which resulted in substantial improvement in the female–male welfare ratio. These trends remain the same, however, when k takes values that are different from zero (see Figure 11.4). Thus, it can be concluded that the introduction of the legislation for equal pay for women had significant impact in improving the welfare disparity between female and male wage earners, particularly in the first year of its introduction.

Further note that the welfare ratio decreases monotonically as k increases from 0 to 1.0. This indicates that if we take into account the welfare loss due to envy, the disparity of welfare between the two sexes increases substantially. For instance, the welfare ratio of 61.49 in May 1974 is reduced to only 32.57 when k increases from zero to unity. Thus, comparisons of mean incomes alone may substantially underestimate the true disparity of welfare between female and male wage and salary earners.

11.6   Disaggregation of aggregate welfare according to socioeconomic and demographic characteristics of households

This section analyzes how the total welfare of the society is distributed among households differing in various socioeconomic and demographic characteristics. The household characteristics considered are sex and age of household head.

Suppose that households are divided into k mutually exclusive groups according to some socioeconomic or demographic characteristics of households, then the aggregate welfare enjoyed by individuals can be written as (see equation 11.22):

$$W = \sum_{i=1}^{k} a_i W_i \qquad (11.23)$$

where W_1 is the expected welfare enjoyed by individuals in the ith group – and a_i is the proportion of individuals in the ith group. This equation will be the basis for analyzing the contribution of each group to the total welfare of the society.

Sex of household head

The disaggregation of welfare according to the sex of the household head is presented in Table 11.6. The results clearly indicate that households headed by males enjoy considerably higher welfare than those headed by females. The disparity of welfare between female- and male-headed households increases substantially as k increases from 0.0 to 1.0. This can be seen by comparing the female–male welfare ratio, which on the basis of original income is reduced from 69.49 percent to only 27.35 percent as k increases from zero to unity. Such a dramatic increase in the welfare disparity between the two sexes does not occur, however, when government cash benefits are added to the original income; the welfare ratio on the basis of gross income is reduced from 86.69 percent to 72.17 percent. The increase in welfare disparity is even lower when income tax is subtracted from the gross income. Thus the disparity of welfare between the female- and male-headed households increases as the welfare measure becomes sensitive to the sense of envy felt by individuals because of income differences. The magnitude of this increase is reduced substantially, however, as a result of government cash benefits and income tax.

Government cash benefits increase the per equivalent-adult income per person in households with a female head by 31.12 percent whereas the income tax reduces it by 8.69 percent. But when we do welfare comparisons, the effect of government cash benefits is considerably greater, increasing

Table 11.6. *Disaggregation of welfare, by sex of household head:*
Australia 1975-6

	Female head	Male head	Total population
$k = 0.0$			
Average welfare based on			
original income	69.08	99.41	96.20
gross income	90.58	104.49	103.01
disposable income	82.77	90.48	89.66
% share of welfare based on			
original income	7.60	92.40	100.00
gross income	9.31	90.69	100.00
disposable income	9.78	90.22	100.00
% change in welfare due to			
government benefits	31.12	5.11	7.08
taxes	−8.62	−13.44	−12.96
combined taxes and benefits	19.82	−8.98	−6.80
$k = 1.0$			
Average welfare based on			
original income	18.46	67.49	62.29
gross income	53.56	74.21	72.01
disposable income	54.05	65.58	64.36
% share of welfare based on			
original income	3.14	96.86	100.00
gross income	7.88	92.12	100.00
disposable income	8.89	91.11	100.00
% change in welfare due to			
government benefits	190.14	9.96	15.60
taxes	.91	−11.63	−10.62
combined taxes and benefits	192.80	−2.83	3.32

the welfare of persons in these households by as much as 190.14 percent. It is interesting to note that the income tax increases rather than decreases the welfare of persons in female-headed households, although the magnitude of this increase is small. These observations tend to support the conclusion that the Australian tax-transfer system plays a major role in improving the welfare of female-headed households compared to that of male-headed households. As a result, the welfare disparity between female- and male-headed households is considerably reduced.

Age of household head

The disaggregation of welfare according to the age of the household head is presented in Table 11.7. It can be seen that the welfare levels of all age

Table 11.7. *Disaggregation of welfare, by age of household head:*
Australia 1975-6

	Age groups				
	15–25	25–45	45–65	65 and over	All house-holds
Percentage of persons	6.56	52.66	31.25	9.53	100.00
$k = 0.0$					
Average welfare based on					
original income	116.85	96.42	106.07	48.46	96.20
gross income	119.74	99.56	112.92	78.16	103.02
disposable income	106.57	86.28	97.74	70.25	89.66
% share of welfare based on					
original income	7.97	52.78	34.46	4.79	100.00
gross income	7.62	50.89	34.25	7.24	100.00
disposable income	7.80	50.67	34.07	7.46	100.00
% change in welfare due to					
government benefits	2.47	3.26	6.46	61.31	7.08
taxes	−11.00	−13.34	−13.44	−10.12	−12.96
combined effect of taxes and benefits	−8.80	−10.52	−7.85	44.96	−6.80
$k = 1.0$					
Average welfare based on					
original income	92.55	63.76	77.08	−15.16	62.29
gross income	95.56	67.14	86.76	34.30	72.01
disposable income	87.58	59.47	76.61	35.19	64.36
% share of welfare based on					
original income	9.75	53.90	38.67	−2.32	100.00
gross income	8.71	49.10	37.65	4.54	100.00
disposable income	8.93	48.66	37.20	5.21	100.00
% change in welfare due to					
government benefits	3.25	5.30	12.56	–	15.60
taxes	8.35	−11.42	−11.70	2.59	−10.62
combined effect of taxes and benefits	−5.37	−6.73	−.61	–	3.32

groups are reduced as k increases from zero to unity. But the magnitudes
of reductions are not uniform across the age groups. The 65-and-over
age group suffers the greatest welfare loss as a result of the envy felt by
individuals.

Government cash benefits increase substantially the welfare share of
the 65-and-over age group. The tax payments also increase the share of
this group in welfare but the magnitude of increase is considerably lower.
Despite these increases, this group has the lowest level of average welfare.

Table 11.8. *Disaggregation of welfare, by age of household head, when people compare their incomes only within their own age groups: Australia 1975-6*

| | Age groups | | | | |
	15-25	25-45	45-65	65 and over	Total population
$k = 1.0$					
Average welfare based on					
original income	83.63	64.97	72.88	19.30	64.31
gross income	87.72	69.34	82.60	52.17	73.05
disposable income	79.14	61.49	73.43	49.24	65.21
% share of welfare based on					
original income	8.53	53.20	35.41	2.86	100.00
gross income	7.88	49.99	35.34	6.79	100.00
disposable income	7.96	49.66	35.19	7.19	100.00
% change in welfare due to					
government benefits	4.89	6.73	13.34	170.31	13.59
taxes	−9.78	−11.32	−11.10	−5.62	−10.73
combined effect of taxes and benefits	−5.37	−5.36	.75	155.13	1.40

It is interesting to note that the 15-25 age group enjoys the highest level of welfare. This is an unexpected finding because this age group did not have the highest average household income. The major reason for this result is that these households have to support on average a smaller number of persons.

It may be argued that people make comparisons of their incomes only within their own age groups. This argument may be justified on the grounds that people expect incomes to be different at different ages. As pointed out in Section 9.2, when a person is young, he goes through an apprenticeship or training phase during which he is paid relatively little. After this training phase, his income increases gradually as he acquires experience in his chosen career until it reaches the peak when he is in his forties. He remains at his peak income until about the age of 55 and then his income starts declining. At the age of 65, he faces a sharp decline in his income as he retires from the work force. These life-cycle income differences do exist but the issue is whether people accept them and do not feel envious when they discover someone, not belonging to their own age group, enjoying higher income than theirs. Although this issue cannot be resolved here, it is still worthwhile to present alternative calculations of welfare under the assumption that people compare their incomes only within their own age group. These calculations are presented in Table 11.8.

The welfare levels of the 25–45 and 65-and-over age groups increase and those of the remaining two age groups decrease as a result of these new calculations. The average welfare of all households is now increased, although the magnitude of increase is very small. Government cash benefits increase the social welfare by 13.59 percent whereas the income tax reduces it by 10.73 percent. The combined effect of taxes and government transfers amounts to an increase in welfare by only 1.40 percent. Thus, the Australian tax-transfer system brings about a smaller improvement in welfare under the new assumption of income comparisons.

11.7   Conclusions

This chapter has been concerned with the measurement of welfare which takes into account both the size and distribution of income. In constructing such a welfare measure it was assumed that people compare their incomes with those of others and feel envious when they find their own incomes are lower. So, each person's welfare depends on a parameter k, which measures the degree of envy he feels when he compares his income with the incomes of others; the higher the value of k, the greater is the welfare loss he suffers due to envy. This methodology was then used to analyze the extent and nature of welfare in Australia. Following are some of the conclusions that emerged from this chapter:

1. The welfare measure is quite sensitive to the degree of envy felt by individuals. This is shown by large reductions in welfare values when k exceeds zero.
2. The numerical results indicate that the higher the degree of envy individuals feel, the greater is the inequality in the distribution of economic welfare. Thus, the distribution of welfare measured by average income alone (for which $k = 0.0$) tends to underestimate the true inequality of economic welfare (for which k is greater than zero).
3. Both government cash benefits and taxes tend to improve the distribution of economic welfare for all values of k.
4. The welfare of all persons up to the bottom 50 percent of population is increased as a result of government cash benefits. When income tax is subtracted from the gross income, the welfare of all persons up to the bottom 30 percent population is increased and that of the remaining 70 percent decreased.
5. The numerical results show that any policy that increases the labor share of the functional distribution may decrease rather than increase the total welfare, unless, of course, the distribution of wage income is changed in the favor of poorer households. The adverse

effect of business income on welfare is not as high as it is believed to be, compared to the employment income.

6. The introduction of the legislation for equal pay for women had significant impact in improving the welfare disparity between female and male wage earners particularly in the first year of its introduction.

7. The disparity of welfare between female and male wage and salary earners increases monotonically with the degree of envy felt by individuals. Thus, comparisons of mean incomes alone substantially underestimate the true disparity of welfare between the two sexes.

8. The Australian tax-transfer system plays a major role in improving the welfare of female-head households compared to that of male-headed households. As a result, the welfare disparity between female- and male-headed households is considerably reduced.

9. The households in the 65-and-over age group suffer the greatest welfare loss as a result of the envy felt by individuals. Despite the fact that both government cash benefits and personal income tax substantially increase their welfare share, they still remain the group with the lowest level of average welfare. The 15–25 age group enjoys the highest level of average welfare in spite of the fact that households in this group did not have the highest average household income. The major reason for this result is that they have to support, on average, a smaller number of persons.

We can now turn to some of the limitations of the analysis presented in the chapter. First, the individual welfare function assumes that the welfare loss due to envy is proportional to the difference in incomes. There are many plausible alternative possibilities that have not been explored. Secondly, the parameter k, which measures the degree of envy, has been assumed to be the same for all individuals. This is an important limitation because different people feel different degrees of envy when they make comparisons.

CHAPTER 12

Optimal negative income taxation, when individuals feel envious

Negative income tax (or guaranteed minimum income) is a commonly suggested fiscal measure used to transfer income from rich to poor in order to reduce poverty. The main objective of negative income-tax proposals is to integrate government's income support programs with personal income taxation by extending the income-tax rates beyond zero to negative levels so that families having an income below a break-even level obtain an allowance from the government. A break-even level of income is the level at which a family neither pays an income tax nor receives a cash allowance from the government.

The guaranteed minimum income scheme is also a form of negative income taxation under which every family receives a cash subsidy from the government depending on the family composition and, in turn, each family is subjected to a proportional tax on income, excluding cash benefits. Such a scheme ensures a level of minimum guaranteed income for all families through a fully integrated but simple tax-transfer system.

There has been a considerable amount of public discussion in various countries on the possibility of introducing some form of a negative income scheme. (See for instance, Friedman 1962; Lampman 1964; Smith 1965; Green 1966; Christopher et al. 1970.) In Australia, the Poverty Commission headed by Professor Henderson proposed a guaranteed-minimum income scheme in 1975 that involves a substantial redistribution of income toward those on lower incomes. In the same year, the Australian government's Priorities Review Staff also proposed a guaranteed-minimum scheme almost identical to that of the Poverty Commission. This scheme was aimed at replacing existing pension and benefits but not existing services.

This chapter is concerned with the problem of determining the optimal negative income-tax structure; one that is associated with the maximum social welfare. The main objective of the chapter is to explore how the sense of envy felt by individuals affects the optimal tax structure. The social welfare measures developed in the previous chapter form the basis for this exercise.

12.1   Optimal taxation: a brief review

How progressive should income tax be? As Atkinson (1973) points out, no definite answer can be given to this question without further clarification of social objectives. However, recent literature on optimal taxation attempts to illuminate the basic structure of the problem and clarifies several issues involved in answering the question posed.

The debate on this issue was initiated in 1971 by Mirrlees, whose analysis was based on a particular form of the utility function and a specific density function. In his model, individuals are assumed to maximize identical utility functions that depend on consumption and leisure. He demonstrated that the tax structure that maximized a utilitarian social welfare function would be approximately linear with negative income tax at low incomes. Sheshinski (1972a) continued the debate by working with more general assumptions regarding the form of the utility function, but restricting himself to linear tax functions. He arrived at a conclusion similar to that of Mirrlees, that is, that the optimal tax structure will always be progressive, taking the form of a linear tax function with a lump-sum subsidy.

While making substantial contributions to the theory of optimal income taxation, these papers followed the traditional approach in assuming the social welfare function to be utilitarian. Atkinson (1972) took up this criticism and examined the effect of replacing the utilitarian social objective with the maxi–min objective, suggested by Rawls (1967), of maximizing the welfare of the worst-off individual in the society. Atkinson concluded that the maxi–min goal implied marginal tax rates that were generally higher than those obtained on the basis of the utilitarian objective.

Itsume (1974) extended Atkinson's approach by assuming that the government may maximize the welfare of an individual or group of individuals at any particular location of the welfare distribution, for example, at the mode or median. He found that the optimal tax rate is very sensitive to differences in ability levels.

Most of the optimal-tax literature is based on the assumption that the satisfaction that the individual derives is independent of the consumption of others,[1] but this is a highly restricted assumption because people do compare themselves with others and feel envious of those with higher consumption.[2] Thus, the purpose of this chapter is to explore how the sense of envy felt by individuals affects the optimal tax structure.

Boskin and Sheshinski (1978) explored this aspect of optimal-tax theory by specifying individual welfare as a function of a person's own consumption and the average consumption of the whole population. They constructed an educational-investment model in which the individual's income is determined by his education and demonstrated that increased concern for relative consumption leads to larger income guarantees and higher marginal tax rates. Oswald (1983), analyzing this problem at a general level concludes that "all of the general results of optimal-tax theory can be overturned by the plausible assumption that people look over their shoulders before they decide how happy they feel." He assumed that each person's utility function contains a "comparison" variable α, which is a weighted average of consumption levels elsewhere in the economy. In this chapter, we consider a welfare function in which each individual compares his or her income with all other individuals in the society. The main contribution of this chapter is to provide quantitative results on optimum tax rates under alternative welfare criteria.

We assume first that the government's aim is to maximize the average welfare of the society. This objective is referred to as the utilitarian social objective although since we also assume that individual utilities are independent, the social welfare function implied by it is not additive-separable. We derive formulas for the optimal marginal tax rate and demonstrate that the upper boundary for this rate is less than unity and that it decreases with the minimum elasticity of the labor supply and increases with the degree of envy felt by individuals.

We then propose a generalized maxi–min criterion under which the government aims to maximize the average welfare of, say, the bottom $100h$ percent of the population. The utilitarian social objective and the Rawlsian maxi–min objective are special cases of this approach, the former applying when h is unity and the latter when h takes its lowest possible value of $1/T$, T the number of people in the society. It is interesting, therefore, to examine how the optimal tax rate varies when h takes not only these limiting values, but also values between unity and $1/T$. This is done both analytically and numerically. The numerical estimates of the optimum tax rate are obtained on the basis of both a Pareto and a lognormal distribution of skills.

12.2   A work–leisure choice model

Suppose there are T individuals in an economy whose pre-tax income is determined by the number of hours they work and their skill level, which determines their wage rate. So, the pre-tax income denoted by y_i is given by $y_i = y(n_i, H_i)$, where H_i is the number of hours the ith individual works, and n_i the skill level of that individual. For simplicity this relationship is assumed to be of multiplicative form: $y_i = n_i H_i$, where H_i is normalized so that its upper limit is unity. Let $l_i = 1 - H_i$ be the leisure enjoyed by the ith individual, and its value to him in terms of consumption is given by a function $g(l_i)$ such that $g'(l_i) > 0$ and $g''(l_i) < 0$.

Suppose the government imposes the tax function

$$t_i = -\alpha + (1 - \beta)y_i \tag{12.1}$$

where α is the lump-sum tax levied or the subsidy granted to the ith individual and $(1 - \beta)$ is the marginal tax rate that lies in the range $0 < (1 - \beta) < 1$. Although the consumption of leisure, like the consumption of goods and services, is assumed to give enjoyment to individuals, it is not subject to tax. Total consumption of the ith individual is then given by

$$c_i = \alpha + \beta n_i (1 - l_i) + g(l_i)$$

which consists of two parts: the first, $c_i^* = a + \beta n_i (1 - l_i)$, is the consumption of goods and services and the second, $g(l_i)$, is the consumption of leisure.

Each individual is assumed to maximize c_i with respect to l_i. The first-order condition is

$$g'(\hat{l}_i) = \beta n_i \quad \text{or} \quad \hat{l}_i = l(\beta n_i) \tag{12.2}$$

and the second-order condition is satisfied in view of the assumption that $g''(l_i) < 0$.

Assuming that the solution to (12.2) exists for all n_i, then the optimum total consumption of the ith individual is given by $\hat{c}_i = \hat{c}_i^* + g(\hat{l}_i)$, where $\hat{c}_i^* = \alpha + \beta n_i (1 - \hat{l}_i)$ is the optimum consumption of goods and services (excluding the consumption of leisure) by the ith individual.

It is assumed that the government chooses the values of tax parameters, (α, β), so as to maximize the social welfare function

$$w = w(\hat{c}_1, \hat{c}_2, \ldots, \hat{c}_T) \tag{12.3}$$

subject to the budget constraint

$$\bar{t} = -\alpha + (1 - \beta)\bar{y} = \epsilon \bar{y} \tag{12.4}$$

where

$$\bar{y} = \frac{1}{T} \sum_{i=1}^{T} \hat{y} = \frac{1}{T} \sum_{i=1}^{T} n_i (1 - \hat{l}_i)$$

is the average income of the society and ϵ is the ratio of government revenue net of transfer payments to national income. It is assumed that ϵ is fixed and that the revenue is spent on projects that do not give direct benefits to individuals.

In the light of equation (12.4), the optimum consumption $\hat{c}_i$ can be written as

$$\hat{c}_i = (1 - \beta - \epsilon)\bar{y} + \beta\hat{y}_i + g(\hat{l}_i) \qquad (12.5)$$

which gives the average consumption of the society (including the consumption of leisure) as:

$$\bar{c} = (1 - \epsilon)\bar{y} + \bar{g} \qquad (12.6)$$

where

$$\bar{g} = \frac{1}{T} \sum_{i=1}^{T} g(\hat{l}_i)$$

In order to derive the optimum tax rates we assume a utilitarian social welfare function derived in Chapter 11 (equation 12.9):

$$W = \bar{c}(1 - kG_c) \qquad (12.7)$$

where G_c is the Gini index of the optimum consumption vector $\mathfrak{c} = (\hat{c}_1, c_2, \ldots, \hat{c}_T)$ and k is the parameter measuring the degree of envy felt by individuals. Note that this welfare function implies that individual utilities are interdependent. The government maximizes this function with respect to α and β, subject to (12.4).

To demonstrate how the government does this, we arrange individuals in ascending order of their ability to earn income (or their wage rate), $n_1 \leq n_2 \leq \cdots \leq n_T$. By means of equation (12.2), the first derivatives of $\hat{y}_i$ and $\hat{c}_i$ with respect to n_i are obtained as

$$\frac{\partial \hat{y}_i}{\partial n_i} = (1 - l_i) - n_i \frac{\partial \hat{l}_i}{\partial n_i} > 0$$

and

$$\frac{\partial c_i}{\partial n_i} = \beta(1 - l_i) > 0$$

where $\partial \hat{l}_i / \partial n_i = \beta / g''(l_i) < 0$. These equations imply that the ranking of individuals is the same for ability as it is for y_i and c_i. And, therefore, applying Theorem 8.3 of Kakwani (1980a) to (12.5) gives

$$\bar{c}G_c = \beta\bar{y}G_y + \bar{g}G_g \qquad (12.8)$$

where G_y is the Gini index of the before-tax income vector

$$\mathbf{y} = (\hat{y}_1, \hat{y}_2, \ldots, \hat{y}_T)$$

and G_g is the concentration index of the vector $g = [g(\hat{l}_1), g(\hat{l}_2), \ldots, g(\hat{l}_T)]$, which is given by

$$G_g = \frac{1}{T\bar{g}} \sum_{i=1}^{T} [g(\hat{l}_i) - \bar{g}_i]p_i,$$

where

$$\bar{g}_i = \frac{1}{i} \sum_{j=1}^{i} g(\hat{l}_j) \quad \text{and} \quad p_i = \frac{i}{T}$$

Following Sheshinski (1972), we define the elasticity of the labor supply function as

$$\lambda_i = \frac{\beta}{h_i} \frac{\partial \hat{H}_i}{\partial \beta} > 0$$

which, in conjunction with (12.2), gives

$$\frac{\partial \hat{y}_i}{\partial \beta} = \frac{z_i}{\beta}$$

and

$$\frac{\partial g(\hat{l}_i)}{\partial \beta} = -z_i$$

where $z_i = \hat{y}_i \lambda_i$. These equations immediately lead to

$$\frac{\partial \bar{y}}{\partial \beta} = \frac{z}{\beta}$$

$$\frac{\partial \bar{y} G_y}{\partial \beta} = \frac{1}{\beta} z G_z$$

$$\frac{\partial \bar{g}}{\partial \beta} = -z$$

$$\frac{\partial \bar{g} G_g}{\partial \beta} = -z G_z$$

where $\bar{z}$ and G_z are the mean and the Gini index of the vector

$$\mathbf{z} = [z_1, z_2, ..., z_T]$$

respectively. These together with (12.6) and (12.8) give the first-order condition for a maximum of W in (12.7) as

$$\frac{\partial W}{\partial \beta} = \frac{(1 - \epsilon - \beta)\bar{z}}{\beta} - k\bar{y} G_y = 0$$

Denoting the optimum parameters by $\hat{a}$ and $\hat{\beta}$, we obtain

$$m = 1 - \hat{\beta} = \frac{k\bar{y} G_y + \epsilon \bar{z}}{\bar{z} + k\bar{y} G_y} \tag{12.9}$$

and

$$\frac{\hat{\alpha}}{\bar{y}} = \frac{k\bar{y}G_y(1-\epsilon)}{\bar{z}+k\bar{y}G_y} \tag{12.10}$$

where m is the optimum marginal tax rate. Since $\epsilon \le 1$, these equations imply that the optimum marginal tax rate lies between zero and unity for all values of k and $\hat{\alpha} > 0$, which means that each individual instead of paying a lump-sum tax $\alpha > 0$ must receive a lump-sum subsidy from the government. Thus, the optimum tax function is progressive in the sense that the average tax rate increases monotonically with income.

It can be seen that the optimum marginal tax rate increases monotonically with ϵ, but the magnitude of increase is less than that of ϵ. If the taxation is purely redistributive, $\epsilon = 0$; in that case the optimum marginal tax rate is zero when $k = 0$. This is an interesting result. It means when people do not feel envious of each other, the government should not tax people at all in order to redistribute income. It can be demonstrated that the optimum marginal tax rate increases monotonically with increase in the degree of envy felt by individuals. As $k \to \infty$, $m \to 1$, implying that when individuals feel extremely envious, the government should tax everyone's income at a marginal rate of 100 percent.

The *relative-income guarantee*, as defined by Boskin and Shishinski (1978), is given by $\hat{\alpha}/y$ in (12.10). It can be demonstrated that $\hat{\alpha}/y$ increases monotonically with k, which means that if the degree of envy felt by individuals increases, the lump-sum subsidy as a percentage of average national income given to each individual must also increase. In the case of extreme envy, when $k \to \infty$, α/y approaches $(1-\epsilon)$.

Let $\bar{\lambda}$ be the lowest elasticity of the labor supply, that is,

$$\lambda_i = \frac{\beta}{h_i}\frac{\partial \hat{H}_i}{\partial \beta} \ge \bar{\lambda}$$

then $z_i \ge \bar{\lambda}\hat{y}_i$. Substituting this inequality in (12.9) and (12.10) and using the fact that $G_y \le 1$, we obtain

$$m \le \frac{k+\bar{\lambda}\epsilon}{\bar{\lambda}+k} \tag{12.11}$$

which demonstrates that the optimum marginal tax rate has an upper boundary that is higher the smaller the minimum elasticity of the labor supply and the greater the degree of envy felt by individuals.

The upper bound on the relative-income guarantee is similarly obtained as

$$\frac{\hat{\alpha}}{\bar{y}} \le \frac{k(1-\epsilon)}{\bar{\lambda}+k}$$

which is also an increasing function of k and decreasing function of $\bar{\lambda}$.

12.3   Numerical estimates of optimum tax rates: utilitarian case

In order to obtain numerical estimates of optimum tax rates, we need to specify a functional form of $g(l_i)$. Suppose that

$$g(l_i) = a[1 - (1 - l_i)^{1+\delta}] \tag{12.12}$$

where a and δ are parameters. It can be easily verified that $g'(l_i) > 0$ and $g''(l_i) < 0$ for all values of $\delta > 0$. When $l_i = 1$, $g(l_i) = a$; a being the value of enjoyment one derives from the maximum feasible consumption of leisure. Also, $g(l_i) = 0$ for $l_i = 0$.

Using (12.2), one derives the optimum labor supply

$$\hat{H}_i = \left[\frac{\beta n_i}{a(1+\delta)} \right]^{1/\delta} \tag{12.13}$$

which implies that the elasticity of the labor supply function is constant and is equal to $1/\delta$. This equation immediately gives the optimum marginal tax rate as

$$m = \frac{k\delta G_\phi + \epsilon}{1 + k\delta G_\phi} \tag{12.14}$$

where G_ϕ is the Gini index of the vector $\phi = (\phi_1, \phi_2, \ldots, \phi_T)$, ϕ_i being equal to $n_i^{1+1/\delta}$.

Let us assume that individual ability to earn income, denoted by n, is a random variable distributed lognormally with parameters μ and σ^2. The distribution function of such a distribution is usually denoted by $\Lambda(\mu, \sigma^2)$. Then, from Theorem 2.1 of Aitchison and Brown (1957), we obtain the distribution function of $n^{1+1/\delta}$ as $\Lambda[(1+1/\delta)\mu, (1+1/\delta)^2\sigma^2]$.

Theorem 2.7 of Aitchison and Brown (1957) shows that the Gini index of a variable distributed as $\Lambda(\mu, \sigma^2)$ depends only on σ^2 and is given by $2N(\sigma/\sqrt{2} \mid 0, 1) - 1$, where $N(x \mid 0, 1)$ is the distribution function of a standard normal variate with mean zero and variance unity. This result immediately gives the Gini of $n^{1+1/\delta}$ as

$$G_\phi = 2N\left[\frac{(1+1/\delta)\sigma}{\sqrt{2}} \,\middle|\, 0, 1 \right] - 1$$

Since the integral of a standard normal variate $N(x \mid 0, 1)$ is widely tabulated, it is not difficult to compute G_ϕ for different values of δ and σ. Equation (12.14) then provides the optimum marginal tax rates for different parameter values. The numerical results are presented in Table 12.1.

As expected, the optimum marginal tax rate increases monotonically with k. These increases are quite significant as k increases from zero to

Table 12.1. *Marginal tax rates for alternative parameter values (lognormal distribution)*

Values of δ		Values of k		
		0.0	0.5	1.0
$\epsilon = 0.0$	0.75	0.00	.134	.237
	1.00	0.00	.159	.275
	1.25	0.00	.176	.299
$\epsilon = 0.1$	0.75	0.10	.221	.313
	1.00	0.10	.243	.347
	1.25	0.10	.258	.347
$\epsilon = 0.2$	0.75	0.20	.307	.389
	1.00	0.20	.327	.420
	1.25	0.20	.340	.439
$\sigma = .45$ *(Gini index of ability = .25)*				
$\epsilon = 0.0$	0.75	0.00	.168	.288
	1.00	0.00	.192	.322
	1.25	0.00	.212	.350
$\epsilon = 0.1$	0.75	0.10	.251	.359
	1.00	0.10	.273	.390
	1.25	0.10	.291	.415
$\epsilon = 0.2$	0.75	0.20	.335	.431
	1.00	0.20	.353	.458
	1.25	0.20	.369	.480
$\sigma = 1.0$ *(Gini index of ability = .52)*				
$\epsilon = 0.0$	0.75	0.00	.259	.402
	1.00	0.00	.296	.457
	1.25	0.00	.332	.499
$\epsilon = 0.1$	0.75	0.10	.326	.462
	1.00	0.10	.366	.511
	1.25	0.10	.399	.549
$\epsilon = 0.2$	0.75	0.20	.401	.522
	1.00	0.20	.437	.565
	1.25	0.20	.466	.599

unity. It can be concluded that the optimum marginal tax rates are extremely sensitive to variations in the degree of envy felt by individuals. The sensitivity is, however, reduced as ϵ takes nonzero values.

The parameter σ can be interpreted as a measure of inequality of ability to earn income. It can be seen that the marginal tax rate is also very sensitive to variations in σ; the higher the inequality of individual ability the greater are the optimum marginal tax rates. Consider, for example, the case where ϵ is zero, when $\sigma = .35$ the Gini index of ability is about .20, and the optimum marginal tax rate increases from 23.7 percent to 29.9 percent as δ rises from .75 to 1.25. But when σ increases to 1.0 the Gini index of ability rises to .52, and the optimum tax rate ranges from 40.2 percent to 49.9 percent for the same variation in δ.

The numerical results indicate that the optimum marginal tax rate increases monotonically with δ. It means that the higher is the elasticity of labor supply, the lower is the optimum marginal tax rate. It should be noted, however, that this monotonic relationship between m and δ does not always hold. This can be seen by differentiating (12.14) with respect to δ:

$$\frac{\partial m}{\partial \delta} = \frac{(1-\epsilon)}{1+k\delta G_\phi} G_\phi + \delta \frac{\partial G_\phi}{\partial \delta}$$

where

$$\frac{\partial G_\phi}{\partial \delta} < 0.$$

Hence it is not possible to say in general whether m increases (or decreases) monotonically with δ. Nonetheless, the numerical results show that the marginal tax rate is sensitive to variations in δ and that the sensitivity becomes even greater as the inequality of ability is increased.

In order to see whether the optimum tax parameters are sensitive to the form of the distribution function of ability, we assume a Pareto density function:

$$f(n) = \theta n_1^\theta n^{-\theta-1}, \quad n \geq n_1 \tag{12.15}$$

where $\theta > 0$ and $n_1 > 0$ are parameters, the latter denoting the lowest ability level. The Gini index of the ability under this distribution is given by (Kakwani 1980a):

$$G = \frac{1}{2\theta - 1}$$

but we require the Gini index of $n^{1+1/\delta}$, which can be derived from (8.12) of Kakwani (1980a). This index, given by

$$G_\phi = \frac{(1+\delta)}{2\delta\phi - 1 - \delta},$$

forms the basis of the numerical results given in Table 12.2.

Again, it is seen that the optimum marginal tax rates are sensitive to both the degree of envy felt by individuals and the inequality of the distribution of ability to earn. Although the optimum marginal tax rate increases

Table 12.2. *Marginal tax rates for alternative parameter values (Pareto distribution)*

Government expenditure as fraction of national ε income	δ	Values of k		
		0.0	0.5	1.0
$\theta = 2.5$ *(Gini index of ability = .25)*				
$\epsilon = 0.0$	0.75	0.00	.247	.396
	1.00	0.00	.250	.400
	1.25	0.00	.260	.413
$\epsilon = 0.1$	0.75	0.10	.322	.457
	1.00	0.10	.325	.460
	1.25	0.10	.334	.471
$\epsilon = 0.2$	0.75	0.20	.398	.517
	1.00	0.20	.400	.520
	1.25	0.20	.408	.530
$\theta = 3.0$ *(Gini index of ability = .20)*				
$\epsilon = 0.0$	0.75	0.00	.193	.323
	1.00	0.00	.200	.333
	1.25	0.00	.211	.349
$\epsilon = 0.1$	0.75	0.10	.273	.391
	1.00	0.10	.280	.400
	1.25	0.10	.290	.414
$\epsilon = 0.2$	0.75	0.20	.354	.458
	1.00	0.20	.360	.467
	1.25	0.20	.369	.479

monotonically with δ, its sensitivity with respect to variation δ is considerably lower for the Pareto than for the lognormal distribution of ability.

Since the optimum tax parameters are sensitive to the inequality of ability, any comparison of numerical results for the two distributions must ensure that their parameters correspond to the same inequality of ability. These corresponding comparisons indicate that the optimum marginal tax rate differs enormously for the two distributions. In fact, the Pareto distribution gives considerably higher values of the optimum marginal tax rate than does the lognormal distribution. These results emphasize the importance of selecting an appropriate distribution function for ability for the purpose of computing the optimum tax parameters.

12.4   A generalized maxi–min criterion

As an alternative to the utilitarian welfare function, the Rawlsian objective criterion (termed maxi–min) has also been used in the optimal-taxation literature. According to this criterion, the government's aim is to maximize the welfare of the worst-off individual in the society. An obvious extension of this criterion is to maximize the average welfare of say, the bottom $100h$ percent of population in the society. In this section, we derive the optimum tax rates by maximizing the welfare function derived in Theorem 11.4.

The average welfare of the bottom $100h$ percent of the population defined in terms of optimal consumption is given by

$$W_k(h) = \bar{c}_h - k[(\bar{c} - \bar{c}_h) + h\bar{c}_h G_{ch}] \tag{12.16}$$

where c_h and G_{ch} are the mean and the Gini index of the optimum consumptions of the bottom $100h$ percent population and c is the average consumption of the whole society. Applying Theorem 8.3 of Kakwani (1980a) to (3.5) for a subgroup of the bottom $100h$th percent population gives

$$\bar{c}_h G_{ch} = \beta \bar{y}_h G_{yh} + \bar{g}_h G_{gh} \tag{12.17}$$

where

$$\bar{c}_h = (1 - \beta - \epsilon)\bar{y} + \beta \bar{y}_h + \bar{g}_h$$

$\bar{y}_h$ and G_{yh} being the mean and the Gini index of the before-tax (money) incomes of the poorest $100h$ percent individuals and $\bar{g}_h$ and G_{gh} are the mean and the concentration index of the value of leisure for this subgroup of the population.

Differentiating (12.17) and (13.18) with respect to β leads to the first-order condition for a maximum of $W_k(h)$ in (12.16) as

$$\frac{\partial W_k(h)}{\partial \beta} = (\bar{y}_h - \bar{y}) + (1 - \beta - \epsilon)\frac{z}{\beta} - k[\bar{y} - \bar{y}_h + h\bar{y}_h G_{yh}] = 0 \tag{12.18}$$

and denoting the optimum parameters by $\tilde{\alpha}$ and $\tilde{\beta}$, we obtain

$$m^* = 1 - \tilde{\beta} = \frac{\epsilon \bar{z} + kh y_h G_{yh} + (1 + k)(\bar{y} - \bar{y}_h)}{\bar{z} + kh \bar{y}_h G_{yh} + (1 + k)(\bar{y} - \bar{y}_h)} \tag{12.19}$$

and

$$\frac{\tilde{\alpha}}{\bar{y}} = \frac{(1 - \epsilon)[kh\bar{y}_h G_{yh} + (1 + k)(\bar{y} - \bar{y}_h)]}{\bar{z} + kh\bar{y}_h G_{yh} + (1 + k)(\bar{y} - \bar{y}_h)} \tag{12.20}$$

Since $\epsilon \le 1$, these equations imply that the optimum marginal tax rate m^* under the generalized maxi–min criterion also lies between zero and unity for all values of k and $\tilde{\alpha} > 0$, which means that each individual must receive a lump-sum subsidy from the government. Further, it can be demonstrated that the optimum marginal tax rate and the relative-income guarantee increase monotonically (for all values of h in the range $0 < h \le 1$)

as the degree of envy felt by individuals increases. In the case of extreme envy, $k \to \infty$, $m^* \to 1$ and $\tilde{\alpha}/y \to (1-\epsilon)$.

When $\epsilon = 0$ (i.e., the taxes are purely redistributive), the optimum marginal tax rate is nonzero for $0 < h < 1$, even if $k = 0$. It means that even if people do not feel envious, the government must tax people in order to redistribute income. In the utilitarian situation, we observed that the optimal policy for the government was to have no tax at all when people do not feel envious. Thus, these two social objectives, in which the government is concerned with the poorest $100h$ percent of the population in the one case and with the social welfare of the entire society in the other case, have different implications for distribution policy, particularly when people do not feel envious of each other.

If we substitute $h = 1.0$, $\bar{y}_h = \bar{y}$, and $G_{yh} = G_y$ in (12.19) and (12.20), we obtain the optimum marginal tax rate and relative-income guarantee as derived in (12.9) and (12.10), respectively. Thus, the optimum tax parameters derived with a utilitarian social objective follow as a special case of the generalized maxi–min criterion. As a matter of fact the Rawlsian maxi–min objective criterion must also be a special case of the generalized maxi–min criterion. In order to obtain optimum tax parameters under this criterion, we need to substitute $h = 1/T$, $G_{yh} = 0$, and $y_h = \hat{y}_1$ in (12.19) and (12.20). Thus, the maxi–min objective criterion leads to the following optimum tax parameters:

$$m_1^* = \frac{\epsilon \bar{z} + (1+k)(\bar{y}-\hat{y}_1)}{\bar{z} + (1+k)(\bar{y}-\hat{y}_1)} \tag{12.21}$$

$$\frac{\tilde{\alpha}_1}{\bar{y}} = \frac{(1+k)(1-\epsilon)(\bar{y}-\hat{y}_1)}{\bar{z} + (1+k)(1-\epsilon)(\bar{y}-\hat{y}_1)} \tag{12.22}$$

Since $z \geq \bar{\lambda} y$, $\bar{\lambda}$ being the lowest elasticity of the labor supply, and the ratio of the lowest to the average before-tax income is less than unity, the upper bound on the optimum marginal tax rate is

$$m_1^* \leq \frac{(1+k)+\epsilon\bar{\lambda}}{\bar{\lambda}+(1+k)} \tag{12.23}$$

which, in view of $\epsilon < 1$, shows that the upper-boundary optimum marginal tax rate with a maxi–min objective criterion also decreases with the minimum elasticity of the labor supply and increases with the degree of envy felt by individuals. It can be seen that the upper bound on m_1^* is greater than that on m – as given in (12.11) with a utilitarian objective – for all values of ϵ and k.

Let us now assume that $g(l_i)$ is of the form (12.12) in which the elasticity of labor supply is constant and equal to $1/\delta$. Then the optimum marginal tax rate m^* in (12.19) becomes

$$m^* = \frac{\epsilon\bar{\phi} + \delta kh\bar{\phi}_h G_h + (1+k)\delta(\bar{\phi} - \bar{\phi}_h)}{\bar{\phi} + \delta kh\phi_h G_{\bar{\phi}h} + (1+k)\delta(\bar{\phi} - \bar{\phi}_h)} \tag{12.24}$$

where $\bar{\phi} = 1/T(\sum_{i=1}^{T} n^{1+1/\delta})$, $\bar{\phi}_h = 1/Th(\sum_{i=1}^{Th} n^{1+1/\delta})$ and $G_{\phi h}$ is the Gini index of the vector $(\phi_1, \phi_2, \ldots, \phi_{Th})$, $\phi_i = n_i^{1+1/\delta}$ when individuals are arranged according to levels of their ability.

In order to see how the optimum tax rate in (12.24) varies with h we need to differentiate m^* in (12.24) with respect to h. Since individuals are ranked according to their income-earning abilities, then from (11.10), it can be demonstrated that

$$(1+k)\frac{\partial\bar{\phi}_h}{\partial h} > k\frac{\partial}{\partial h}(h\bar{y}_h G_{\phi h}) \tag{12.25}$$

Differentiating (12.24), with respect to h, yields

$$\frac{\partial m^*}{\partial h} = -\frac{\delta(1-\epsilon)\bar{\phi}[(1+k)(\partial\bar{\phi}_h/\partial h) - k(\partial h\bar{y}_h G_{\phi h}/\partial h)]}{[\bar{\phi} + \delta kh\bar{\phi}_h G_{\phi h} + (1+k)\delta(\bar{\phi} - \bar{\phi}_h)]^2} \tag{12.26}$$

which in view of (12.25) is negative. *Thus, if the elasticity of labor supply is constant, the optimum marginal tax rate decreases monotonically with* h, *implying that the maxi-min welfare objective leads to the highest marginal tax rate and the utilitarian welfare objective to the lowest marginal tax rate.* This result is valid for all values of k and ϵ.

12.5 Numerical estimates of optimal tax rates with a generalized maxi-min objective

In order to compute the optimum marginal tax rate as derived in (12.19) for different values of h, we assume $f(n)$ to be the Pareto distribution (see 12.15). The Lorenz curve of $\phi = n^{1+1/\delta}$ can then be derived from equation (8.12) of Kakwani (1980a):

$$L(p) = 1 - (1-p)^{\frac{\theta\delta - 1 - \delta}{\theta\delta}} \tag{12.27}$$

which, on integration with respect to p in the range $0 \leq p \leq h$, yields

$$G_{\phi h} = 1 - \frac{2(\theta\delta - 1 - \delta)}{(2\theta\delta - 1 - \delta)L(h)} + \frac{2(1-h)\theta\delta}{(2\theta\delta - 1 - \delta)h}$$

where $L(h) = 1 - (1-h)^{(\theta\delta - 1 - \delta)/\theta\delta}$. From the definition of the Lorenz curve it follows that

$$\frac{\bar{\phi}_h}{\bar{\phi}} = \frac{L(h)}{h}.$$

Table 12.3. *Marginal tax rates for alternative parameter values:*
generalized maxi-min criterion with a Pareto distribution of ability

Value of k	Value of δ	Max–min criterion	Values of h				Utilitarian criterion for which h = 1.00
			.2	.4	.6	.8	
Pareto parameter θ = 2.5 (Gini index of ability .25)							
0.0	0.75	.41	.409	.407	.403	.395	0.000
	1.00	.44	.438	.431	.419	.396	0.000
	1.25	.47	.465	.455	.438	.406	0.000
0.5	0.75	.51	.510	.508	.504	.498	0.247
	1.00	.54	.539	.533	.522	.503	0.250
	1.25	.57	.566	.557	.542	.516	0.260
1.0	0.75	.58	.580	.579	.576	.570	0.396
	1.00	.61	.609	.603	.594	.578	0.400
	1.25	.64	.635	.626	.614	.592	0.413
Pareto parameter θ = 3.0 (Gini index of ability .20)							
0.0	0.75	.37	.363	.355	.342	.319	0.000
	1.00	.40	.390	.379	.360	.325	0.000
	1.25	.43	.418	.402	.379	.337	0.000
0.5	0.75	.47	.461	.452	.441	.420	0.193
	1.00	.50	.490	.479	.461	.431	0.200
	1.25	.53	.519	.504	.483	.447	0.211
1.0	0.75	.54	.533	.525	.514	.495	0.323
	1.00	.57	.562	.551	.535	.508	0.333
	1.25	.60	.590	.576	.557	.525	0.349

These two equations together with (12.24) can be used to derive numerical estimates of optimum marginal tax rates for different values of h. The results are presented in Table 12.3 for $\epsilon = 0.0$ (i.e., when taxes are purely redistributive).

The numerical results indicate that the maxi–min marginal tax rates are considerably higher than those obtained on the basis of the utilitarian welfare function. Both sets of rates are fairly sensitive to variations in the degree of envy felt by individuals.

As might be anticipated, the optimum tax rate decreases monotonically with h. What may not be expected, however, is the sharp change in the rate at which the marginal tax rate falls. The rate decreases quite slowly as h approaches .8 but then drops sharply as h approaches unity. This is an important finding. Intuitively, the maxi–min objective, under which the government's aim is to maximize the welfare of the worst-off individual in the society, would seem to be considerably more egalitarian than that under which the government is concerned with the bottom 80 percent of the population; but the difference between the two tax rates is very slight.

A policy implication of this result is that the government need not know the exact proportion of the population that is poor in order to arrive at the tax structure that maximizes the average welfare of the poor.

12.6   Conclusions

The aim of this paper has been to explore the effect of envy among individuals on the optimal tax structure. The individual welfare function used for this purpose assumes that people compare their incomes with those of others and feel envious when they find their own incomes are lower. This welfare function depends on a parameter k which measures the degree of envy; the higher the value of k, the greater the envy felt by individuals. Following are some of the implications for tax policies that emerge from this analysis.

1.   The optimum linear tax function is progressive for all values of $k > 0$.
2.   The optimum marginal tax rate is bounded above by a fraction that decreases with the minimum elasticity of the labor supply function and increases with the degree of envy felt by individuals.
3.   The optimum marginal tax rate and the relative-income guarantee increase monotonically with the increase in the degree of envy felt by individuals. These increases are very substantial as k increases from zero to unity. Even the utilitarian social objective, which is considered by many to be not egalitarian enough, may yield a highly progressive tax function when people feel envious.
4.   In the case of the utilitarian social objective, if people do not feel envious of each other, the government should not tax people at all in order to redistribute income. But if the government follows the generalized maxi–min social objective, which calls for maximization of the average welfare of the poorest $100h$ percent of the population, then the marginal tax rate must be positive even when people do not feel envious. Thus, the two social objectives have different implications for public policy in the field of income redistribution.
5.   If the elasticity of the labor supply is constant, the optimum marginal tax rate decreases monotonically with h. This implies that the maxi–min welfare objective leads to the highest and the utilitarian welfare objective to the lowest marginal tax rate. In fact

the numerical results based on a Pareto distribution of ability show that the marginal tax rates are substantially higher for the maxi–min than for the utilitarian social objective.

6.   The numerical results indicate that the government does not need to know the exact proportion of the poor in order to arrive at the tax structure that maximizes the average welfare of the poor.

7.   The numerical results confirm the earlier finding by Mirrlees that the optimum marginal tax rate is highly sensitive to the inequality of individual ability to earn income; the higher the degree of inequality, the greater the optimum marginal tax rate.

Some of the limitations of the analysis must also be pointed out. First, the individual welfare function used has many limitations, which have been highlighted in the previous chapter. Secondly, the value of leisure function $g(l)$ has been assumed to be the same for all individuals. It will be interesting for future research to relax this assumption. Thirdly, the chapter deals with the taxation of earned income and not with the taxation of investment income, which introduces quite different considerations. Finally, a most important limitation is that the tax function considered takes no account of the different needs of the people.

CHAPTER 13

The impact of taxes and cash benefits on poverty

Poverty has been in existence in the world for many centuries. But an awareness of its existence in Western societies has increased only recently.[1] Social attitudes toward poverty have changed and, increasingly, it is being realized that the government could play an important role in eliminating poverty. It is also being increasingly realized that the developing countries will continue to need outside assistance to eliminate poverty, or at least to reduce its intensity.[2] The prior problem, however, is to identify the poor and to measure the intensity of their poverty, so that methods can be devised to wage a war against it.

During the 1970s, considerable attention was paid to the problem of poverty in Australia. The Commission of Inquiry into Poverty (1975), headed by Professor R. F. Henderson, was set up by the federal government to inquire into the legal and sociological, as well as economic, aspects of poverty in Australia. The importance of government income-support programs to reduce, if not eliminate, poverty was increasingly recognized. How far this objective is achieved should be an issue of utmost importance to policy makers. This chapter attempts to measure the impact of personal income tax and government cash transfers on the overall level of poverty. The results of a breakdown of aggregate poverty according to the several socioeconomic and demographic characteristics of households considered in Chapter 9 are also analyzed in this chapter.

13.1 Specification of the poverty line

In the measurement of poverty, the first problem is the identification of the poor. The poor are those who lack resources to obtain the minimum necessities of life. The *poverty line* is the level of income that is sufficient to buy the so-called minimum necessities of life. A person is poor if his or her income falls below that line.[3]

One of the earlier studies on poverty was done by Rowntree (1901), who defined families to be in primary poverty if their total earnings are insufficient to obtain the "minimum necessities of merely physical efficiency." He estimated the minimum money costs for food would satisfy the average nutritional needs of families of different sizes. To these costs he added the rent paid and certain minimum amounts for clothing, fuel, and sundries to arrive at a poverty line for a family of given size. This poverty line based on the concept of physical subsistence involves a number of serious problems.[4]

One of the main criticisms against this concept of poverty is that it does not take into account the current living standards of the society. This concept of poverty may be valid in the developing countries, where the malnutrition is still widely prevalent, but in developed countries, poverty rarely means starvation or near starvation. The old standards of poverty are not relevant to contemporary society (Wedderburn 1974: 1). The new approach to the definition of poverty is based on the concept of *relative deprivation*, which denotes feelings of deprivation relative to others.[5] In view of this, it seems best to recognize explicitly that any poverty line will be influenced by current living standards and should only be defined in relation to the living standards of a particular society at a particular date (Atkinson 1974a: 48).[6]

Sen (1979), recognizing these different aspects of poverty, defined two poverty lines, viz., (1) the nutritional poverty line and (2) the cultural poverty line; the first corresponds to the level of income at which the consumption level of an individual or of a family is nutritionally adequate, and the second identifies the level of income adequate for meeting necessities, defined in terms of the overall living standards of that society. It seems useful to define a single poverty line that takes into account both these aspects of poverty. One such poverty line is:

$$z(\beta) = z_0 + \beta(m - z_0) \tag{13.1}$$

where z_0 is the nutritional poverty line income and m denotes either the median or the mean income of the society. β lies in the range $0 \le \beta \le 1$, which implies that the poverty line can neither be lower than z_0 (which represents a standard of minimum subsistence) nor higher than the mean or median income of the society.[7] The value of β depends on the society's value judgment about the minimum standard of living that all its members must enjoy. The problem is that of obtaining social preferences about the alternative values of β from the individual preferences. This is discussed in the next section.

13.2   A probabilistic approach to measuring poverty[8]

Suppose, in a society, there are n families who are arranged in ascending order of their incomes $x_1 \le x_2 \le \cdots \le x_n$. These incomes are denoted by a vector $\mathbf{x} = (x_1, x_2, \ldots, x_n)$. If $z(\beta)$ is the poverty line, then the poverty index $\theta[\mathbf{x}, z(\beta)]$ is defined to be a unique function of $x_1, x_2, \ldots, x_n$ and

$z(\beta)$, satisfying certain axioms. Assume that β takes m alternative values $\beta_1, \beta_2, ..., \beta_m$ (all of which lie in the range $0 \le \beta \le 1$), which lead to m alternative poverty lines, as defined in (13.1). Each individual in the society has certain preferences among alternative poverty lines, which are summarized by individual probability vector

$$\mathbf{p}_i = (p_{i1}, p_{i2}, ..., p_{im}); \quad p_{ij} \ge 0, \text{ all } i, j; \quad \sum_{j=1}^{m} p_{ij} = 1, \text{ for all } i$$

where p_{ij} is the probability that an individual i will choose the poverty line $z(\beta_j)$.[9] Let the social probability vector $\mathbf{p}$ derived from individual probability vectors $\mathbf{p}_1, \mathbf{p}_2, ..., \mathbf{p}_n$ is given by

$$\mathbf{p} = (\mathbf{p}_1, \mathbf{p}_2, ..., \mathbf{p}_m); \quad p_j \ge 0, \text{ all } j; \quad \sum_{j=1}^{m} p_j = 1$$

where p_j is the probability that the society will choose the poverty line $z(\beta_j)$.

The problem is, then, one of obtaining the social probability vector $\mathbf{p}$ from the individual vectors $\mathbf{p}_i$. To tackle this problem, the following three axioms are proposed.[10]

Axiom 13.1 (Existence of social probabilities): *Given any set of n non-negative vectors $\mathbf{p}_i$ with unit sums, there exists a non-negative vector, $\mathbf{p}$, such that meaningful individual probabilities will yield meaningful social probabilities.*

Axiom 13.2 (Unanimity preserving for a loser): *If all individuals reject a poverty line with certainty then so does society (i.e., if $p_{ij} = 0$ for all i, then $p_j = 0$). Similarly, if all individuals accept a poverty line with certainty so does society (i.e., if $p_{ij} = 1$ for all i, then $p_j = 1$).*

Axiom 13.3 (Strict and equal sensitivity to individual probabilities): *Social probabilities are strictly sensitive to individual probabilities in that an increase (decrease) in the probability that any one individual will choose a particular poverty line always increases (decreases) the probability that society will choose this poverty line.*

Given these axioms, Intriligator (1973) proved that there is a unique rule for determining social probabilities, the average rule, according to which the social probabilities are simple averages of individual probabilities, that is,[11]

$$p_j = \frac{1}{n} \sum_{i=1}^{n} p_{ij}, \quad \text{for all } j = 1, 2, ..., m$$

There are m poverty indices $\theta_j = \theta[x, z(\beta_j)]$, each of which is associated with a social probability p_j, which is derived from individual probabilities. A weighted average of all these poverty indices is given by

$$E(\theta) = \sum_{j=1}^{m} \theta_j p_j = \frac{1}{n} \sum_{j=1}^{m} \sum_{i=1}^{n} \theta_j p_{ij}$$

provides an aggregated index of poverty, which incorporates the value judgments (expressed in terms of probabilities) of all the members of a society.[12]

13.3   The poverty line used

The poverty line should be determined on the basis of society's value judgment about the minimum standard of living that all its members must enjoy. Ideally these social values should be formed from individual preferences. This is a gigantic task and cannot be accomplished as yet. In this study we adopted the poverty line recommended by the Poverty Inquiry Commission, which suggested that a household consisting of head, dependent wife, and two children will be in poverty if its income falls short of 56.6 percent of seasonally adjusted average weekly earning for Australia. According to this definition, the poverty line for a household of husband, wife, and two children was computed to be $92.56 per week during the year 1975-6.

The poverty line that the commission originally used consisted of the basic wage plus child endowment (rounded up to the nearest whole dollar) for a standard family of husband, wife, and two children. This amounted to $33 per week in 1966. Since this figure turned out to be 56.6 of the seasonally adjusted average earning in Australia in that year, the commission set the same poverty norm for other years. Thus the poverty line has been updated so that the line for the standard family remained at 56.6 percent of the before-tax adjusted average weekly earning.

In order to determine the poverty lines for households other than the standard ones, the commission used the equivalent-income scales calculated from the 1954 "Family Budget Standard" of the community council of Greater New York. This scale, as pointed out in Section 2.6, is inappropriate for the present-day Australian lifestyle. The Poverty Inquiry Commission recognized this problem and recommended that "further inquiry be instituted to derive a set of relative rates of pension–benefit for different income-unit sizes appropriate to Australian conditions."

In view of uncertainty inherent in the estimation of equivalent-income scales, it seems best to measure poverty using alternative scales. In this chapter the effect of adopting alternative scales on the level of poverty is investigated.

13.4   Measures of poverty used

The intensity of poverty suffered by those below the threshold income must be measured, once the poverty line is specified. Most of the literature on poverty concerns the number of individual households or persons below the poverty line. The percentage of population below the poverty line (known as the head-count ratio), as such, does not reflect the intensity of poverty suffered by the poor. The problem is, How poor are the poor? They may have incomes that approximate the threshold level or they may have incomes of almost zero. If the deviation of a poor person's income from the poverty line is proportional to the degree of misery suffered by that person, the sum total of these deviations divided by the number of poor may be considered a desirable measure of poverty. This index, which has been used by the U.S. Social Security Administration, is called the poverty gap. It indicates the average short-fall of income from the poverty line of all the poor taken together. There are two main drawbacks with this index: (1) it is completely insensitive to the number of poor, and (2) it does not take into account the inequality of income among the poor.

In order to overcome these deficiencies, Sen (1976) defined a general measure of poverty as

$$\theta = \sum_{i=1}^{q} g_i v_i \tag{13.2}$$

where $g_i = (z - x_i)/z$ is the poverty gap of the ith poor and v_i is the weight attached to his or her poverty gap. It should be understood that v_i has been defined as a function of the whole income distribution and not the income of the ith individual alone, which implies a more general welfare function than the one that is additive-separable.[13] One could also define poverty measure as the sum total of disutilities arising from being poor. This definition would correspond to the utilitarian welfare function and, in that case, v_i must depend only on the income x_i of the ith person and not also on the incomes of others. Sen (1979) dismissed this approach because it misses the idea of relative deprivation, which is rather central to the notion of poverty. Instead, he determines the weight v_i on the basis of ranking of poor individuals, which in some way captures the relative-deprivation aspect of the poverty.[14] Using this rank-order weighting in conjunction with some other less demanding axioms, Sen (1976) derived the following poverty index:

$$S = F(z)[z - \mu^*(1 - G)]/z \tag{13.3}$$

where z is the poverty threshold income, μ^* is the mean income of the poor, G^* is the Gini index of the income distribution among the poor, and $F(z)$ is the percentage of poor.

The index S is zero when nobody is below the poverty line and it is unity when everyone in the population is below the poverty line and has zero income. When there is no inequality among the poor, clearly G^* is zero, and S will be equal to the product of two poverty indicators, viz., the percentage of the poor and the poverty gap. Thus, the poverty index is sensitive to three factors, viz., the percentage of poor, the poverty gap, and the inequality of income among the poor, all of which are essential indicators of the aggregate poverty.

Sen's rank-order axiom makes the weight v_i on the poverty gap of person i depend on the number of persons among the poor who are richer than i, thus ignoring completely their actual income.[15] Kakwani (1980a) proposed an axiom, alternative to Sen's, which makes the i's sense of deprivation depend on the actual income enjoyed by those who are richer than i but still belonging to the category of poor. He arrived at an alternative poverty index K given by

$$K = F(z)[z - \mu^*/(1 + G^*)]/z \tag{13.4}$$

which has essentially the same properties as S. But the two indices differ with respect to their characterization of the relative deprivation among the poor: while S concentrates on persons, K focuses on income.

Sen (1979) believes that the sense of relative deprivation is more readily captured by knowing how many people are richer than in knowing what their aggregate income happens to be. He, therefore, prefers S over K. There may be some who might believe that the aggregate income of the richer rather than their number is more important in capturing the deprivation aspect of poverty. This issue cannot be easily resolved here. Thus, the empirical investigation of poverty presented in this chapter is based on both these indices.[16]

13.5   Numerical results of various poverty measures

Table 13.1 presents the numerical results of various poverty measures based on different income concepts. These estimates have been obtained by ranking households by their per equivalent-adult income. Eight alternative equivalent-income scales have been used for this purpose. Several interesting findings emerge from the tables.

The numerical results based on adjusted original income show that the percentage of persons in poverty range from the minimum of 16.06 to the maximum of 16.59. The variation in poverty based on Sen's and Kakwani's indices is slightly greater than that based on head-count ratio. It is interesting to note that per capita income indicates the highest poverty on the basis of head-count ratio but the lowest poverty on the basis of Sen's and Kakwani's indices. This is an important observation because all the earlier

Table 13.1. *Poverty measures based on different income concepts, and with different weights given to second and subsequent adult and each child: Australia 1975-6*

Weights								
λ_1	1.0	.9	.8	.8	.8	.7	.7	.7
λ_1	1.0	.5	.5	.4	.3	.5	.4	.3
Original income								
Sen's poverty index	10.74	12.36	12.27	12.52	12.30	12.21	12.50	12.60
Kakwani's index	10.35	11.48	11.44	11.63	11.21	11.41	11.63	11.69
% persons in poverty	16.59	16.37	16.19	16.43	16.42	16.18	16.45	16.06
% children in poverty	15.44	14.16	14.00	14.08	13.27	13.99	14.24	13.49
% adults in poverty	17.21	17.55	17.36	17.68	18.10	17.35	17.63	17.43
% households in poverty	21.11	21.99	21.80	22.08	22.24	21.80	22.08	21.92
Number of persons in poverty (millions)	2.13	2.10	2.08	2.11	2.11	2.08	2.11	2.06
Number of households in poverty (millions)	.88	.91	.91	.92	.92	.91	.92	.91
Gross income								
Sen's poverty index	4.03	3.67	3.72	3.57	3.34	3.67	3.69	3.34
Kakwani's index	3.69	3.13	3.35	3.31	3.24	3.35	3.37	3.24
% persons in poverty	6.82	5.66	5.71	6.53	8.66	5.94	6.07	8.61
% children in poverty	11.40	8.81	8.95	8.61	7.59	7.98	8.01	7.67
% adults in poverty	4.37	3.98	3.98	5.42	9.24	4.85	5.03	9.12
% households in poverty	4.57	3.97	4.04	6.98	10.77	6.37	6.66	10.70
Number of persons in poverty (millions)	.88	.73	.73	.84	1.11	.76	.78	1.11
Number of households in poverty (millions)	.19	.17	.17	.29	.45	.27	.28	.45
Disposable income								
Sen's poverty index	4.40	3.82	4.17	3.98	3.62	4.18	4.12	3.87
Kakwani's index	4.05	3.57	3.83	3.71	3.55	3.86	3.81	3.75
% of persons in poverty	7.02	6.22	7.19	6.88	9.28	7.17	6.92	9.09
% of children in poverty	11.69	9.81	9.81	9.17	8.08	9.79	9.23	8.38
% of adults in poverty	4.52	4.31	5.79	5.65	9.92	5.78	5.68	9.47
% of households in poverty	4.73	4.40	7.39	7.28	11.46	7.42	7.35	11.15
Number of persons in poverty (millions)	.90	.80	.92	.88	1.19	.92	.89	1.17
Number of households in poverty (millions)	.20	.18	.31	.30	.48	.31	.31	.46

poverty studies carried out in Australia are based on crude indicators of poverty.

All poverty indicators show that the poverty is substantially reduced when government benefits are added to the original income. This can be seen by observing that the percentage of persons in poverty varies from 5.66 to 8.66 when the adjusted gross income is used as a basis for measuring poverty. Both Sen's and Kakwani's indices also show considerable reduction in poverty as a result of government cash transfers; the magnitude of reduction depending on the equivalent-income scale used. On the basis of adjusted original income, the number of persons living in poverty is just over 2 million. But when government benefits are added to the original income, this number varies from 727,000 to 1.11 million. Thus, it can be concluded that the number of persons in poverty is reduced by about 50 percent as a result of government cash transfers.

As can be seen from the table, the incidence of poverty for individuals is much less than that for households. This reflects the higher incidence of poverty among one-person households, which may partly be explained by the higher incidence of poverty among the old. If this explanation is correct, the differences in incidence of poverty for individuals and for households must become smaller after benefits because the old people receive larger benefits in the form of pensions. This indeed seems to be the case; the percentage of households in poverty varies from 21.11 to 22.24 before benefits but the variation is from 3.97 to 10.77 after benefits, indicating that government cash transfers have considerably greater impact in reducing the incidence of poverty for households than that for individuals.

On the basis of adjusted original income, the percentage of children in poverty varies from the minimum of 13.27 to the maximum of 15.44, depending on the equivalent-income scale used. The similar variation in the percentage of adults in poverty is from 17.21 to 18.10, indicating considerably greater poverty among adults than among children. This situation is reversed, however, when cash benefits are added to the original income. For the adjusted gross income, the head-count ratio for children varies from 8.08 percent to 11.69 percent, whereas the similar variation for adults is from 4.31 percent to 9.92 percent. From these results we may conclude that the reduction in the incidence of poverty for adults due to government benefits is far greater than that for children.

The most important finding from the table concerns the effect of personal income tax on the overall incidence of poverty. All poverty indicators show an increase in poverty as a result of taxation. For example, from column 7 we observe that the percentage of persons in poverty increases from 6.07 to 6.92, and Sen's measure increases from 3.69 to 4.12 when the personal income tax is subtracted from the gross income. About 110,000 individuals, living in 29,000 households, are driven to poverty as a result of taxation. This result is in complete contrast to the following judgment of the Taxation Review Committee:

In the Committee's judgement there will be almost universal agreement that overall taxation should be progressive at the upper end of the scales of income and

Table 13.2. *Poverty measures, by sex by household head: Australia 1975-6*

Poverty measures	Female head	Male head	All households
Adjusted original income			
% of persons in poverty	43.80	13.38	16.45
% of children in poverty	51.11	11.67	14.24
% of adults in poverty	41.51	14.35	17.63
% of households in poverty	50.71	15.99	22.08
Sen's poverty index	32.00	9.53	12.50
Adjusted gross income			
% of persons in poverty	11.26	5.40	6.07
% of children in poverty	9.57	7.91	8.01
% of adults in poverty	11.79	4.63	5.03
% of households in poverty	16.14	5.24	6.66
Sen's poverty index	4.74	3.40	3.69
Adjusted disposable income			
% of persons in poverty	11.32	6.61	6.92
% of children in poverty	9.74	9.07	9.23
% of adults in poverty	11.81	4.89	5.68
% of households in poverty	16.15	5.52	7.35
Sen's poverty index	4.96	4.08	4.12

wealth, and that at the other extreme poverty and threats of poverty reflecting situations of special need should be relieved of taxation or assisted by social service payments.

13.6 A breakdown of aggregate poverty according to the socioeconomic and demographic characteristics of households

This section focuses on the results of a breakdown of aggregate poverty according to various socioeconomic and demographic characteristics of households. The analysis is based on the equivalent-income scale that gave weights of unity to the household head, .7 to the second and subsequent adults, and .4 to each child in the household. The poverty measures were computed on the basis of all the equivalent-income scales, considered in the previous section but not reported here because they resulted in more or less the same broad conclusions.

The breakdown of households according to the sex of household head is presented in Table 13.2. The results clearly indicate that households headed by females are subject to a higher incidence of poverty than those headed by males. If there were no government transfers, the 43.8 percent of persons in households with female heads would have been living in poverty, but this percentage is reduced to only 11.26 percent as a consequence of the income support provided by the government. The percentage of poor is slightly increased to 11.32 as a result of the personal income tax paid by these households. The percentage of those living in male-headed households who are poor is reduced from 13.38 to 5.40 because of government transfers but then it is increased to 6.61 due to income taxes paid to the government.

It is interesting to note that the percentage of children belonging to female-headed households who are poor is reduced drastically from 51.11 to 9.57 as a consequence of government transfers to these households. The similar reduction in the case of male-headed households is from 11.67 to 7.91. Thus, government transfers have far greater effect in reducing the incidence of poverty for children in female-headed households than that in male-headed households. As a result, the male-headed households have a greater percentage of children living in poverty than adults. But the reverse is the case for female-headed households.

Next the decomposition of poverty according to the age of the household head is considered. It is generally believed that there is a high incidence of poverty among households where the head is over 65 years old. This is indicated by Table 13.3. If government pensions did not exist, the percentage in these households who were poor would have been as much as 56.69. This percentage is reduced to only 6.02 as a consequence of the government age pension. Income tax, however, increases the percentage of poor to 7.05. Clearly, the government income-support programs play a major role in reducing poverty among the aged households.

It is interesting to note that the poverty among households in the 25–45 age group is higher than the national level. This is an unexpected finding because this age group had the highest average household income. The major reason for this result is that these households have to support, on average, a larger number of equivalent-adults. These households are in the time span of bearing and rearing children and have an average of 2.17 children per household, as against 1.07 in the entire population. The higher incidence of poverty in this age group implies a higher proportion of children living in poverty. It seems that the family allowance, designed to help families with children, is not large enough to have significant impact on poverty among children. It is worth pointing out that in real terms the family allowance paid per child has decreased substantially since 1976. It is likely that the incidence of poverty among children has become even worse.

The decomposition of poverty according to the employment status of the household head is presented in Table 13.4, which shows that the maxi-

Table 13.3. *Poverty measures, by age of household head: Australia 1975-6*

Poverty measures	15-25	25-45	45-65	over 65	All households
Adjusted original income					
% of persons in poverty	7.08	12.23	13.68	56.69	16.45
% of children in poverty	15.22	15.24	13.39	34.04	14.24
% of adults in poverty	5.05	9.40	13.77	57.47	17.63
% of households in poverty	5.73	10.37	18.74	63.69	22.08
Adjusted gross income					
% of persons in poverty	5.77	8.51	3.84	6.02	6.07
% of children in poverty	11.66	10.40	4.43	3.80	8.01
% of adults in poverty	4.31	6.73	3.65	6.09	5.03
% of households in poverty	4.34	6.92	5.41	9.47	6.66
Adjusted disposable income					
% of persons in poverty	5.96	9.30	4.32	7.05	6.92
% of children in poverty	12.13	11.25	5.35	6.88	9.23
% of adults in poverty	4.43	7.46	3.99	7.06	5.68
% of households in poverty	4.49	7.64	5.75	11.03	7.35

Table 13.4. *Poverty measures, by employment status of household head: Australia 1975-6*

Poverty measures	Employees & self-employed	Unemployed head	Retired head	Others
Adjusted original income				
% of persons in poverty	5.81	76.64	71.31	63.52
% of children in poverty	7.95	91.76	45.52	68.07
% of adults in poverty	4.49	64.75	72.55	61.96
% of households in poverty	4.72	72.86	75.68	72.38
Sen's poverty index	3.64	71.21	52.31	50.17
Adjusted gross income				
% of persons in poverty	3.98	63.56	4.62	19.73
% of children in poverty	5.71	79.21	4.50	23.36
% of adults in poverty	2.91	51.26	4.63	18.49
% of households in poverty	3.09	57.84	6.56	24.12
Sen's poverty index	3.45	61.20	5.25	16.01
Adjusted disposable income				
% of persons in poverty	5.28	64.91	5.59	21.61
% of children in poverty	7.15	80.66	7.28	27.58
% of adults in poverty	4.13	52.53	5.51	19.56
% of households in poverty	4.37	59.30	8.14	24.92
Sen's poverty index	3.91	63.10	6.01	17.10

Table 13.5. *Poverty measures, by marital status of household head: Australia 1975-6*

Poverty measures	Never married	Married	Widowed, divorced, separated
Adjusted original income			
% of persons in poverty	17.18	13.35	41.75
% of children in poverty	17.99	12.15	39.94
% of adults in poverty	17.12	14.07	42.34
% of households in poverty	20.80	15.39	50.98
Adjusted gross income			
% of persons in poverty	6.12	6.04	11.21
% of children in poverty	9.67	8.04	8.31
% of adults in poverty	5.86	4.55	12.16
% of households in poverty	6.40	5.01	16.71
Adjusted disposable income			
% of persons in poverty	7.09	6.61	11.26
% of children in poverty	16.72	9.61	8.46
% of adults in poverty	6.38	4.78	12.17
% of households in poverty	7.19	5.27	16.72

mum concentration of poverty occurs among the households whose heads are unemployed. About 65 percent of persons in these households are poor, the percentage of children in poverty being over 80 percent. This may be regarded as an extremely high level of poverty in a country as affluent as Australia. Government benefits reduce the poverty from 76.64 percent to 63.56 percent but then taxes increase it to 64.91 percent. These results demonstrate the ineffectiveness of the unemployment benefits to have a significant impact on the level of poverty. It must be stressed that unemployment benefits per recipient have not kept pace with inflation; as a result, their real value has been reduced drastically since 1976. This must have accentuated the already severe poverty among these households. An extremely high incidence of poverty among children suggests that the government should provide greater assistance to these households either by giving additional family allowance or by revising the structure of unemployment benefits so that households with children receive more benefits.

The breakdown of the population according to the marital status of the household head is presented in Table 13.5. It can be seen that married households have the least poverty and that poverty among widowed, di-

Table 13.6. *Poverty measures, by predominant source of household income: Australia 1975-6*

Poverty measures	Wages and salaries	Business income	Interest, dividends, and rent	Govt. benefits	Other income
Adjusted original income					
% of persons in poverty	1.71	16.08	29.93	99.34	40.76
% of children in poverty	2.64	19.37	47.12	98.58	60.97
% of adults in poverty	1.18	13.59	27.32	99.52	28.25
% of households in poverty	1.28	14.19	28.55	99.53	26.62
Adjusted gross income					
% of persons in poverty	.89	13.24	25.98	20.48	33.34
% of children in poverty	1.26	17.22	38.17	47.54	47.52
% of adults in poverty	.69	10.23	24.13	14.08	24.57
% of households in poverty	.76	10.92	26.12	15.36	22.54
Adjusted disposable income					
% of persons in poverty	1.91	17.59	27.23	23.17	44.81
% of children in poverty	3.00	20.71	40.42	47.54	53.86
% of adults in poverty	1.29	15.23	25.23	17.41	39.20
% of households in poverty	1.39	16.19	26.73	20.51	40.72

vorced, or separated individuals is significantly higher than that of the other two groups. Among married households, the percentage of children in poverty is lower than that of adults in poverty. This situation is reversed, however, when government cash transfers are added to the original income.

The decomposition of poverty according to the predominant source of household income is presented in Table 13.6, which shows that the poverty is lowest among households whose predominant source of income is wages and salaries. Only 1.91 percent of individuals in this group are poor as against 40.72 percent in households dependent principally on other income. The most surprising finding, however, is the poverty level of 17.59 percent among households whose principal income comes from business. This high poverty level may be attributed to the greater disparity of income among these households.

Table 13.7 focuses on the distribution of poverty according to the length of residence of the household head in Australia. It is indicated that the highest incidence of poverty is among migrants who have lived from 5 to 10 years in the country. One possible explanation of it may be that many of these migrants may be elderly but are not eligible for the age pension

Table 13.7. *Poverty measures, by period of residence of household head: Australia 1975-6*

Poverty measures	Australian born	Less than 2 years	2-5 years	5-10 years	10 years or more
Adjusted original income					
% of persons in poverty	17.18	.29	8.90	10.12	16.05
% of children in poverty	14.04	.33	11.07	13.46	14.83
% of adults in poverty	18.83	.27	7.61	7.71	16.69
% of households in poverty	23.34	.48	7.64	9.17	21.39
Adjusted gross income					
% of persons in poverty	6.18	.21	6.59	8.91	6.88
% of children in poverty	7.94	.35	6.43	12.71	9.71
% of adults in poverty	5.26	.15	6.68	6.19	5.39
% of households in poverty	7.09	.17	6.72	6.21	6.92
Adjusted disposable income					
% of persons in poverty	7.51	1.36	7.12	11.05	7.37
% of children in poverty	8.86	.11	7.16	16.14	10.71
% of adults in poverty	6.80	1.88	7.09	7.39	5.61
% of households in poverty	8.60	2.20	7.03	7.43	7.15

because of a minimum requirement of 10 years' residence. Those who have lived in Australia for less than 2 years have the lowest incidence of poverty; only 1.36 percent individuals living in poverty. This finding has an important implication for immigration policy.

The distribution of poverty according to the country of birth of household head is presented in Table 13.8. The households with a head born in Asia have the highest incidence of poverty, the poverty among children being considerably higher than that among adults. One explanation of it is the high incidence of unemployment among these households. The incidence of poverty is least among households whose head is born in countries other than those listed in the table. No explanation can be offered for this phenomenon due to nonavailability of further information. Households whose head is born in the United Kingdom, Ireland, or America also have very low levels of poverty. It is interesting to note that poverty among households with head born in Australia is higher than that at the national level.

The distribution of poverty according to region is presented in Table 13.9. It can be seen that poverty among rural households is significantly higher than that of the other two groups. More than 19 percent of individuals in such households live in poverty as against 6.92 percent at the national level.

Table 13.8. *Poverty measures, by country of birth of household head: Australia 1975–6*

Poverty measures	Australia	U.K. and Ireland	Italy, Greece, and Yugoslavia	Germany and Netherlands	Other Europe	Asia	Oceania, including New Zealand	America	Others
Adjusted original income									
% of persons in poverty	17.18	13.09	13.09	18.42	12.73	23.58	15.01	10.66	7.81
% of children in poverty	14.04	7.64	16.00	22.67	14.90	33.59	13.03	6.39	9.73
% of adults in poverty	18.83	15.64	11.05	15.60	11.61	17.47	15.91	12.83	6.78
% of households in poverty	23.34	19.97	12.85	17.20	15.57	21.94	20.69	16.58	9.67
Adjusted gross income									
% of persons in poverty	6.18	3.32	9.41	12.23	4.65	18.03	8.04	4.32	1.90
% of children in poverty	7.94	4.23	10.88	15.65	7.68	28.10	11.54	6.43	1.08
% of adults in poverty	5.26	2.89	8.37	9.96	3.09	11.88	6.46	3.25	2.34
% of households in poverty	7.09	3.48	9.40	10.27	4.24	12.72	6.63	3.19	4.22
Adjusted disposable income									
% of persons in poverty	7.51	3.98	11.81	12.28	5.37	22.30	8.21	4.32	1.90
% of children in poverty	8.86	5.98	14.73	15.74	10.01	36.08	13.09	6.43	1.08
% of adults in poverty	6.80	3.04	9.75	9.98	2.98	13.88	6.01	3.25	2.34
% of households in poverty	8.60	3.10	10.98	10.29	3.58	14.95	6.52	3.19	4.22

Table 13.9. *Poverty measures, by regions: Australia 1975-6*

Poverty measures	Metropolitan	Urban	Rural
Adjusted original income			
% of persons in poverty	13.68	19.14	31.39
% of children in poverty	12.26	13.90	30.98
% of adults in poverty	14.40	22.05	31.65
% of households in poverty	18.40	27.14	35.25
Adjusted gross income			
% of persons in poverty	4.64	6.10	18.80
% of children in poverty	6.58	7.43	22.83
% of adults in poverty	3.65	5.35	16.29
% of households in poverty	5.13	7.39	18.25
Adjusted disposable income			
% of persons in poverty	5.79	8.21	19.39
% of children in poverty	8.40	7.77	23.89
% of adults in poverty	4.45	8.46	16.59
% of households in poverty	5.95	10.27	18.66

Table 13.10. *Percentage of poor, by states and territories: Australia 1975-6[a]*

States or territories	Adjusted original income	Adjusted gross income	Adjusted disposable income
N.S.W.	17.82	7.75	8.78
	(23.53)	(7.94)	(8.44)
Victoria	15.42	5.66	7.28
	(20.67)	(6.40)	(8.15)
Queensland	19.60	8.93	9.93
	(24.97)	(9.47)	(10.73)
South Australia	13.23	2.83	3.91
	(20.79)	(2.73)	(5.21)
Western Australia	13.06	6.16	6.83
	(18.94)	(6.60)	(7.20)
Tasmania	18.91	6.52	8.92
	(23.04)	(4.65)	(6.16)
Northern Territory	4.30	2.88	5.82
	(3.98)	(2.54)	(4.18)
A.C.T.	4.21	1.96	3.29
	(5.87)	(2.38)	(3.27)

[a] Figures in parentheses give the percentage of households in poverty.

Table 13.11. *Percentage of poor, by capital cities of Australia: 1975-6*[a]

Capital cities	Adjusted original income	Adjusted gross income	Adjusted disposable income
Sydney	14.16	6.43	7.50
	(18.04)	(6.53)	(7.03)
Melbourne	14.12	5.20	6.38
	(19.24)	(5.89)	(7.14)
Brisbane	14.53	5.56	6.62
	(19.20)	(5.48)	(6.06)
Adelaide	10.73	2.45	2.45
	(18.01)	(3.52)	(3.55)
Perth	11.72	4.55	5.20
	(17.51)	(4.58)	(5.04)
Hobart	13.57	3.23	3.47
	(17.56)	(2.50)	(3.10)
Darwin	4.56	3.19	5.16
	(4.82)	(3.01)	(4.11)
Canberra	4.21	1.96	3.29
	(5.87)	(2.38)	(3.27)

[a] Figures in parentheses give the percentage of households in poverty.

It must be stressed that we may have overestimated the degree of poverty in the rural areas because of differences in consumer price levels in the rural, urban, and metropolitan areas. Some evidence exists to the effect that average income levels and average price levels are positively correlated (Taussig 1973: 22). We do not have the necessary information to test this hypothesis here. If this hypothesis is valid, regional as well as national inequalities of income and welfare reported in the previous chapters will overstate the inequality of real incomes.

The results given in Table 13.10 indicate that Queensland has the highest incidence of poverty, just under 10 percent of people living in poverty. In contrast, the Australian Capital Territory has the lowest poverty, with only 3.29 percent of people living in poverty. South Australia also has a low level of poverty (3.91 percent) despite the fact that its mean income is not high compared with other states. After Queensland, Tasmania, New South Wales, and Victoria are the other three states where the poverty is higher than the national level.

Table 13.11 presents the distribution of poverty according to the capital cities. It indicates that poverty in the three major capital cities, viz.,

Table 13.12. *Percentage of poor, by household size and composition: Australia 1975-6*

Household composition groups	Original income	Gross income	Disposable income
1 adult	53.61	19.54	20.01
2 adults	27.34	3.08	3.83
3 or more adults	5.53	1.29	2.09
1 adult, 1 child	35.15	1.35	1.35
1 adult, 2 children	34.50	9.23	13.72
1 adult, 3 or more children	61.98	25.35	25.54
2 adults, 1 child	5.84	4.09	4.09
2 adults, 2 children	8.02	6.03	7.59
2 adults, 3 children	12.16	11.55	11.79
2 adults, 4 children	15.30	10.17	14.75
2 adults, 5 children	31.61	28.64	34.33
2 adults, 6 or more children	38.92	20.19	20.19
3 or more adults, 1 child	4.01	1.59	1.64
3 or more adults, 2 children	6.30	2.08	2.11
3 or more adults, 3 or more children	12.47	1.58	2.28

Sydney, Melbourne, and Brisbane, is considerably higher than that in the remaining capital cities. Sydney has the highest percentage of poor, whereas Melbourne has the highest percentage of households in poverty. Poverty, measured by percentage of poor, is lowest in Adelaide, but Canberra has the lowest percentage of households falling below the poverty line.

Table 13.12 concerns the decomposition of total poverty according to household size and composition. It was noted earlier that government income-support policies brought the maximum reduction of income inequality to households with one adult and three or more children. Despite the sizable income redistribution, the results in the table indicate that these households suffer from severe poverty. If the government income-support programs did not exist, the percentage of persons living in poverty would have been 61.98 but this percentage is reduced to 25.54 as a consequence of government transfers.

Poverty among households with two adults is relatively low but it increases steadily as children are added. The most severe poverty is among households with 2 adults and 5 children. The least poverty is observed among households with three or more adults. Again, these observations cast doubt on the effectiveness of the family allowance to reduce poverty among households with large numbers of children.

13.7   Summary of policy conclusions

This chapter has been concerned with the measurement of poverty, the main objective being the investigation of the effectiveness of government income-support programs on the overall level of poverty. Although many of the policy conclusions emerging from this chapter will be valid for many other developed countries, it is outside the scope of this study to provide comparisons. However, we summarize below some of the important conclusions that may have bearing on policies in other countries.

1. The degree of poverty was found to be sensitive to the equivalent-income scales used. The percentage of poor based on adjusted disposable income varied from the minimum of 6.22 to the maximum of 9.28.

2. Poverty is substantially reduced when government benefits are added to the original income. Without these benefits an additional 8 to 9 percent of population would be below the poverty line. But the reduction in the incidence of poverty for adults is far greater than that for children. It seems that the family allowance, designed to help families with children, does not have significant impact on poverty among children.

3. The incidence of poverty for individuals is much less than that for households. This reflects a higher incidence of poverty among smaller households (particularly one-person households). These differences in poverty levels are reduced, however, as a result of government cash transfers (which have considerably greater impact in reducing the incidence of poverty for households than for individuals).

4. All poverty indicators show increase in poverty as a result of personal income taxation. This result is in complete contrast to the norm set by the Taxation Review Committee that the people in poverty should be relieved of taxation.

5. The government income-support programs play a major role in reducing poverty among the aged households. The percentage of poor living in these households is reduced from 56.69 to only 6.02 as a consequence of the government age pensions. Income tax, however, increases the percentage of poor to 7.05.

6. The most severe poverty was observed among households whose head was unemployed. About 65 percent of persons in these households are poor, the percentage of children in poverty being over 80 percent. This is an extremely high level of poverty in a country as affluent as Australia. Government benefits reduce the

poverty in this group from 76.64 percent to 63.56 prcent but the personal income tax increases it to 64.91 percent. These results demonstrate the ineffectiveness of unemployment benefits to have a significant impact on the level of poverty.

7.   Households with one adult and two or more children and with two adults and five or more children are characterized by low incomes.

8.   The households with head born in Asia have the highest incidence of poverty, poverty among children being considerably higher than that among adults. One reason for this is the high incidence of unemployment among these households.

Data sources and their accuracy

Australia is one of the small number of countries where relatively few surveys have been undertaken to collect information on income and expenditure patterns of households. This poor data base is perhaps the major reason for our inadequate knowledge and understanding of poverty and income inequality in this country.

Although the first official survey, entitled "Inquiry into the Cost of Living in Australia," was undertaken by the then Commonwealth Bureau of Census and Statistics (now the Australian Bureau of Statistics) as early as 1910–11, it was immediately abandoned because of the poor response rate from the households. In 1913, the bureau conducted a further expenditure inquiry which also suffered from a poor response rate.

After these limited attempts in 1910–11 and 1913, no major survey was carried out in Australia for more than 50 years. The Survey of Consumer Finances and Expenditure 1966–8 was a nationwide survey undertaken by the joint efforts of two universities in conjunction with Computer Dynamics, Ltd. (formerly, The Survey Research Centre Pty. Ltd.).[1] A detailed analysis of distributions of income and wealth in Australia based on this survey was carried out by Podder (1972), Podder and Kakwani (1976), and more recently by Kakwani (1980a). This survey also formed the basis of a redistribution study undertaken by Podder and Kakwani (1975a) commissioned by the Australian Review Committee, and a poverty report prepared by Podder (1978) on the behalf of the Australian Government Commission of Inquiry into Poverty. These studies provided a base for an extensive debate on the issues of income distribution and poverty in Australia, and generated considerable demand for more up-to-date income and expenditure surveys.

In view of this demand, the Australian Bureau of Statistics conducted a feasibility study to assess, by pilot testing, whether or not a full-scale survey could be conducted in Australia, and to calculate estimates of the cost and accuracy of such a survey. After the completion of the 1969–70 feasibility study, it was not until 1973 that the bureau gained approval from the Treasurer for a full-scale survey of approximately 10,000 responding households over the year 1974–5, to be followed in 1975–6 by a smaller survey of approximately 6,500 responding households.

The Household Expenditure Surveys 1974–5 and 1975–6 were completed as planned, but unfortunately researchers working outside the bureau could not obtain access to the data because of confidentiality reasons. The bureau published some data in group form, but this is only of limited use. The data in these publications are grouped in only six income classes, which involves a considerable loss of information and may even lead to wrong policy conclusions. Moreover, the published data do not provide all the tables necessary for a thorough study of welfare issues. The present study could only be undertaken after the bureau provided the necessary data on tapes, giving detailed breakdowns of households according to various socioeconomic and demographic characteristics.[2]

Although the present study is mainly based on the Household Expenditure Survey 1975–6, extensive comparisons will be made with earlier income-distribution studies based on the Survey of Consumer Finances and Expenditures 1966–8 and Income Surveys conducted by the Australian Bureau of Statistics during the periods 1968–9, 1973–4, and 1978–9. Only the main features of these surveys will be described here; for further details reference should be made to the original sources.

A.1   The Survey of Consumer Finances and Expenditures, 1966–8

The Survey of Consumer Finances and Expenditure was the first nationwide survey of its kind to be carried out in Australia. The survey was conducted in two stages. In the first stage, expenditures on different commodities and total household income along with the sociodemographic characteristics of the households were covered. Most of the interviewing for this stage took place between May 1967 and December 1968 and a total of 5,459 usable responses was obtained.

At the second stage of the investigation the interviewers returned to the households involved in the first stage in order to obtain finance data, but only obtained data from about 50 percent of the initial respondents. In all, 2,757 usable questionnaires were obtained.

The actual sample design was not made available to any researcher. The only information on it is the following paragraph, which appears in an unpublished write-up issued by the Macquarie University Data Archive, Ltd.:

The Sample was drawn according to a design by W. E. Deming involving a number of replications but preserving an equal probability of selection for each household. The number of households approached in each area was proportional to the population, except that a certain amount of over-sampling was carried out in nonmetropolitan areas.

Since this information on the sample design is clearly vague and insufficient, it is not possible to assess the reliability of the data. In an effort

Table A.1. *Standard-error percentages for the survey of Consumer Finances and Expenditures: 1966–1968*

Variable name	Mean	Standard error	Standard-error percentage
Household size	3.52	.03	.9
Original income	$3896.00	64.00	1.6
Gross income	$4183.00	62.00	1.5
Disposable income	$3728.00	48.00	1.3
Income tax	$458.00	17.00	3.7
Cash benefits	$287.00	8.00	2.8
Equity in superannuation	$1358.00	98.00	7.2
Total debts	$2196.00	64.00	2.9
Value of assets	$13822.00	292.00	2.1
Total net worth	$11663.00	283.00	2.4

Source: N. Podder, *The Economic Circumstances of the Poor*, Commission of Inquiry into Poverty, Australian Government Publishing Service, Canberra 1978.

to provide a partial assessment of the data, Podder (1978) computed the standard errors of some variables from the finances data on the assumption that the sample is completely random. These estimates of standard errors are presented in Table A.1.

The third column in the table gives the standard error percentage which has been computed by dividing the standard errors given in Column 2 by the means in Column 1. Although these errors when compared with those given by the Australian Bureau of Statistics for the Household Expenditure Surveys 1974–5 and 1975–6 appear to be quite reasonable, still we cannot conclude that the sample is truly representative of the population. The reason is that these errors may have been underestimated because of the possible high nonresponse rate at both stages of survey. The high nonresponse rate has the effect of making the sample nonrandom, which may have reduced the variability of some variables and consequently underestimated the standard errors.

Since the number of households included at the first stage of the survey is not known, the response rate cannot be determined. However, the low response rate of only 50 percent at the second stage suggests that the nonresponse rate at the first stage may have been high.

A comparison of samples at two stages of survey has been made by Podder and Kakwani (1976). A statistical test carried out by them suggested that the first age group (under 30) is underrepresented at the second stage of the survey. But the same test carried out on household size did not show significant difference between the two samples. It appears that these tests do not provide any conclusive evidence for the bias due to nonresponse in the finance sample. However, the nonresponse error at the first stage can introduce bias at both stages of the survey. Unfortunately, the extent of this bias cannot be determined.

A.2   Income surveys, 1968–9, 1973–4, and 1978–9

In order to meet the growing demand for income distribution statistics, the Australian Bureau of Statistics conducted three income surveys during the periods 1968–9, 1973–4, and 1978–9.[3] The first survey began in November 1969 when questions on income for the year 1968–9 were asked in respect of each person aged 15 years or over in a sample of one-half of the dwellings included in the quarterly population survey in that month. The sample roughly corresponds to one-half of 1 percent of the Australian population.

The definition of income in the surveys is gross income before taxation and other deductions from all sources. The main categories of income are wages and salaries; own business, farm, profession, etc. (net income); share of net income in partnership; government social security and welfare benefits; superannuation payments, interest, dividend, and rent (excluding imputed rent); and other sources (e.g., trust or will, maintenance or alimony). Some lump sum payments, employer contribution to superannuation, and reimbursements for expenses are not included as income.

The income recipient used is either individual (any person over 15 in receipt of an income) or the family. The family concept used is defined as two or more persons living together in a household related by marriage, blood, or adoption except where that person is either married or accompanied by his or her own children. The distribution of income for one-person families was not provided for the 1968–9 survey and as a consequence overall distribution of family incomes could not be derived. This information was made available, however, for the subsequent surveys.

It has been pointed out by the bureau that income information from these surveys (particularly from the first two) may not be totally reliable. Although respondents were asked to refer to records wherever possible, in fact answers were based on memory in about half of all cases, and frequently on the memory of one person, generally the housewife. (See Ingles 1981.) This situation was corrected, however, in the 1978–9 survey by ensuring that interviews were conducted with each adult member of the selected dwellings and that information about all income sources was thoroughly checked. Hence, information from this survey must be considerably more accurate than that from the previous two.

The data from these surveys have been published for both individuals and families in the form of closed income intervals with an open terminal income group. This presentation not only involves a considerable loss of information but also is the source of technical difficulties in the calculation of welfare measures. Hence, these surveys cannot be used for a detailed analysis of distribution income and welfare unless the bureau provides considerably more disaggregated data to the researchers.

A.3   Household Expenditure Survey, 1975–6

The Household Expenditure Survey (HES) 1974–5 was confined to the six state capital cities and Canberra. But the 1975–6 survey was extended to include other urban areas, including Darwin, and also rural areas. This is the only survey so far available that covers the whole of Australia except remote and sparsely settled areas.

The 1975–6 survey was designed to obtain details of expenditures, income, and a wide range of demographic characteristics of private households. But some categories of households, like foreign diplomats and their staff, foreign servicemen stationed in Australia and their families, visitors staying with the household for less than six weeks after the initial interview, and persons from overseas countries, were excluded from the survey. However, children under 15 years of age who were away at boarding school or away for less than six weeks were included as members of a household.

Out of 9,600 dwellings initially selected, only 8,017 households living in them were eligible for inclusion in the survey. Of these 8,017 households, 73.2 percent of the households fully cooperated, giving the effective sample size of 5,869 households. The response rate of 73.2 percent was considered to be satisfactory considering the nature of the survey.

Expansion factors ("weights") were inserted in respondent household records to enable the data provided by these households to be expanded to obtain estimates for the defined population. The weight given to each respondent household was determined by its probability of selection within a stratum adjusted to take account of nonresponding households. So, the total of 12.843 million persons living in 4.159 million households was covered by the survey.

The general methodology of the 1975–6 survey was identical to that of 1974–5, with only minor changes to diaries and interview questionnaires.[4] Therefore there is no need to give further details of this survey, except a comparison of standard-error percentage of the two surveys. The numerical results are presented in Table A.2.

The standard error percentages for the 1974–5 survey were computed on the basis of a sample size of 5,800 households and are, therefore, comparable with that of 1975–6 figures which are based on 5,869 households. From this comparison, it is not possible to conclude if one survey is superior to the other on the basis of standard error percentage.

Table A.2. *Standard-error percentages for total household income and income sources for the 1974-5 and 1975-6 Household Expenditure Surveys*

Source of income	1974-5 survey	1975-6 survey
Wages and salaries	1.1	1.3
Self-employment	5.5	6.2
Government benefits	4.6	3.4
Interest, rent, and dividends	5.5	4.2
Other regular income	4.6	4.2
Total	1.2	1.1

Source: The 1974-5 survey figures were computed from the graph given on page 40 of Bulletin 3, "Standard Errors" of the Household Expenditure Survey 1974-1975. The 1975-6 survey figures were taken from Table 1.19 of Bulletin 1, "Summary of Results" of the Household Expenditure Survey 1975-6.

Table A.3. *The standard-error percentages for the total household income and income sources for the United Kingdom household survey, 1971*

Sources of income	Average weekly household income	Standard error (%)	Households recording income
Wages and salaries	28.43	1.4	5352
Self-employment	2.80	5.9	1331
Investment	1.40	6.5	3729
Annuities and pensions (other than Social Security benefits)	.83	6.2	955
Social Security benefits	3.42	1.7	4344
Subletting and imputed income from owner/rent-free occupancy	1.19	2.8	3598
Other sources	.41	6.9	1137
Total	38.48	1.1	7238

The standard error percentage of the total household income and sources of income for the United Kingdom survey in 1971 are presented in Table A.3. This table provides some broad comparisons of the errors in the Australian surveys with those of the United Kingdom. The figures suggest that the sampling errors are of similar magnitude in the two countries.

Table A.4. *Some population characteristics according to the 1976 census and the Household Expenditure Survey, 1975–1976*

	HES 1975–6	Census 1976
Average size of the household	3.09	3.04
Sex ratio (males per 100 females)	99.35	100.02
Broad age distribution of population		
under 2 years	3.9	3.3
2 years and under 5 years	6.1	5.5
5 years and under 18 years	24.6	24.0
18 years and under 65 years	57.3	58.3
65 years and over	8.1	8.9
Nature of housing occupancy		
Owner occupied	33.14	34.31
In the process of purchase/renting	36.84	38.23
Renting	30.02	27.46
All households	100.00	100.00

The quality of the survey data can further be assessed by comparing the survey data with those of census of population. Such a comparison is possible here because the Census of Population and Housing was conducted in 1976 enumerating every person in Australia including those on vessels in or between Australian ports, on board long-distance trains, buses, or aircraft, and every dwelling, whether occupied or unoccupied. The adjustment for underenumeration to the census figures "as recorded" is estimated to be 2.71 percent for Australia as a whole.[5]

Table A.4 provides the basic information to compare the Household Expenditure Survey 1975–6 with those of 1976 Census of Population and Housing. The data pertain to only three demographic characteristics and the nature of housing occupancy. Although the census provides a variety of characteristics, counts of the population classified by sex, the information was not directly comparable with that obtained from the Household Expenditure Survey.

The average size of household according to the Household Expenditure Survey was about the same as reported by the 1976 census. However, instead of a 0.02 percent excess of males indicated by the census, the HES shows a deficit of males of the order of 0.65 percent. This difference with respect to the sex composition could be due to the fact that the population coverage by households in the Household Expenditure Survey was marginally higher for females than for males.

Comparing the age distribution of population, we note that the two sources give somewhat different results. These differences mainly occur in the age groups under 2 years and 65 years and over. The available information is insufficient to provide definitive explanation for such deviations. Similarly, some deviations are also evident with respect to the nature of housing occupancy. But these deviations are not sufficiently significant to cast doubt on the reliability of the Household Expenditure Survey data.

A.4   Conclusions

The sample surveys are the major source of information to analyze the distribution of income and welfare. The measurement of socioeconomic phenomena, which these surveys provide, can never be exact. In this appendix, an attempt has been made to assess the quality of the Household Expenditure Survey used in the present study by comparing it with other data sources. These comparisons do not cast serious doubts on the reliability of the survey.

In conclusion it must be pointed out that although the Household Expenditure Survey 1975–6 provides the most detailed information on expenditures, income, and a wide range of demographic characteristics of private households, it contains no information whatsoever on assets, debt, and net worth. This is a major drawback of this survey because such information is extremely useful in gaining insights into aspects of poverty and inequality in Australia.

Notes

Chapter 1. Introduction

1. A detailed discussion of this survey and its limitations is provided in the appendix.
2. For a more detailed comparison of the Australian tax structure with those of other OECD countries, see Mathews 1980: 96.
3. The government introduced tax indexation in 1976–7, but it did not continue with this policy for long. In fact, from 1977–8 onwards, only half-indexation was allowed. In April 1981, the government completedly abandoned tax indexation as of July 1, 1982.
4. See Horn (1981), who points out that a rise in exemption limits may partly counteract this effect.
5. The failure of the government to adjust family allowances with inflation may have significantly reduced the advantage for low-income earners in the later years.
6. Imputed rents were taxed from 1915 until 1923, when assessable income included 5 percent of the capital value of a residence (Cass 1982).
7. See Mathews (1980) and Cass (1982), who conclude that since 1976 the effective tax burden has shifted away from those who derive substantial income from property or business toward wage and salary earners.
8. The author is not aware of any empirical evidence in Australia for the argument that higher taxes reduce work effort.
9. Groenewegen (1984) points to increases in avoidance and evasion as a major change perceived in Australian taxation between the 1960s and 1980s. Also see Swan (1983), who advocates a proportional income-tax system.
10. It should be pointed out, however, that the ability of a country like Australia to place an effective tax on capital may be quite limited. Australia is a small economy subject to considerable international capital mobility. Higher taxes on capital may simply lead to an outward movement of capital until after-tax rates of return in Australia rise again to the world level. In other words, capital may succeed in escaping the burden of the tax completely.
11. For a detailed discussion of the Australian Social Security System see Saunders (1982).

Chapter 2. Income-recipient units and their differing needs

1. Edwards (1981) has conducted a survey of 50 married couples in Queanbeyan, N.S.W. (Australia) to study the financial arrangements within families, but her findings do not throw any light on the issue raised here.

267

2. Becker (1974a) makes this assumption to show that intrahousehold redistribution will not affect individual or aggregate welfare.
3. The utilitarian welfare function of the family is defined as the sum of the utilities of individual family members.
4. Sen (1973a) makes this point in connection with the social welfare function.
5. The household concept adopted here is the same as the definition of the *1980 World Population Census Program* given in the UN "Draft Principles and Recommendations for Population and Housing Census." E/CN 3/515/add 2, 1978 para. 73-4.
6. A discussion of the utility basis of the Prais-Houthakker model is given in Muellbauer (1980).
7. Cramer (1969) provides a clear exposition of the identification problem in the Prais-Houthakker model.
8. McClements (1977, 1978) attempts to overcome the identification problem by using the commodity scales for food, derived from nutritional requirements, and estimates the remaining commodity scales and the general scale subject to this prior restriction. For a critical evaluation of this approach see Muellbauer (1978).
9. Note that here we are specifying a household preference function as distinct from individual preference functions. For a discussion of this issue see Samuelson (1956), Lancaster (1975), and Becker (1974b). An interesting discussion of welfare comparisons and equivalence scale is given in Pollak and Wales (1979).
10. Brown (1954) proposed to estimate equivalent-income scales using log-linear Engel curves, which turns out to be exactly consistent with the Barten form of the log-linear demand function.
11. The data from the Survey of Consumer Finances and Expenditures 1966-8 were available at that time but the commission did not make an attempt to estimate the equivalent-income scale.
12. Statistics Canada uses a procedure in the construction of its poverty lines where an equivalence scale is constructed by seeing at what income level the expenditure share on food, shelter, and clothing combined drops below a specific level. This procedure requires that the expenditure share on these items must be a monotonically increasing function of total expenditure in each of the household composition group. Our experience with household expenditure surveys indicates that this may not be valid. Moreover, there is so much quality variation in shelter and clothing that one may get completely nonsensical results using this procedure.

Chapter 3. Income concept in the analysis of income distribution

1. A detailed income questionnaire is given in Appendix 6 of Household Expenditure Survey 1974-5, Bulletin 1, issued by the Australian Bureau of Statistics, Canberra.
2. Thurow (1975) has suggested that although wives' earnings were once a factor leading to an equalization of family incomes, they are now "becoming a source of family inequality."

3. *Family Expenditure Survey* 1971, Department of Employment, Her Majesty's Stationery Office, London 1972, page 131.
4. Podder's conclusion that the inclusion of imputed rent in income has an equalizing effect on income distribution may still be valid, the reason being that all houses are not alike and, therefore, their imputed rents may vary widely in various income ranges. In order to refute or support this conclusion conclusively, we require the information on imputed rents which is not available in either the 1974–5 or the 1975–6 survey.
5. Podder and Kakwani (1976) have analyzed the distribution of wealth in Australia using this data base. Two recent survey articles written on this subject are those by Nevile and Warren (1984) and Piggott (1984).
6. Among the important contributions in the field are those of Lampman (1973), Friedman (1957), Nordhaus (1973), Kuznets (1974), Thurow (1975), Atkinson (1974b), and Taussig (1976).
7. Lillard (1977) estimates inequality in lifetime income using the longitudinal data on earnings but such data are not available in Australia.
8. A detailed discussion of the Gini index is provided in the next chapter.

Chapter 4. On the measurement of income inequality

1. For an illuminating discussion of relative inequality measures in terms of social welfare see Blackorby and Donaldson (1978).
2. Runciman (1966) defined relative deprivation as "we can roughly say that a person is relatively deprived of X when (i) he does not have X; (ii) he sees some other person or persons, which may include himself at some previous or expected time, as having X (whether or not this is or will be in fact the case); (iii) he wants X; and (iv) he sees it as feasible that he should have X." Yitzhaki (1979, 1982) has in fact provided an interpretation of the Gini index that is consistent with this theory.
3. The rank-order weighting has been widely used in voting theory (see, for instance, Borda 1781; Black 1958; Fine and Fine 1974; Fishburn 1975; Gardenfors 1973; and Hansson 1973).
4. Yitzhaki (1980) has demonstrated that the generalized Gini index has the basic properties of Atkinson's (1970) index while its main advantage over the latter is that it can be expressed as a function of the Lorenz curve.
5. See Kakwani (1980a), who demonstrated that Schutz and Kuznets' measures are identical to the relative mean deviation.
6. See Fishlow (1972) for application of these measures to U.S. data.
7. Cowell and Kuga (1981) introduce a further axiom of sensitivity which leads to Theil's measure I_1 alone.
8. Mookherjee and Shorrocks (1982) have analyzed the trend in U.K. income inequality using these decomposition equations.
9. Sen (1973a) does not consider this criticism to be a serious one since the ordering of Dalton's measure would not be affected by taking positive linear transformations. He argues that what is really significant with these measures is the ordering property.
10. The measure of relative risk aversion is defined as

$$R = -\frac{u''(x)x}{u'(x)}$$

which can be interpreted as equal to minus times the elasticity of the marginal utility $u'(x)$ with respect to x. For further details see Arrow (1965).

Chapter 5. Measures of redistribution and equity

1. This chapter is based on Kakwani (1984c).
2. For an illuminating discussion of the principle of horizontal equity and its relationship with utilitarianism, see Stiglitz (1982).
3. For a discussion of difficulties associated with the measurement of horizontal equity, see King (1983).
4. Jakobsson (1976) also prefers this measure of progressivity but gives no further justification.
5. Government cash transfers may be regarded as the negative tax, therefore the measure of progressivity of a government cash benefit will be given by $G-C$ where C is the concentration index of the government cash benefit under consideration.
6. The graph of $C(p)$ and $L(p)$ is called the relative concentration curve of $T(x)$ with respect to x. For further details see Kakwani (1977b, 1980a).
7. It seems reasonable to choose the simplest functional form in the absence of a convincing case for any alternative forms.
8. Recently King (1983) has developed a normative index of horizontal inequality by defining a social welfare function that is sensitive to changes in ranking of individuals in the society. But his index cannot be empirically estimated unless some strong assumptions are made about the form of the social welfare function.
9. It is interesting to note that Plotnick (1981) has also suggested an index of horizontal equity that is similar to H but he does not discuss its relationship with the measures of progressivity and income redistribution. This relationship, equation (5.9), is important because it provides the quantitative framework to analyze the contribution of horizontal and vetical equity to the total redistributive effect of taxes.
10. Note that the indices of horizontal and vertical equity for government cash benefits are the same as above except that P in this case is measured by $G-C$ instead of $C-G$ as was the case for taxes.

Chapter 6. Distribution of income in Australia

1. The inconsistency between the national accounts and household survey data on the importance of different income components is very significant. The available information is insufficient to provide a definitive explanation for such deviations. One reason may be due to the differences in definitions of various income components between the two data sources. Secondly, income estimates of national accounts are based on income-tax statistics, which are

notoriously unreliable. Third, household survey data may itself be subject to errors, particularly "business income" and "other income," which are likely to contain larger error terms than other income components.

2. Examining this methodology in more general terms, Shorrocks (1982a) has proposed a number of basic principles of decomposition that provide considerable insight into this problem.

3. Note that in Chapter 5 we defined the concentration curve for taxes paid. The concentration curve for a factor income is similarly constructed by arranging households accoding to the total household income. The concentration index for a factor income is then given by one minus twice the area under the concentration curve for that factor income.

4. For a detailed discussion of various income components see Chapter 3.

5. See, for instance, Kuznets (1976) and Visaria (1979). Danziger and Taussig (1979), using the U.S. data, found that the distribution of households by per capita household income was more equal in 1976 but more unequal in 1967 than that by household income.

6. It may be recalled that I_2 is equal to the square of the coefficient of variation – a measure criticized by Sen (1973a) on the grounds that it is equally sensitive to transfers at all levels of income.

Chapter 7. Tax rates and government benefit rates by income ranges

1. For an excellent survey of the literature, see Mieszkowski (1969).

2. Many leading economists, such as Hahn (1981) and Blaug (1980), have argued that the practical value of general equilibrium analysis is virtually zero (see Groenewegen 1983).

3. See Barlow (1974), who computed the relative tax burden using the U.S. data.

Chapter 9. Redistribution of income within and between socioeconomic and demographic groups

1. Throughout this chapter, the inequality is measured with respect to the distribution of individuals (not of households) by adjusted or per equivalent-adult income, which is derived by giving weights of unity to the first adult, .7 to the second and subsequent adults, and .4 to each child in the household.

2. The between-group Gini index was computed by assuming that the inequality of income within each household group is zero.

3. Note that this hypothesis is different from the one discussed in Chapter 6, which suggests a positive association between the size of household and total income per household.

Chapter 10. Progressivity of sales tax on individual expenditure items

1. It is not being suggested here that indirect taxes are necessarily inflationary. The relationship between the two is rather complex and has, as yet, not been empirically investigated in Australia.

2. Apart from the extension of the base, the 1981-2 budget also raised some existing rates and removed a number of anomalies in existing sales tax legislation.
3. This result follows immediately from the fact that the concentration curve of a function is independent of the mean value of the function. For further details see Theorem 8.3 of Kakwani (1980a).
4. Note that this condition is equivalent to the demand theory restriction that the weighted sum of income elasticities is equal to 1.
5. The Industries Assistance Commission (1980), however, has estimated the implicit tax effects of tariffs and quantity restrictions on 16 household expenditure items. This study is restricted also to allocating only the total tax components to household income classes. It would have been more useful if the tax component of each of the 16 expenditure items had been allocated to income classes.
6. Indirect taxes can be made progressive, however, by taxing only a few expenditure items for which the progressivity index is positive. But in that case the tax base will be so small that not enough revenue will be collected even with high tax rates.
7. A tax of 10 percent has been levied on wine in the recent 1984-5 federal budget.
8. Note that the excise duty collected on crude oil used in industry is not included in this item.

Chapter 11. Distribution of welfare in Australia

1. For a general discussion of equity and efficiency aspects of the welfare function see Graaff (1977).
2. Moreover, this approach poses a number of problems, which are discussed by several economists in Krelle and Shorrocks (1982).
3. For proof, see Lemma 5.9 on page 78 of Kakwani (1980a).
4. It is interesting to note that Pyatt's (1980) formulation of individual welfare based on the feeling of guilt (when aggregated over the whole population) also leads to Sen's social welfare measure.
5. The task of computing E_{12} and E_{21} from the grouped data is extremely difficult. But equations (11.20) and (11.21) express these quantities in terms of the Gini indices, which can be computed fairly acccurately from the grouped observations (Gastwirth 1972).
6. Note that this measure is sensitive to the formulation of the individual welfare. Pyatt's (1980) formulation in terms of guilt feelings gives different values of the measure.

Chapter 12. Optimal negative income taxation, when individuals feel envious

1. Note that we have not attempted to review here the entire optimal-taxation literature because of space limitation. Other important studies not mentioned above are those of Atkinson and Stiglitz (1972); Diamond and Mirrlees (1971); Heady and Mitra (1980); Stern (1976); Sandmo (1976); and Tuomala (1984).
2. There is considerable literature in economics that supports the view that individual utilities are interdependent; see for instance Layard (1980), Duesenberry (1949), Runciman (1966), Sen (1966), Schall (1972), and Brennan (1973).

Chapter 13. The impact of taxes and cash benefits on poverty

1. Harrington (1962) was perhaps the first to emphasize the poverty issue in the United States. For other outstanding contributions on the subject of poverty in advanced countries, since 1962, see Atkinson (1969); Ferman, Kornbluh, and Haber (1965); Fishman (1966); Townsend (1954, 1962, 1965); Tobin (1965); and Budd (1967). There is also a considerable amount of excellent work done on poverty in India for which Bardhan and Srinivasan (1974) is the best reference. An international comparison of poverty is provided by Kakwani (1980a).

2. For a number of years, the World Bank has been particularly interested in financing projects in the developing countries leading to a reduction in poverty.

3. Van Praag, Hagenaars, and Van Weeren (1980) define poverty in terms of welfare. A person is called poor if his or her welfare or utility level falls below a certain level. So they derive a poverty line from the relation between welfare and income.

4. These problems have been discussed at length by Townsend (1954, 1962). For a brief but illuminating discussion, see Sen (1979).

5. The term relative deprivation was coined by Stouffer (1949) and subsequently developed by Merton (1957) and Runciman (1966). This term is used here in a narrower sense meaning a level of income sufficiently low to be regarded as creating hardship in terms of society's current living standards.

6. For an excellent discussion of *relative* versus *absolute* poverty, see Sen (1983).

7. Fuschs (1969) argues that the poverty standard should be linked to the median income. Drewnowski (1977) suggests the poverty line be equal to the mean income of the society. Under this definition, the poor are those who gain when income becomes more evenly distributed, and the nonpoor are those who lose.

8. This approach to measuring poverty has been suggested by Kakwani (1984a).

9. Note that this procedure of assigning probabilities to the alternative poverty line takes into account the intensity of preferences of individuals (i.e., it introduces an element of cardinality). If an individual feels very strongly for a poverty line, then she will choose the most preferred line with probability unity and the probability assigned to the remaining poverty lines will then be zero.

10. These are basically Intriligator's axioms slightly modified for the poverty line.

11. In addition to Axioms 13.1, 13.2, and 13.3, the average rule satisfies a number of other important conditions which are discussed by Intriligator (1973). Note that this collective-choice rule violates one of Arrow's (1963) conditions, the condition of "independence of irrelevant alternatives." This is because each pairwise comparison is affected by the probabilities assigned to the remaining poverty lines.

12. The determination of the poverty line on the basis of value judgments of all the members of the society or its representatives is not new. Goedhart et al. (1977) proposed an approach in which family heads are asked what they consider a minimum income level for their own family. For each family size they estimated an income level at which a respondent's stated minimum income is equal to his actual income. This level was taken as a definition of the poverty line.

13. Clark, Hemming, and Ulph (1981), following a welfare-based approach, have proposed two new indices of poverty by employing the group welfare function which is additive-separable in individual welfares. But this is a strong assumption. Sen (1973a) has discussed the restrictions implied by additive-separability – namely, that the relative social valuation of the incomes of two individuals is independent of the levels of any other incomes. In view of these shortcomings, these measures have not been used in the present study.

14. See Chapter 4 for a discussion of the rank-order weighting.

15. Kakwani (1980b) proposed a generalization of Sen's rank-order axiom which makes the weight v_i kth power of the number of persons who are richer than i. The generalization was motivated by the failure of Sen's measure to satisfy certain transfer-sensitivity axioms. Other variations of Sen's measure are given in Takayama (1979) and Thon (1979). For a thorough synthesis of alternative poverty measures see Ray (1984).

16. Both these measures as well as their variants are not additively decomposable in the sense that total poverty is a weighted average of the subgroup poverty levels. Foster, Greer, and Thorbecke (1984) have proposed a class of poverty measures which are in fact additively decomposable. But the welfare function implied by these measures must be additive-separable, which is a serious drawback of these measures.

Appendix. Data sources and their accuracy

1. This study was financed primarily by the Australian Research Grants Committee, with additional support from the Reserve Bank of Australia, the Social Science Research Council, the Australian Council of Trade Unions (ACTU), and a number of private companies. Professors Drane and Edwards of Macquarie University and Professor Gates of Queensland University directed the operation of the survey and the Macquarie University Data Archive, Ltd. filed the voluminous data in a form that was accessible by computer to researchers.

2. The final data tape was received in June 1980.

3. Murray (1978, 1981) has analyzed the sources of income inequality in Australia based on Income Surveys 1968-9 data.

4. This is documented in *Household Expenditure Survey* 1974-5, A.B.S. Bulletin 1 "An Outline of Concepts, Methodology and Procedures," Reference No. 17.19, page 15.

5. Australian Bureau of Statistics, "Population and Dwellings: Summary Tables," 1976 *Census of Population and Housing,* Catalogue No. 2417.0.

References

Adams, D. W. (1980), *The Distributional Effects of VAT in the United Kingdom, Ireland, and Germany,* Three Bank Reviews, No. 128, London: Midland Bank Review.

Adelman, I. and Morris, C. (1971), *An Anatomy of Pattern of Income Distribution in Developing Nations,* Part III of final report, Evanston, Illinois: Northwestern University.

Aitchison, J. and Brown, J. A. C. (1957), *The Lognormal Distribution,* Cambridge, Cambridge University Press.

Arrow, K. (1963), *Social Choice and Individual Values,* 2nd edition, New Haven: Yale University Press.

(1965), *Aspects of the Theory of Risk-Bearing,* Helsinki: Yrjö Jahnssonin Säätiö.

Atkinson, A. B. (1969), *Poverty in Britain and the Reform of Social Security,* Cambridge: Cambridge University Press.

(1970), On the Measurement of Inequality, *Journal of Economic Theory* 2, 244–63.

(1972), *Maxi-min and Optimal Income Taxation.* Paper presented at the Budapest Meeting of the Econometric Society.

(1973), How Progressive Should Income Tax Be?, in M. Parkin (ed.), *Essays on Modern Economics,* London: Longman, 1973.

(1974a), Poverty and Income Inequality in Britain, in Dorothy Wedderburn (ed.), *Poverty, Inequality, and Class Structure,* Cambridge: Cambridge University Press.

(1974b), *Unequal Shares,* revised ed., Harmondsworth, U.K.: Penguin.

(1980), Horizontal Equity and the Distribution of Tax Burden, in H. Aaron and M. J. Boskin, *The Economics of Taxation,* Washington, D.C.: Brookings Institute.

Atkinson, A. B. and Stiglitz, J. E. (1972), The Structure of Indirect Taxation and Economic Efficiency, *Journal of Public Economics,* 1, 97–119.

Bardhan, P. K. and Srinivasan, T. N., editors (1974), *Poverty and Income Distribution in India,* Calcutta: Statistical Publishing Society.

Barlow, R. (1974), The Incidence of Selected Taxes by Income Classes, in J. N. Morgan (ed.), *Five Thousand American Families: Patterns of Economic Progress,* Institute for Social Research, The University of Michigan.

Barlow, R., Brazer, H. E., and Morgan, J. N. (1966), *Economic Behavior of the Affluent,* Washington, D.C.: The Brookings Institute.

Barten, P. (1964), Family Composition, Prices, and Expenditure Patterns, in P. Hart, G. Mill, and J. Whittaker (eds.), *Econometric Analysis for National Economic Planning,* London: Butterworth.

276   **References**

Becker, G. S. (1965), A Theory of Allocation of Time, *The Economic Journal,* 75, 493–517.

(1974a), A Theory of Marriage: Part II, *Journal of Political Economy,* 82, 511–26.

(1974b), A Theory of Social Interactions, *Journal of Political Economy,* 82(6), 1063–93.

Bentley, P., Collin, D. J., and Drane, N. T. (1974), The Incidence of Australian Taxation, *Economic Record,* 50, 489–510.

Bentley, P., Collin, D. J., and Rutledge, D. J. S. (1977), *Estimating the Distributional Effects of Taxation,* Research Paper No. 147, Sydney, Australia: School of Economics and Financial Studies, Macquarie University.

Benus, Jacob and Morgan, J. N. (1975), Time Period, Unit of Analysis, and Income Concept in the Analysis of Income Distribution, in James D. Smith (ed.), *The Personal Distribution of Income and Wealth,* New York: Columbia University Press.

Bhatia, K. B. (1974), Capital Gains and Distribution of Income, *Review of Income and Wealth,* 20.

Black, D. (1958), *The Theory of Committees and Elections,* Cambridge: Cambridge University Press.

Blackorby, C. and Donaldson, D. (1978), Measures of Relative Equality and their Meaning in Terms of Social Welfare, *Journal of Economic Theory,* 18, 59–80.

Blaug, M. (1980), *The Methodology of Economics,* Cambridge: Cambridge University Press.

Borda, J. C. (1781), Memoire sur les Elections au Scrutin, in *Memoires de l'Academie Royale de Sciences,* Paris.

Boskin, M. J. and Sheshinski, E. (1978), Optimal Redistributive Taxation when Individual Welfare Depends upon Relative Income, *Quarterly Journal of Economics,* 43, 589–601.

Bourguignon, F. (1979), Decomposable Income Inequality Measures, *Econometrica,* 47, July, 901–20.

Brady, D. (1958), Individual Incomes and the Structure of Consumer Units, *American Economic Review,* 48, 267–78.

Break, G. F. (1957), Income Taxes and Incentive to Work: An Empirical Study, *American Economic Review,* 47, 529–49.

Brennan, G. (1973), Pareto Desirable Redistributions: The Case of Malice and Envy, *Journal of Public Economics,* 2, 173–83.

Bresciani-Turroni, C. (1910), Di un Indice Misuratone della Disugaglianza dei Redditi, Studi in onone di B. Brugi, Palermo: 54–61.

Brown, H. P. (1957), Estimation of Income Distribution in Australia, Chapter 7, *Income and Wealth, Series VI,* London: Bowes and Bowes.

Brown, J. A. C. (1954), The Consumption of Food in Relation to Household Composition and Income, *Econometrics,* 22, 444–60.

Bryze, Jeannine (1982), The Estimation of Welfare Levels of a Cardinal Utility Function, *European Economic Review,* 17, 325–32.

Budd, E. (1967), *Inequality and Poverty,* New York: Norton.

Cass, B. (1982), Family Policies in Australia: Contest over the Social Wage, *Social Welfare Research Centre Report No. 21,* Australia: the University of New South Wales.

Champernowne, D. G. (1974), A Comparison of Measures of Inequality of Income Distribution, *Economic Journal,* 84, 787–816.

Chipman, J. S. (1974), The Welfare Ranking of Pareto Distribution, *Journal of Economic Theory,* 9, 275–82.

Christopher, A., Polanyi, G., Seldon, A., and Shenfield, B. (1970), *Policy for Poverty,* Research Monograph No. 20, London: Institute for Economic Affairs.

Clark, S., Hemming, R., and Ulph, D. (1981), On Indices for the Measurement of Poverty, *The Economic Journal,* 91, 515–26.

Commission of Inquiry into Poverty (1975), *Poverty in Australia,* First Main Report, Canberra: Australian Government Printing Service.

Cowell, F. A. and Kiyoshi Kuga (1981), Additivity and the Entropy Concept: An Axiomatic Approach to Inequality Measurement, *Journal of Economic Theory,* 25, 131–43.

Cramer, J. S. (1969), *Empirical Econometrics,* Amsterdam: North-Holland.

Dagum, C. (1980), Inequality Measures between Income Distributions with Applications, *Econometrica,* 48, 1791–803.

Dalton, H. (1920), The Measurement of Inequality of Income, *Economic Journal,* 30, 348–61.

(1936), *Principles of Public Finance,* London: George Routledge & Sons, Ltd.

Danziger, S. R. H. (1976), Conference Overview: Conceptual Issues, Data Issues, and Policy Implications, *Conference on the Trend in Income Inequality in the United States,* Institute for Research on Poverty, University of Wisconsin.

Danziger, S. R. H. and Smolensky, E. (1977), The Measurement and Trend of Inequality: Comment, *American Economic Review,* 67, 505–12.

Danziger, S. R. H. and Taussig, M. (1979), The Income Unit and the Anatomy of Income Distribution, *Review of Income and Wealth,* 25, 365–75.

Dasgupta, P., Sen, A. K., and Starrett, D. (1973), Notes on the Measurement of Inequality, *Journal of Economic Theory,* 6, 180–7.

David, M. (1959), Welfare Income and Budget Needs, *Review of Economics and Statistics,* 41, 393–9.

Diamond, P. (1975), A Many-Person Ramsey Tax Rule, *Journal of Public Economics,* 4, 335–42.

Diamond, P. and Mirrlees, J. A. (1971), Optimal Taxation and Public Production, *American Economic Review,* 61, 8–27, 261–78.

Dodge, D. A. (1975), Impact of Tax Transfer and Expenditure Policies of Government on the Distribution of Personal Income in Canada, *Review of Income and Wealth,* 21, 1–52.

Drewnowski, D. (1977), Poverty: Its Meaning and Measurement, *Development and Challenge,* 8, 183–208.

Duesenberry, (1949), *Income, Saving, and the Theory of Consumer Behavior,* Cambridge, Mass.: Harvard University Press.

278   References

Edwards, M. (1981), *Income Distribution within Families: Findings of a Survey and Some Policy Issues,* Paper for Workshop on Income Security in Australia, University of Melbourne, 31 July.

Elteto, O. and Frigyes, E. (1968), New Inequality Measures as Efficient Tools for Causal Analysis and Planning, *Econometrica,* 36, 383-96.

Epstein, A. L. (1969), Measuring the Size of the Low-Income Population, *Six Papers on the Size Distribution of Wealth and Income,* Lee Soltow (ed.), New York: National Bureau of Economic Research.

Fei, J. C. H., Ranis, G., and Kao, S. W. Y. (1978), Growth and the Family Distribution of Income by Factor Components, *Quarterly Journal of Economics,* XCII, 17-53.

Feldstein, M. S. (1976), On the Theory of Tax Reform, *Journal of Public Economics,* 6, 77-104.

Ferman, L., Kornbluh, J., and Haber, A. (1965), *Poverty in America,* Ann Arbor, Michigan: University Press.

Fields, G. S. (1979), Income Inequality in Urban Colombia: A Decomposition Analysis, *Review of Income and Wealth,* 25, 327-41.

Fields, G. S. and Fei, J. C. H. (1974), *On Inequality Comparisons,* Discussion Paper No. 202, New Haven, Conn.: Economic Growth Center, Yale University.

Fine, B. and Fine, K. (1974), Social Choice and Individual Ranking, *Review of Economic Studies,* 41, 303-22 & 459-75.

Fishburn, P. C. (1975), *Theory of Social Choice,* Princeton, N.J.: Princeton University Press.

Fishlow, A. (1972), Brazilian Size Distribution of Income, *American Economic Review,* 62, 391-402.

Fishman, L. (1966), *Poverty amid Affluence,* New Haven, Conn: Yale University Press.

Forsyth, F. J. (1960), The Relation between Family Size and Family Expenditure, *Journal of Royal Statistical Society,* Series A, 124.

Foster, J., Greer, J., and Thorbecke, E. (1984), A Class of Decomposable Poverty Measures, *Econometrica,* 52, no. 3, 761-6.

Friedman, M. (1952), A Method of Comparing Incomes of Families Differing in Composition, *Studies in Income and Wealth,* New York: National Bureau of Economic Research.

(1957), *A Theory of the Consumption Function,* Princeton, N.J.: Princeton University Press.

(1962), *Capitalism and Freedom,* Chicago: University of Chicago Press.

Fuschs, V. (1969), Comment, in L. Soltow (ed.), *Six Papers on the Size Distribution of Income and Wealth,* New York: National Bureau of Economic Research.

Gardenfors, P. (1973), Positional Voting Functions, *Theory and Decision,* 4, 1-24.

Gastwirth, J. L. (1972), The Estimation of the Lorenz Curve and Gini Index, *Review of Economics and Statistics,* 54, 306-16.

Geary, R. C. (1950-1), A Note on a Constant Utility Index of the Cost of Living, *Review of Economic Studies,* 18, 65-6.

Gillespie, W. I. (1965), The Effect of Public Expenditures on the Distribution of Income, in R. A. Musgrave (ed.), *Essays in Fiscal Federalism,* Washington, D.C.: Brookings Institute.

Goedhart, T., Halberstady, V., Kapteyn, A., and van Praag, B. (1977), The Poverty Line Concept and Measurement, *Journal of Human Resources,* 4, 503–20.

Graaff, J. De V. (1977), Equity and Efficiency as Components of General Welfare, *South African Journal of Economics,* 45(4), 362–75.

Green, C. (1966), *Negative Taxes and Poverty Problem,* conference monograph, prepared for the Brookings Institute Studies in Government Finance, Washington, D.C.: Brookings Institute.

Groenewegen, P. D. (1976), *The Taxable Capacity of Local Governments in New South Wales,* Research Monograph No. 13, Canberra, Australia: Centre for Research on Federal Financial Relations.

(1982), *Australian Taxation Policy Survey 1965–1980,* Sydney, Australia: the Taxation Research and Education Trust.

(1983), The Australian Wholesale Sales Tax in Perspective, in John Head (ed.), *Taxation Issues of the 1980s,* Sydney, Australia: Australian Tax Research Foundation.

(1984), Rationalizing Australian Taxation Revisited, *The Economic Record,* 60, no. 169, 113–27.

Hahn, F. (1981), Reflections on the Invisible Hand, Fred Hirsh Memorial Lecture, Working Paper No. 196, University of Warwick, England.

Hansson, B. (1973), The Independence Condition in the Theory of Social Choice, *Theory and Decision,* 4, 25–50.

Harrington, Michael (1962), *The Other America,* New York: Macmillan.

Head, J. G., editor (1983), *Taxation Issues of the 1980s,* Chapter 1, Sydney, Australia: Australian Tax Research Foundation.

Heady, C. J. and Mitra, P. K. (1980), The Computation of Optimum Linear Taxation, *The Review of Economic Studies,* XLVII, no. 3, 567–86.

Henderson, A. M. (1949), The Cost of Children, *Population Studies,* 3, 130; 4, 267.

Henderson, R. F., Harcourt, A., and Harper, R. J. A. (1970), *People in Poverty: A Melbourne Survey,* Melbourne, Australia: Melbourne University Press.

Henderson Report (1975), *Poverty in Australia,* 1, Commission of Inquiry into Poverty, Canberra, Australia: Australian Government Publishing Service.

Horn, R. V. (1981), Fiscal Welfare Effects of Changes in Australian Income Tax, 1972–1973 to 1980–1981, Social Welfare Research Centre Report No. 9, Sydney, Australia: University of New South Wales.

Horne, Donald (1964), *The Lucky Country,* Sydney, Australia: Penguin Books.

Howe, H. J. (1974), *Estimation of the Linear and Quadratic Expenditure System: A Cross-Section Case for Colombia,* unpublished Ph.D. dissertation, University of Pennsylvania.

Industries Association Commission (1980), *Tariffs as Taxes: An Analysis of Some of the Effects of Tariffs and Quotas on Consumers and Consuming Industries,* Information Paper No. 2, Canberra, Australia: Australian Government Publishing Service.

Ingles, David (1981), *Statistics on the Distribution of Income and Wealth in Australia,* Research Paper No. 14, Canberra, Australia: Research & Statistics Branch, Development Division, Department of Social Security.

Intriligator, M. (1973), A Probabilistic Model of Social Choice, *Review of Economic Studies,* 553-60.

Itsumi, Yoshitaka (1974), Distributional Effect of Linear Income-Tax Schedules, *Review of Economic Studies,* 41, 371-81.

Jakobsson, U. (1976), On the Measurement of Degree of Progression, *Journal of Public Economics,* 12, 161-8.

Johnson, William R. (1977), The Measurement and Trend of Inequality: Comment, *American Economic Review,* 67, June, 502-4.

Kakwani, N. (1977a), Measurement of Tax Progressivity: An International Comparison, *Economic Journal,* 87, 71-80.

(1977b), Applications of Lorenz Curves in Economic Analysis, *Econometrica* 45, 719-27.

(1977c), On the Estimation of Consumer-Unit Scale, *Review of Economics and Statistics,* 59, 507-10.

(1979), Measurement of Tax Progressivity: A Reply, *The Economic Journal,* 89, 653-5.

(1980a), *Income Inequality and Poverty: Methods of Estimation and Policy Application,* New York: Oxford University Press.

(1980b), On a Class of Poverty Measures, *Econometrics,* 48, 437-46.

(1981a), Welfare Measures: An International Comparison, *Journal of Development Economics,* 8, 21-45.

(1981b), Note on a New Measure of Poverty, *Econometrics,* 49, no. 2/March, 205-6.

(1983a), Progressivity Index of Sales Tax on Individual Expenditure Items in Australia, *Economic Record,* March, 61-79.

(1983b), *Redistributive Effects of Income Tax and Cash Benefits in Australia,* Centre for Applied Economic Research Paper No. 18, Australia: the University of New South Wales.

(1984a), Issues in Measuring Poverty, *Economic Inequality: Measurement and Policy,* Advances in Econometrics, 3, Greenwich, Conn.: JAI Press.

(1984b), Welfare Ranking of Income Distribution, in *Economic Inequality Measurement and Policy,* Advances in Econometrics, 3, Greenwich, Conn.: JAI Press.

(1984c), On the Measurement of Tax Progressivity and Redistributive Effect of Taxes with Applications to Horizontal and Vertical Equity, in *Economic Inequality: Measurement and Policy,* Advances in Econometrics, 3, Greenwich, Conn.: JAI Press.

(1984d), The Relative Deprivation Curve and Its Applications, *Journal of Business and Economic Statistics,* 2, October, 384-94.

(1984e), Reply, *Journal of Business and Economic Statistics,* 2, October, 400-5.

(1985), Measurement of Welfare with Applications to Australia, *Journal of Development Economics* (in press).

Kapteyn, A. (1977), *A Theory of Preference Formation,* Ph.D. thesis, Leyden University, The Netherlands.

Kats, A. (1972), On the Social Welfare Function and Parameters of Income Distribution, *Journal of Economic Theory,* 5, 90–1.

Kay, J. A. and Keen, M. J. (1980), Consumption, Expenditure, and Interpretation of Household Budget Data, I.F.S. Working Paper No. 14; London.

Kemsley, W. F. F. (1975), A Study of Differential Response Based on a Comparison of the 1971 Sample with the Census, *Statistical News,* 31.

King, M. A. (1983), An Index of Inequality: With Applications to Horizontal Equity and Social Mobility, *Econometrica,* 51, no. 1, 99–116.

Kolm, S.-Ch. (1976), Unequal Inequalities, *Journal of Economic Theory,* 12, 416–42; 13, 82–111.

Kravis, I. B. (1960), International Differences in the Distribution of Income, *Review of Economics and Statistics,* 42, 408–16.

(1962), *The Structure of Income: Some Quantitative Essays,* Philadelphia: University of Pennsylvania Press.

Krelle, W. and Shorrocks, A. F., eds. (1978), *Personal Income Distribution,* Amsterdam, North-Holland.

Kurien, John (1977), The Measurement and Trend of Inequality, *American Economic Review,* 67, June, 517–19.

Kuznets, S. (1955), Economic Growth and Income Inequality, *American Economic Review* 45, 1–28.

(1957), Quantitative Aspects of the Economic Growth of Nations, II: Industrial Distribution of National Product and Labor Force, *Economic Development and Cultural Change,* supplement to 5, 1–80.

(1963), Quantitative Aspects of the Economic Growth of Nations: Part VIII, Distribution of Income by Size, *Economic Development and Cultural Change,* 11, 1–80.

(1974), Demographic Aspects of the Distribution of Incomes among Families: Recent Trends in the United States, in Willy Sellekaerts (ed.), *Econometrics and Economic Theory: Essays in honour of Jan Trinbergen,* London: Macmillan Press Ltd., 223–45.

(1976), Demographic Aspects of the Size Distribution of Income: An Exploratory Essay, *Economic Development and Cultural Change,* 25, 1–94.

(1981), Children and Adults in the Income Distribution, Yale Economic Growth Center Discussion Paper No. 379, New Haven, Conn.: Yale University Press.

Lampman, Robert (1954), Recent Changes in Income Inequality Reconsidered, *The American Economic Review,* XLIV, June, 251–68.

(1964), Prognosis for Poverty, National Tax Association, Proceedings of the 57th Annual Conference, 71–81; Pittsburgh, Pa.

(1973), Measured Inequality of Income: What Does It Mean and What Can It Tell Us, *The Annals,* 409, September 9, 81–91.

Lancaster, K. J. (1975), The Theory of Household Behaviour: Some Foundations, *Annals of Economic and Social Measurement,* 4, 5–21.

Layard, R. (1980), Human Satisfaction and Public Policy, *Economic Journal,* 90, 737–50.

Lillard, L. A. (1977), Inequality Earnings versus Human Wealth, *American Economic Review,* LXVII, 42–53.

Lluch, C. (1973), The Extended Linear Expenditure System, *European Economic Review*, 4, 21–32.

Lorenz, M. C. (1965), Methods of Measuring the Concentration of Wealth, *Publications of the American Statistics Association*, 9, 209–19.

Lydall, H. (1965), The Dispersion of Employment Incomes in Australia, *Economic Record*, 41, no. 96, December, 549–69.

Mathews, R. L. (1980), The Structure of Taxation, in E. Wilkes (ed.) *The Politics of Taxation*.

McClements, L. D. (1977), Equivalence Scales for Children, *Journal of Public Economics*, 8, 191–210.

(1978), *The Economics of Social Security*, London: Heinemann.

McElroy, (1970), Capital Gains and the Theory and Measurement of Income, unpublished Ph.D. dissertation, Evanston, Illinois: Northwestern University.

Meade, J. E. (1976), *The Just Economy: Principles of Political Economy*, London: George Allen & Unwin.

Merton, R. K. (1957), *Social Theory and Social Structure*, Chicago: Chicago University Press.

Mieszkowski, P. (1969), Tax Incidence Theory, *Journal of Economic Literature*, December, 7, 1103–24.

Minarik, Joseph J. (1977), The Measurement and Trend of Inequality: Comment, *American Economic Review*, 67, June, 513–16.

Mirrlees, J. A. (1971), An Exploration in the Theory of Optimum Taxation, *Review of Economic Studies*, 38, 175–208.

Mookherjee Dilip and Anthony Shorrocks (1982), A Decomposition Analysis of the Trend in U.K. Income Inequality, *The Economic Journal*, 92, December, 886–902.

Morgan, J. (1962), The Anatomy of Income Distribution, *Review of Economics and Statistics*, 44, 270–83.

(1965), Measuring the Economic Status of the Aged, *International Economic Review*, 6, no. 1.

(1968), The Supply of Effort, the Measurement of Well-being, and the Dynamics of Improvement, *American Economic Review*, 58, 31–9.

Morgan, James and James D. Smith (1969), Measures of Economic Well-offness and Their Correlations, *American Economic Review*, 59, 450–62.

Morgan, James, David, M., Cohen, W., and Brazer, H. (1962), *Income and Welfare in the United States*, New York: McGraw-Hill.

Muellbauer, J. (1974), Household Composition, Engel Curves, and Welfare Comparisons between Households, *European Economic Review*, 5, 103–22.

(1975), Identification and Consumer-Unit Scale, *Econometrica*, 43, 807–9.

(1977), Testing the Barten Model of Household Composition Effects and the Cost of Children, *Economic Journal*, 87, 460–87.

(1978), McClements on Equivalence Scales for Children, *Journal of Public Economics*, 9.

(1980), The Estimation of the Prais–Houthakker Model of Equivalence Scales, *Econometrica*, 48, 153–76.

Murray, David (1978), Sources of Income Inequality in Australia 1968–1969, *Economic Record*, 54, 159–69.

(1981), The Inequality of Household Incomes in Australia, *The Economic Record*, March, 57, 12–22.

Musgrave, R. A. (1959), *The Theory of Public Finance*, New York: McGraw-Hill.

(1964), Estimating the Distribution of the Tax Burden, in C. Clark and G. Stuvel (eds.) *Income Redistribution and the Statistical Foundations of Economic Policy*, London: Bowes and Bowes.

Musgrave, R. A. and Thin, T. (1948), Income-Tax Progression 1929–1948, *Journal of Political Economy*, 56, 498–514.

Nelson, Eric R. (1977), The Measurement and Trend of Inequality: Comment, *American Economic Review*, 67, June, 513–16.

Neutze, M. (1977), State and Local Property Taxes, in R. L. Mathews (ed.), *State and Local Taxation*, Canberra, Australia: ANU Press.

Nevile, J. W. and N. A. Warren (1984), How Much Do We Know about Wealth Distribution in Australia?, Working Paper No. 62, Australia: Centre for Applied Economic Research, University of New South Wales.

Newbery, D. (1970), A Theory on the Measurement of Inequality, *Journal of Economic Theory*, 2, 264–6.

Nicholson, J. L. (1949), Variations in Working-Class Family Expenditures, *Journal of the Royal Statistical Society*, 122, 359.

(1974), The Distribution and Redistribution of Income in the United Kingdom, in D. Wedderburn (ed.), *Poverty, Inequality, and Class Structure*, London: Cambridge University Press.

(1977), How Should Indirect Taxes Be Allocated when Estimating the Redistribution of Income?, in A. J. Culyer and J. Wiseman (eds.), *Public Economics and Human Resources*, Paris: Cujas.

Nordhaus, William D. (1973), The Effects of Inflation on the Distribution of Economic Welfare, Journal of Money, Credit, and Banking, no. 1, part 2: 465–504.

OECD (1981), The Impact of Consumption Taxes at Different Income Levels, *OECD Studies in Taxation*, Paris.

Oswald, A. J. (1983), Altruism, Jealousy and the Theory of Optimal Non-linear Taxation, *Journal of Public Economics*, 20, 77–87.

Paglin, M. (1975), The Measurement and Trend of Inequality: A Basic Revision, *American Economic Review*, 65, September, 598–609.

Pechman, J. A. and Okner, B. A. (1974), *Who Bears the Tax Burden?*, Washington, D.C.: Brookings Institute.

Piggott, John (1983), Some General Equilibrium Implications of Tax Substitutes: A Numerical Assessment for Australia, in John Head (ed.), *Taxation Issues of the 1980s*, Sydney: Australian Tax Research Foundation.

(1984), The Distribution of Wealth in Australia – A Survey, *Economic Record* (in press).

Piggott, J. R. and J. Whalley (1981), A Summary of Some Findings from a General Equilibrium Tax Model of the United Kingdom, in K. Brunner and A. Meltzer (eds.), *Carnegie-Rochester Conference Series on Public Policy*, 14, Spring.

Plotnick, Robert (1981), A Measure of Horizontal Inequity, *The Review of Economics and Statistics*, 63, 283–88.

Podder, N. (1971), The Estimation of an Equivalent-Income Scale, *Australian Economic Papers,* December, 175–87.

(1972), Distribution of Household Income in Australia, *Economic Record,* 48, 187–98.

(1978), *The Economic Circumstances of the Poor,* Commission of Inquiry into Poverty Study, Canberra: Australian Government Publishing Service.

Podder, N. and N. Kakwani (1975a), Distribution and Redistribution of Household Income in Australia, Study No. 4, Australia: Taxation Review Committee, 111–51.

(1975b), Incidence of Indirect Taxes and Company Income Tax, Study No. 4, Australia: Taxation Review Committee, 201–10.

(1976), Distribution of Wealth in Australia, *Review of Income and Wealth,* series 22, 75–91.

Pollak, R. A. and T. J. Wales (1979), Welfare Comparisons and Equivalence Scales, *American Economic Review,* 69, no. 2, 216–21.

Prais, S. J. and H. S. Houthakker (1955), *The Analysis of Family Budgets,* Cambridge: Cambridge University Press.

Projector, Dorothy S. and Weiss, G. S. (1969), Income Net-Worth Measures of Economic Welfare, *Social Security Bulletin,* 32(11) (November, 1969), 14–17.

Pyatt, G. (1976), On the Interpretation and Disaggregation of Gini Coefficients, *Economic Journal,* 86, 243–55.

(1980), Poverty and Welfare Measures Based on the Lorenz Curve, mimeographed paper: Development Research Centre, Washington, D.C.: The World Bank.

Pyatt, G., Chau-Nan Chen, and John Fei (1980), The Distribution of Income by Factor Components, *The Quarterly Journal of Economics,* 94, 451–73.

Ranadive, K. R. (1965), The Equality of Income in India, *Bulletin of the Oxford Institute of Statistics,* 27, 119–34.

Rao, V. M. (1969), Two Decompositions of Concentration Ratio, *Journal of the Royal Statistical Society,* Series A, 132, 418–25.

Rawls, J. (1967), Distributive Justice, in P. Laslett and W. G. Runciman (eds.), *Philosophy, Politics, and Society,* 3rd series, Oxford: Blackwell.

Ray, Ranjan (1984), On Measuring Poverty in India: A Synthesis of Alternative Measures, mimeographed, University of Manchester: Faculty of Economic and Social Studies, Department of Econometrics and Social Statistics.

Reynolds, Morgan and Smolensky, E. (1974), The Past Fisc Distribution: 1961 and 1970 compared, Discussion Paper 191–74, Madison: Institute for Research on Poverty, University of Wisconsin.

Richardson, S. (1979), Income Distribution, Poverty, and Redistribution Policies, *Survey of Australian Economics,* edited by F. H. Gruen, Sydney, Australia: George Allen & Unwin.

Roberti, P. (1978), Income Inequality in Some Western Countries: Patterns and Trends, *International Journal of Social Economics,* 5(1).

Rosen, Harvey S. (1978), An Approach to the Study of Income Utility and Horizontal Equity, *Quarterly Journal of Economics,* XCII, 367–22.

Rothbarth, E. (1943), Note on a Method of Determining Equivalent Income for Families of Different Composition, Appendix IV to *War-Time Pattern of Saving and Spending* by Charles Madge, New York: Cambridge University Press.

Rothschild, M. and Stiglitz, J. E. (1973), Some Further Results on the Measurement of Inequality, *Journal of Economic Theory*, 6, 188–204.

Rowntree, S. (1901), *Poverty: A Study of Town Life*, London: Macmillan.

Runciman, W. G. (1966), *Relative Deprivation and Social Justice*, Routledge and Kegan Paul, London.

Samuelson, P. A. (1956), Social Indifference Curves, *Quarterly Journal of Economics*, 70, 1–22.

Sandmo, Agnar (1976), Optimal Taxation: An Introduction to Literature, *Journal of Public Economics*, 6, 37–54.

Saunders, Peter (1980), Introduction: Poverty and the Poverty Line, from *The Poverty Line: Methodology and Measurement*, paper given at a seminar held on 12 June, 1980 at the University of New South Wales, Australia, the Social Welfare Research Centre.

(1982), *Equity and the Impact on Families of the Australian Tax-Transfer System*, Monograph No. 2, Melbourne, Australia: Institute of Family Studies.

Schall, L. D. (1972), Interdependent Utilities and Pareto Optimality, *Quarterly Journal of Economics*, 86, 19–24.

Schnitzer, Martin (1974), *Income Distribution: A Comparative Study of the United States, Sweden, West Germany, East Germany, the United Kingdom, and Japan*, New York: Praeger.

Schutz, R. R. (1951), On the Measurement of Income Inequality, *American Economic Review*, 41, 107–22.

Sebel, R. (1976), Poverty in Australia: A Methodological Review, Economic Monograph No. 50, Sydney, Australia: Economics Society of Australia and New Zealand.

Sen, A. K. (1966), Labour Allocation in a Co-operative Enterprise, *Review of Economic Studies*, 33, 361–71.

(1972), Utilitarianism and Inequality, *Economic and Political Weekly*, 7, 54–7.

(1973a), *On Economic Inequality*, Oxford: Clarendon Press.

(1973b), On the Development of Basic Income Indicators to Supplement G.N.P. Measures, *U.N. Economic Bulletin for Asia and the Far East*, 24, 1–11.

(1974), Informational Bases of Alternative Welfare Approaches: Aggregation and Income Distribution, *Journal of Public Economics*, 4, 387–403.

(1976), Poverty: An Ordinal Approach to Measurement, *Econometrica*, 44, no. 2, March, 219–31.

(1979), Issues in the Measurement of Poverty, *Scandinavian Journal of Economics*, 81, 285–307.

(1981), *Poverty and Famines: An Essay on Entitlement and Depreciation*, Oxford: Clarendon Press.

(1983), Poor, Relatively Speaking, *Oxford Economic Papers*, 35, 153–69.

Sheshinski, E. (1972a), The Optimal Linear Income Taxation, *Review of Economic Studies*, 39, 297–302.

(1972b), Relation between a Social Welfare Function and the Gini Index of Inequality, *Journal of Economic Theory,* 4, 98-100.

Shorrocks, A. F. (1980), The Class of Additively Decomposable Inequality Measures, *Econometrica,* 48, No. 3, 613-26.

(1982a), Inequality Decomposition by Factor Components, *Econometrica,* 50, no. 1, 193-212.

(1982b), On the Distance between Income Distributions, *Econometrica,* 50, 1337-41.

(1983), Ranking Income Distributions, *Economica,* 50, 3-18.

Singh, B. and A. L. Nagar (1973), Determination of Consumer-Unit Scales, *Econometrics,* 41, 347-56.

Slitor, R. E. (1948), The Measurement of Progressivity and Built-in Flexibility, *Quarterly Journal of Economics,* 62, 309-13.

Smith, D. B. (1965), A Simplified Approach to Social Welfare, *Canadian Tax Journal,* 13, 260-5.

Stanton, David (1980), Determining the Poverty Line, Social Security Quarterly, Canberra: Australian Government Printing Service.

Stark, T. (1972), *The Distribution of Personal Income in the United Kingdom, 1949-1963,* Cambridge University Press: London.

Stern, N. H. (1976), On the Specification of Models of Optimum Income Taxation, *Journal of Public Economics,* 6, 123-62.

Stiglitz, J. E. (1982), Utilitarianism and Horizontal Equity, *Journal of Public Economics,* 18, 1-33.

Stone, J. R. N. (1954), Linear Expenditure Systems and Demand Analysis: An Application to the Pattern of British Demand, *Economic Journal,* 64, 511-27.

Stouffer, S. A. (1949), *The American Soldier,* Princeton, N.J.: Princeton University Press.

Suits, D. B. (1977), Measurement of Tax Progressivity, *American Economic Review,* 67, 747-52.

Swan, P. L. (1983), Reforming the System: An Economist's View, (N.S.W. Branch) conference paper on Tax Avoidance and the Economy (4 March, 1983), Sydney, Australia.

Takayama, N. (1979), Poverty, Income Inequality, and their Measures: Professor Sen's Axiomatic Approach Reconsidered, *Econometrica,* 47, no. 3, 747-60.

Taussig, Michael K. (1973), *Alternative Measures of the Distribution of Economic Welfare,* Princeton, N.J.: Industrial Relations Section, Department of Economics, Princeton University.

(1976), Trends in Inequality of Well-Offness in the United States since World War II, Conference on the Trend in Income Inequality in the United States, Madison: Institute for Research on Poverty, University of Wisconsin, October 29-30, 1976.

Taxation Review Committee (the Asprey Committee) (1975), *Full Report,* Canberra: Australian Government Publishing Service.

Theil, H. (1967), *Economics and Information Theory,* Amsterdam, North-Holland.

Theo Goedhart, Victor Halberstadt, Arie Kapteyn, and Bernard Van Praag (1977), The Poverty Line: Concept and Measurement, *The Journal of Human Resources,* 12, 503-20.

Thon, Dominique (1979), On Measuring Poverty, *Review of Income and Wealth,* 25.

Thurow, Lester C. (1975), *Generating Inequality,* New York: Basic Books.

Titmuss, R. M. (1962), *Income Distribution and Social Change,* London: George Allen and Unwin.

Tobin, J. (1965), Improving the Economic Status of the Negro, *Daedalus,* 94, 878-98.

Townsend, P. (1954), Measuring Poverty, *British Journal of Sociology,* V, reprinted in Townsend (1973).

(1962), Meaning of Poverty, *British Journal of Sociology,* XIII, reprinted in Townsend (1973).

(1965), The Scale and Meaning of Poverty in Contemporary Western Society, *Dependency and Poverty,* Colloquium Series Paper, Brandeis University.

(1973), *The Social Minority,* London: Allen Land.

Tuomala, Matti (1984), On the Optimal Income Taxation: Some Further Numerical Results, *Journal of Public Economics,* 23, 351-66.

Van Praag, B. M. S. (1968), *Individual Welfare Function and Consumer Behaviour,* North-Holland.

(1971), The Welfare Function of Income in Belgium: An Empirical Investigation, *European Economic Review,* 2, 337-69.

(1977), The Perception of Welfare Inequality, *European Economic Review,* 10, 189-207.

(1978), The Perception of Income Inequality, in Krelle, W. and Shorrocks A. F. (eds.), Amsterdam: North-Holland.

Van Praag, B. M. S. and A. Kapteyn (1973), Further Evidence on the Individual Welfare Function of Income: An Empirical Investigation in the Netherlands, *European Economic Review,* 4, 33-62.

Van Praag, B. M. S., A. J. M. Hagenaars, and J. Van Weeren (1982), Poverty in Europe, *Review of Income and Wealth,* 28, 345-59.

Visaria, P. (1979), Demographic Factors and the Distribution of Income: Some Issues, in *Economic and Demographic Change: Some Issues for the 1980s,* Liege: Iussp, 289-320.

Wedderburn, D. (ed.) (1974), *Poverty, Inequality, and Class Structure,* Cambridge: Cambridge University Press.

Weisbrod, Burton A. and Hansen, W. Lee (1968), An Income Net Worth Approach to Measuring Economic Welfare, *American Economic Review,* 58, 1315-29.

Weisskoff, R. (1970), Income Distribution and Economic Growth in Puerto Rico, Argentina, and Mexico, *Review of Income and Wealth,* 16, 303-32.

Yitzhaki, Shlomo (1979), Relative Deprivation and Gini Index, *Quarterly Journal of Economics,* 93, 321-4.

(1980), On an Extension of the Gini Inequality Index, Discussion Paper No. 8013, Jerusalem: Falk Institute.

(1982), Relative Deprivation and Economic Welfare, *European Economic Review,* 17, 99-113.

Yntema, D. W. (1933), Measures of the Inequality in the Personal Distribution of Wealth or Income, *Journal of the American Statistical Association,* 28, 423-33.

Author index

289

Subject index

Lightning Source UK Ltd.
Milton Keynes UK
UKHW011845161020
371545UK00001B/226

9 780521 126311